MERE READING

D1606509

MERE READING

The Poetics of Wonder in Modern American Novels

Lee Clark Mitchell

Bloomsbury Academic
An imprint of Bloomsbury Publishing Inc

B L O O M S B U R Y
NEW YORK · LONDON · OXFORD · NEW DELHI · SYDNEY

Bloomsbury Academic

An imprint of Bloomsbury Publishing Inc

1385 Broadway	50 Bedford Square
New York	London
NY 10018	WC1B 3DP
USA	UK

www.bloomsbury.com

BLOOMSBURY and the Diana logo are trademarks of Bloomsbury Publishing Plc

First published 2017

Library of Congress Cataloging-in-Publication Data
Names: Mitchell, Lee Clark, 1947- author.
Title: Mere reading : the poetics of wonder in modern American novels /
Lee Clark Mitchell.
Description: New York : Bloomsbury Academic, 2017. |
Includes bibliographical references and index.
Identifiers: LCCN 2016041961 (print) | LCCN 2017001942 (ebook) |
ISBN 9781501329654 (hardback) | ISBN 9781501329647 (paperback) |
ISBN 9781501329661 (ePDF) | ISBN 9781501329678 (ePUB) Subjects: LCSH:
American fiction–20th century–History and criticism. | American fiction–21st
century–History and criticism. | Wonder in literature. | Books and reading. | Criticism. |
BISAC: LITERARY CRITICISM / Books & Reading. | LITERARY CRITICISM /
Semiotics & Theory. | LITERARY CRITICISM / American / General.
Classification: LCC PS379 .M496 2017 (print) | LCC PS379 (ebook) |
DDC 813/.509–dc23
LC record available at https://lccn.loc.gov/2016041961

ISBN:	HB	978-1-5013-2965-4
	PB:	978-1-5013-2964-7
	ePub:	978-1-5013-2967-8
	ePDF:	978-1-5013-2966-1

Cover design: Eleanor Rose
Cover image © Ron Blunt

Typeset by RefineCatch Limited, Bungay, Suffolk, UK
Printed and bound in the United States of America

The house was quiet and the world was calm.
The reader became the book; and summer night

Was like the conscious being of the book.
The house was quiet and the world was calm.

The words were spoken as if there was no book,
Except that the reader leaned above the page,

Wanted to lean, wanted much most to be
The scholar to whom his book is true, to whom

The summer night was like a perfection of thought.
The house was quiet because it had to be.

The quiet was part of the meaning, part of the mind:
The access of perfection to the page.

And the world was calm. The truth in a calm world,
In which there is no other meaning, itself

Is calm, itself is summer and night, itself
Is the reader leaning late and reading there.

—Wallace Stevens (1954)

What is this special use of language, and what makes it so special?
... It is, first of all, a use of language which refuses to be a use. Mere
use is abuse. That should be the motto of every decent life. So it
treats every word as a wonder, and a world in itself. ... And it does
not care to get on, but it dwells; it makes itself, as Rilke wrote, into a
thing, mute as the statue of an orator. It reaches back into the
general darkness we—crying—came from, retouches the terrors
and comforts of childhood, but returns with a magician's skills to
make the walls of the world dance.

—William Gass (235)

There is less to be said about literature than has been said, and this
book adds a little more.

—J. V. Cunningham (vii)

For Carl

CONTENTS

ACKNOWLEDGMENTS

Close reading might initially seem an intensely private activity, in the tilting, transforming immediacy of reader and book ("The reader became the book . . . the reader leaning late"). But the experience hardly ends there. For just as literature challenges casual assumptions while evoking a sense of wonder, so too do others' responses alter our sense of what we have read. In that regard, reading is strangely akin to those alleged "team" activities that actually consist of multiple individual encounters: Davis Cup tennis, say, or chess meetups, or swimming competitions. None of these depend on anything like a collaborative performance, though participants inspire each other to excel by their example.

Close reading works the same way, at least at its best: beginning in solitary delight at verbal thickets and narrative conundrums; then coming together with others to test out rickety insights, hone half-certain arguments; only to be persuaded by startling glimpses and unforeseen judgments. For me (and for that reason), the wonder of teaching has always occurred less often in lecture than in seminar, listening to others' responses, pressing back sometimes defensively, mulling over insights, being challenged to explain one's own. I have been blessed at Princeton with decades of students and colleagues who give the lie to those Cassandras worried over the future of literary delight. In fact, reading continues as a largely healthy, unwaveringly contested, deeply unstable activity, as we continue each semester to test ourselves and each other with the mutual disruptions of books that read us as intently as we read them.

Among those inspiring me in this ever-shifting conversation, I think most immediately of four impressive current graduate students: Carolina Alvarado, Brian Gingrich, Antonio Iannarone, and Jesse McCarthy. But I have also learned immensely from others nearly as recent: Timothy Anderson, Ellie Green, Jenny Huang, Jeffrey Lawrence, Dave Molk, Francisco Robles, Ron Martin Wilson. And as the following pages show, undergraduates have not shrunk from provoking and persuading. Among the most passionate in recent years (often on the subject of this book) have been Fareed ben-Youssef, Sally Butler, Justin Cahill, Claire Fallon, Elinor Flynn, Ben Goldman, Victoria Gruenberg, Aranya Jain, Michael Juel-Larsen, Catherine Keyser, Lillian Li, John

Marshal, Sarah Paige, Cameron Platt, David Pugliese, Emily Weigel, and Mona Zhang. I only hope they keep pressing me, now long after classes past. Which reminds me of fond voices elsewhere that patiently, sometimes acerbically, have prompted me to rethink even when they least suspected: Gene McHam, Barbara Lundy, Diane Somers, Michael Lundy, Lingyun Zhu. And last, but also importantly first, are those conversations with colleagues themselves who were kind enough to always be there at resonant moments, often simply to read, but always to respond generously: Carolyn Abbate, Maria DiBattista, Jeff Dolven, Sarah Rivett, and Anne Sobel.

Four of the following chapters have appeared earlier in different versions: Chapter 1 as "'Strangely Static": Wonder and Possession in *The Professor's House*,' in *Literary Imagination* 16(3) (2014): 289–308; Chapter 3 as '"A Regime of Small Kindnesses": *Housekeeping*'s Stylistic Hospitalities,' in *Style* 49.2 (2015): 153–80; Chapter 4 as 'A Book "Made Out of Books": The Humanizing Violence of Style in McCarthy's *Blood Meridian*,' in *Texas Studies in Literature and Language* 57.3 (2015): 259–81; and Chapter 5 as '"Make It Like Talk That You Imagine": The Mystery of Language in Cormac McCarthy's *The Road*,' in *Literary Imagination* 17.2 (2015): 204–27.

ABBREVIATIONS

BM	McCarthy, Cormac. *Blood Meridian: or, the Evening Redness in the West*. New York: Vintage, 1985.
BWL	Díaz, Junot. *The Brief Wondrous Life of Oscar Wao*. New York: Riverhead Books, 2007.
CH	Page, Norman (ed.). *Nabokov: The Critical Heritage*. London: Routledge & Kegan Paul, 1982.
E&L	Emerson, Ralph Waldo. *Essays and Lectures*. New York: Library of America, 1983.
F&S	Emerson, Ralph Waldo. *Essays: First and Second Series*. New York: Library of America, 1990.
H	Robinson, Marilynne. *Housekeeping*. New York: Farrar, Strauss, 1980.
L	Nabokov, Vladimir. *The Annotated Lolita: Revised and Updated,* edited by Alfred Appel, Jr. New York: Random House, Inc., 1991.
OW	Cather, Willa. *On Writing: Critical Studies on Writing as an Art*. Lincoln, NE: University of Nebraska Press, 1976.
PH	Cather, Willa. *The Professor's House*. New York: Vintage Classic, 1990.
R	McCarthy, Cormac. *The Road*. New York: Alfred A. Knopf, 2006.
SO	Nabokov, Vladimir. *Strong Opinions*. New York: McGraw-Hill, 1973.

INTRODUCTION: SLOWING DOWN

Mere reading, it turns out, prior to any theory, is able to transform critical discourse in a manner that would appear deeply subversive to those who think of the teaching of literature as a substitute for the teaching of theology, ethics, psychology, or intellectual history. Close reading accomplishes this often in spite of itself because it cannot fail to respond to structures of language which it is the more or less secret aim of literary teaching to keep hidden.

—Paul de Man (24)

Alliteration does more than candor can to justify God's ways to man.

—William Gass (*Tests of Time* 8)

Student explains that when reading a novel he likes to skip passages 'so as to get his own idea about the book and not be influenced by the author.'

—Vladimir Nabokov (*Strong Opinions* 30)

One of the odd experiences of my reading life occurred in adolescence when my mother seized on a newly-touted offering in our town that promised to "double your reading speed. Learn to read as fast as you can flip the page." That advertisement, still luring them in online today, prompted her to plunk down what at the time was a hefty sum to enroll us in a night course promoted by the schoolteacher-turned-entrepreneur, Evelyn Woods. The opening session began with a brief exercise timed to measure reading speed, followed by a multiple choice exam of facts culled from the text, purporting to measure comprehension (calibrated as a percentage of correct answers). Then, over a handful of weeks, a suitably bespectacled instructor offered a set of visual exercises coupled with patterned hand gestures to be practiced while reading at home, a procedure he promised would improve initial benchmark numbers for speed as well as comprehension. The underlying premise of the exercises was to avoid any "regressions, ... the rereading of the paragraphs, sentences or phrases from the text," and to learn to skim a text through "meta-guiding" by using a finger to sweep over the page, effectively pacing one's eyes. One learned how "to read groups of words or complete thoughts, rather than one word at a time." The promise heralded by the instructor was that even normally fast readers (say, 600 words a minute, or more than two double-spaced typewritten pages) could improve to anywhere upwards of the purported world-champion level of 4,700 words (nearly nineteen pages) per minute with a dazzling 67% comprehension. Only much later would I realize that Evelyn Woods was proposing to update for sedentary readers of the mid-twentieth century the corrective practices of seventy years earlier devised for casual manual laborers: Frederick Winslow Taylor's vision of "scientific management" as a stop-watch means of eradicating casual gestures, unnecessary movements, or anything else that might interfere with getting the job of brick-laying or hod-carrying done most efficiently.

Yet even this mildly nerdy high school sophomore lost interest after a session or two, although our paid tuition mandated for my mother that I complete the course along with her (who, as it happened, never abandoned the technique, never allowing her finger to slow as it crossed the pages of *Time Magazine*). And I lost interest for what seemed to me an obvious reason: the absence of any evident pleasure in this forced-march procedure, whose very premise seemed awry. Apart from the fact that the scoring seemed rigged for obvious answers to broad questions (Where does the opening of *Great Expectations* take place? A graveyard!), the one-size-fits-all program for reading legal depositions and lyrical novels, love letters and licensing agreements, meant that whole realms of verbal experience shriveled up amid the effort to "comprehend" at a simple mechanical level. The idea of gleaning grains of sense scattered joylessly through arid textual fields, of screening nouns (and occasional verbs) from "all types of reading material, regardless of difficulty," became for me an experience precisely the opposite of what I had enjoyed, slowly lingering over favorite novels late at night, under covers with the conventional flashlight. And I suppose my entire professional career has been spent, however ironically, in defiance of precepts Evelyn Woods ferreted out, not only in striving for what might be termed "slow reading" but in an ever-growing delight at the recursive habits "corrected" by speed reading's abhorrence of re-reading. Samuel Otter deftly identifies the heart of the matter in citing an inconspicuous passage from *Moby-Dick*, then wondering through a series of increasingly urgent questions at all that is lost in our misplaced passion for readerly efficiency:

When one is reading a line of prose or poetry, where do the eyes pause? When does the mind reflect? And why? Which features require concentration? Among all the verbal possibilities, what counts as evidence? On what bases do we link parts to wholes? Which aspects of the words or their arrangement seem to require that we look beyond the page in order to understand or appreciate them? To invoke the title of Melville's 1857 satire *The Confidence-Man*, where do we get the 'confidence' that our details count? Readers are trained to see, and they also discern with their own peculiar eyes. We seldom pause and reflect on our formal preferences and aesthetic commitments.

Otter 122

Those questions haunt anyone who sees writing as more than a system of transparent signs, a ready-made discursive vehicle for conveying a stark point (shopping list, roadway warning, restroom placard) from the simple message-encoding writer to equally simple message-decoding reader.

I. Slow Reading and Wonder

Turning from Evelyn Woods' strategies I turned completely away, and over the course of a career teaching American novels have become a progressively slower reader (and re-reader), as if my initial glowing speed and comprehension levels had sadly deteriorated year by year, at least according to any end-of-the-text pop quiz. Yet the question that increasingly has come to tantalize me is what it might mean to read a novel so slowly that it becomes akin to reading a poem. Ezra Pound notoriously claimed that "poetry must be *as well written as prose*" (48) even if poets have hardly seemed to need the reminder. But the claim has its counterpart in the notion that prose should be at least as well *read* as poetry, opening up possibilities for what it might mean to treat novels so attentively. How does that slowed-down immersion in prose alter us in the reading, opening us to multiple verbal and epistemological possibilities, unsettling our expectations in the teeterings of diction and knottings of syntax?[1] Of course, not all novels—perhaps not even most—aspire to being read poetically, asking instead to be "read for the plot" rather than for words and sounds, for internal rhymes and verbal iterations, for metaphoric flowerings and disquieting shifts in point of view. And that aspiration makes them no less valuable or enjoyable. As

Roland Barthes observed, in a tone that concedes Evelyn Woods' pseudo-scientific skimming even as it undermines the technique with an argument for "rhythm" and rereading: "we do not read everything with the same intensity of reading . . . we boldly skip (no one is watching) descriptions, explanations, analyses, conversations. . . . it is the very rhythm of what is read and what is not read that creates the pleasure of the great narratives: has anyone ever read Proust, Balzac, *War and Peace*, word for word?" As he promptly adds, however, catching himself parenthetically, it is nonetheless "(Proust's good fortune [that] from one reading to the next, we never skip the same passages)" (Barthes, *Pleasure* 10–11).

Barthes cannot help but acknowledge the pleasures of skittering perusal, of casual leap-frogging across a page of text; but he also cannot fail to savor the greater pleasures that await the reader, at least the reader of different kinds of texts. We all love flipping the pages, breathlessly, of a mystery novel or well-written sci-fi, but that kind of joyride is reserved for a certain plotted escapism that leaves the reader unmoved and certainly unchanged. As Barthes reconsiders his argument in the very essay that celebrates "boldly skip[ping]," he finds himself settling into a more considered division between "two systems of reading" for different kinds of novel: one, for the likes of Jules Verne, in which he finds minimal play of language; and another, for those with a more ambitious sense of verbal possibilities: "the other reading skips nothing; it weighs, it sticks to the text, it reads, so to speak, with application and transport" (*Pleasure* 12). That second reading is prompted by the text itself, and the pressures and suasions it performs on the reader open to linguistic disorientations—a reader who in turn animates words themselves through his own exacting scrutiny. In Barthes' celebrated description of this binary division between enjoyable reading and blissful transformation, the former (Verne) is a "text of pleasure: the text that contents, fills, grants euphoria; the text that comes from culture and does not break with it, is linked to a *comfortable* practice of reading." By contrast, the latter (Proustian) "text of bliss . . . imposes a state of loss, the text that discomforts (perhaps to the point of a certain boredom), unsettles the reader's historical, cultural, psychological assumptions, the consistency of his tastes, values, memories, brings to a crisis his relation with language" (*Pleasure* 14).[2] Here, Barthes commends a mental crisis that one suspects Evelyn Woods happily never felt, in his notion of reading that is transformative not simply for the text being read, but for the very processes by which it is read, the attentiveness it inspires, frustrates, rewards. And this constitutes the dramatic transition in my own (and others') career between speed reading and something more akin to slow or "close reading."

Yet if different kinds of reading are evoked by different kinds of texts, Barthes never clarifies what constitutes the "text of bliss" that has the capacity to elicit from a reader responses commensurate with its more complex verbal demands. His examples ("Proust, Balzac, *War and Peace*") suggest that sheer overarching plot is less at issue than simple (or rather, not so simple) syntax; astonishing scenes would seem to be less compelling than vivid diction or disruptive verbal turns. Moreover, his own practice (especially in *S/Z* [1970], his intensely close reading of Balzac's novel, *Sarrasine*) confirms that his focus was at least as much on reading sentences for their uncanny swerves and breaks as reading larger narrative twists and turns. That emphasis on what Garrett Stewart has termed "narratographic" analysis (in preference to structural or narratological interpretations) involves "the reading of prose fiction for its words, word for word if called upon" (6). By which he means a renewed concern not for the structure of novelistic organization, but for its surface rhythms and glancing cadences, for "narrative writing itself; narrative writing itself out, phrase by phrase" (Stewart 8). Or as he goes on to state, in a nice twist of the usual gesture toward plot as adumbrated stylistically, narratography "offers, in progress, a reading of style for its own plot" (Stewart 33). Even more than traditional stylistics, which "reads novels for recurrent habits, ... what narratography reads for, instead, is the microplot of narrative language itself, tracked at times syllable by syllable across a building sequence" (Stewart 221).[3] As William Keach ventured over a quarter-century ago, in a different vein well worth recalling: "Criticism of Shelley's poetry may be said to have gone beyond formalism without ever having been there—without ever having given the formal features of his writing adequate attention" (xvii). Such a call for the return to close reading may seem initially retrograde until we realize that too often unstable literary effects have been translated, just as often persuasively, by New Historicism and cultural studies into stable thematic renditions that often seem thinner than the texts they explain—and thinner precisely because they resist reading "word for word," preferring to skip over the "formal features" that make those texts of "literary" interest in the first place.

Still, this intensified call for close reading, of reading prose as intently as poetry with the assumption that it is crafted as tightly, tends to ignore the ways prose leads inevitably toward narrative sequence, toward plots larger than the style from which they emerge. Indeed, novels by their very nature resist the micro suasions of narratography even as they do in part submit, refusing to be read only as poems glistening syllabically, phonemically, transegmentally, in their drive toward external representation of characters in plots that narrative promises. The sequence across which we "track" in novels tends to be not syllables, nor even the individual word, but rather words in full sentences, or patterns of words that emerge over the course of a much longer narrative— words, that is, whose larger implications shift in the process of larger chapter developments. Even so, the effort to read "style for its own plot"—which nicely echoes Vladimir Nabokov's long-ago claim that "The best part of a writer's biography is not the record of his adventures but the story of his style" (154–55)—continues to be an intriguing, even inspiring prospect. And the tracking of words across a developing narrative illuminates the contradictions and coalescences among larger themes that emerge from a text. Often, just when we presume we understand a narrative moment, a verbal echo disrupts that understanding, pushing us off balance, reminding us of at least part of what constitutes a disorienting "text of bliss" in its success at initiating "a state of loss" as we read.

As much to the point, such readings themselves can be equally exhilarating, as critics better known for structural insights have sometimes been heard to admit. Consider moments when forceful theoreticians claim to have had most fun in simply slow reading, as when Stanley Fish pauses over a line of Milton:

> For me the reward and pleasure of literary interpretation lie in being able to perform analyses like this. Literary interpretation, like virtue, is its own reward. I do it because I like the way I feel when I'm doing it. I like being brought up short by an effect I have experienced but do not yet understand analytically. I like trying to describe in flatly prosaic words the achievement of words that are anything but flat and prosaic. I like savouring the physical 'taste' of language at the same time that I work to lay bare its physics. I like uncovering the incredibly dense pyrotechnics of a master artificer . . .
>
> Fish, *Professional* 110

Instead of skipping through lines to engage the ostensible sense of a passage, Fish here acknowledges not only the confusion he feels, but the delight (both sensual and intellectual) in words that magically do more than they seem. Charles Altieri has likewise admitted his own enchantment with poetry that has little to do with rational assessment, even though the importance of what we learn is undeniable:

We value the value not because we believe some argument but because we trust in or revel in some state or find ourselves able to relate differently to our surroundings and other persons. There will often be conflict between values arrived at this way and values determined by epistemic processes and social negotiations. Obviously there cannot be a strong rational case why poetry's way of mediating values ought to prevail in these conflicts.

Altieri 268

And this is again because of the "state of loss" we gladly suffer, as we "relate differently to our surroundings" in at least two different ways: first, simply in being captivated by words on the page, sometimes at a microcosmic level of poetic sound, sometimes at less immediate levels involving character transformation and descriptive revelation. But we also "relate differently" to such texts of bliss at a more radically disruptive level, as Barthes observed in finding our deeper "historical, cultural, psychological assumptions" dismantled, set awry.

One way to conceive this process is by analogy with magic, which would seem to share little with verbal performance except in early avatars that rest similarly on the belief in an inherent power of words to influence phenomena, of symbolic structures having a measurable effect in the physical realm. "Abracadabra" signals not simply a magical moment but as a performative gesture itself initiates the magic, actually making it occur.[4] And like the disorientation we feel with magic, complex literary texts place us under a spell, compelling us to wonder how something was done with simple words on a page that have an impact larger than explanation warrants. Like magic as well, we first presume the way in which the upendedness of novelistic writing achieves its hold is by *not* knowing the trick, by being fooled. Even better, however, is to learn the trick at last so as not to be fooled, yet still to feel renewed amazement at its presentation. As the contemporary close-up magician, Jamy Ian Swiss, observes, sounding much like Fish and Altieri: "Magic should be an emotional and aesthetic experience. A puzzle is an intellectual one, an intellectual problem that needs to be solved. Magic is an experience."[5] And that experience continues even in the presence of explanation, which only enhances our fascination. The sensation of mystery and wonder that ensues from magic is akin to what we feel in the midst of novelistic pyrotechnics, as words resonate in unexpected ways that alter what we think we know. My interest in reading closely, then—in attending to the slip and slide of verbal evocation—is intended not as a means of achieving some final or fixed interpretation, some comprehensive paraphrase, but rather in order to assess what happens to words in texts that aspire to be read as much like poetry as possible, even while they necessarily elude such possibility. Again, magic offers another kind of analogy in the problem of "the Too Perfect theory," the trick that goes too far by effortlessly astonishing beyond explanation or conceivable rationale. As Adam Gopnik writes, "What makes a trick work is not the inherent astoundingness of its effect but the magician's ability to suggest any number of possible explanations, none of them conclusive, and none of them quite obvious" (60). What most deeply sustains interest in a magic performance is its very lack of closure, its ability to leave the viewer in a state of irresolution between viable accounts.

II. Symptomatic Reading

Early close readers found this resistance to closure the most compelling evidence that complex texts were suitably complex, valued by the New Critics as the sustaining "tension" in poetry and adumbrated more recently by Andrew Dubois as "the competing meanings in a word" (6).[6] By contrast to some readers who had indulged in relatively straightforward paraphrase, or to those more recently who upgraded such treatment to symptomatic (or sociological) readings, the New Critics embraced a play of differences that anticipated the deconstructionists' engagement with language's necessary self-contradictions. And among the virtues of close reading was its inherent resistance to generalization, in compelling our attention to the contradictory pressures enforced not only at the level of plot but as well at micro-levels of diction and syntax. James Longenbach brashly claims that "*poetry is disjunctive*," which is one way we recognize it as poetry: "A poem unempowered by disjunction would seem as intolerable as a life without change, discovery, or defiance. It would seem content with what it knows" (35). One might claim the same for novels in exactly the same terms, impelling us to tighten our focus on points of disjunction as well as joints of conjunction, but only by ratcheting down to the tonalities of sentences themselves. For as Jane Gallop remarks, on behalf of a more scrupulous approach to reading: "The detail is, I would argue, the best safeguard against projection" ("Close" 16).

Evelyn Woods would of course have protested against this as a waste of time, in the call back to forms of close reading that means even more slowing down, a braking of the impulse to get beyond a text or otherwise to collapse it into packagable terms. As I.A. Richards argued nearly a century ago, instead of speedier perusal we need to re-read, iteratively, recursively, so as to appreciate the ways in which variant meanings emerge half-unsuspected (Guillory 9). The legacy of Richards and the New Critics in the modern classroom has best been summarized by Barbara Johnson, in championing the need to pay attention patiently rather than succumbing to some sort of culturally prescribed version of Attention Deficit Disorder:

> Teaching literature is teaching how to read. How to notice things in a text that a speed-reading culture is trained to disregard, overcome, edit out, or explain away; how to read what the language is doing, not guess what the author was thinking; how to take in evidence from a page, not seek a reality to substitute for it. This is the only teaching that can properly be called literary; anything else is history of ideas, biography, psychology, ethics, or bad philosophy. Anything else does not measure up to the rigorous perversity and seductiveness of literary language.
>
> 140

Ironically, much of what passes for literary teaching at major research institutions (and what constitutes evidence of tenurability) is in fact a "history of ideas, biography, psychology, ethics, or bad philosophy." Still, Johnson defines in the strongest terms the guiding rational behind what should be *literary* analysis, rather than any other kind that would carve out more straightforward or one-sided messages from contestable, complex texts.

For those uncertain about the tantalizing term "literature," moreover, perhaps that should be considered its definition: any text that presents itself (however minimally) as ambivalent, unstable, open to varying interpretations, and in that uncertainty tantalizes the reader into unexpected insights or revelations. Poems achieve that status through their intense compression, inviting one set of understandings that are undone by others that immediately emerge; novels achieve it through their more elaborate digressions and conflicts, in the process once again undoing our readings even as we make them. We are drawn in only to be undone mysteriously by the "perversity and seductiveness" of words constructed poetically, or prosaically, to alter presumptions and re-orient expectations. This is something like the opposite of the usual claims made for "symptomatic readings," most brilliantly argued by Fredric Jameson in *The Political Unconscious* (1981). As Stephen Best and Sharon Marcus recently argue, "Jameson insisted that the 'strong' critic must rewrite narrative in terms of master codes, disclosing its status as ideology, as an imaginary resolution of real contradictions" (13). But the very notion of such a "rewrite," installing the critic's system of "codes," assumes the kind of translatable system that the "literary" itself is pitched towards destabilizing. Johnson's invocation of perversion and seduction—the former a condition knowingly resisted, the latter an invitation unknowingly succumbed to—aptly identifies that dissociative process at the heart of our transformative encounters with literature.

In short, the common propensity for thematic or symptomatic readings, however revealing, tends to ignore the inconsistently resonant, often self-contradictory nature of novels we value as more than pedestrian, more than simply generic. For such readings allow critics to impose agendas onto texts that are more elusive or ambiguous than their agendas permit, giving (for example) a supposed voice to often oppressed identity groups by reading figurative language in a one-to-one allegorical fashion. And the claim for this kind of "surface reading," again as Best and Marcus assert, is supposedly "that the most interesting aspect of a text is what it represses" (3).[7] Making the distinction between what is completely absent from a text and what is merely latent is, of course, the crucial premise in a form of interpretation that has a pedigree extending back to the Gnostic tradition that always began with a faith in certain spiritual essences, not an attention to material facts. Yet reading gaps or silences as plain evidence in a text, or otherwise translating shimmering possibilities into full-fledged declarative truths, tends to impose a narrow construction on meanings elided, and foreclose figurative resonances into single (often flat) notes. Close reading, after all, rests on the premise that passages resonate in multiple ways, often inconsistently, sometimes paradoxically, registering at once more and less than they may at first glance seem to mean. And that multi-dimensional aspect of complex texts is precisely what undoes allegorical readings, since (as deconstruction taught with a vengeance) words are themselves unstable in ways that continue to delight us as readers. The problem of paraphrase (or of any "symptomatic" reading) is that instead of allowing a text to potentially disorient us, we end up imposing our own agendas, stabilizing quicksilver words into clear messages.[8]

Yet how do we escape from the impulse to paraphrase what our readings conclude, even when we slow down to avoid imposing an agenda? The answer is that we do not, but that at least awareness of the propensity should help guard against too ready interpretations, too easy dismissal of other alternatives. Marjorie Levinson has taken note of this salutary effect of the "new formalism," which is not different from the old: that it gives priority (over history, philosophy, sociology, psychology, or any other ideological reading of a text) to the unstable words on the page, which themselves precede and evade ideological discipline:

> Reading, understood in traditional terms as multilayered and integrative responsiveness to every element of the textual dimension, quite simply produces the basic materials that form the subject matter of even the most historical of investigations. Absent this, we are reading something of our own untrammeled invention, inevitably less complex than the products of reading. That complexity (a leitmotif throughout new formalism), which is attributed to the artwork and recoverable only through a learned submission to its myriad textual prompts, explains the deep challenge that the artwork poses to ideology, or to the flattening, routinizing, absorptive effects associated with ideological regimes.
>
> 560[9]

Literary texts, then, can teach us how to read them if only we resist the urge to manhandle them into manageable discourses. And in doing so, they hold out the possibility extolled by Barthes, of moving the reader beyond comfortable reading to an experience that actively distresses, that "brings to a crisis his relation to language" (Pleasure 14).

Those calling for a return to formalism frequently decry the loss of faith over recent decades in the self-transforming potential of literary texts and therefore the explanatory power of close reading. In that, they tend to unduly ignore the many critics who continued in this period to offer sustained close readings, including Jeff Dolven, Richard Godden, Hermione Lee, James Longenbach, John T. Matthews, Samuel Otter, Marjorie Perloff, Vance Smith, Garrett Stewart, Susan Stewart, and Helen Vendler, among others. Yet it is nonetheless true that they have been swimming largely against a tide of critics that rest their claims on identity politics, ethical quandaries, historical representations, and sociological evidence, all at the expense of aesthetic delights and subversions that literature distinctively offers. Indeed, close, formal readings are often dismissed as "mystifications," in refusing to endorse any single set of social truths or cultural behavior. Of course, this emphasis on culture, history, politics, and ideology has much to do with the professionalization of the discipline of English studies, in a turn some decades ago toward more readily measurable standards of reading. And that occurred precisely as questions about the literary canon grew less answerable, less informed by reverence—all of which makes any return to formal criticism seem somewhat fraught. Yet reverence for a canon tied to a bygone era of colonial imperialism need not short-circuit reverence for aesthetic achievement more generally. Although any serious return to close reading remains troubled in the wake of a broadened canon (a broadening that has coincided with the last half-century's theories and historicism), its potential difficulties are off-set by the promise of a return to what we have lost, a promise Aristotle first declared as the fundamental pleasure of wonder in reading (2183). More recently, J. V. Cunningham has interpreted Aristotle's claim for wonder as "not only an effect of a story or of a subject matter, it is also an effect of language and of style. It is precisely the effect of characteristically poetic, or tragic, style, as opposed to the plain straightforward style proper to prose and to dialectic" (63). This may ignore the wondrous evocation possible in a perfectly realistic account, but for Aristotle (as Cunningham continues) "the effect of astonishment or wonder is the natural correlative of unusual diction, as it is of the unusual event. The proper word satisfies by its exactness; the unusual pleases or displeases by its startling effect" (64).

Whether this particular verbal distinction continues to hold matters less than the larger belief that wonder forms a response not only occasionally elicited by literary texts but valued as their single important reason for being. James Longenbach pursues this premise in his poetic analyses, claiming more broadly that "Wonder is the reinvention of humility, the means by which we fall in love with the world. . . . Wonder is most commonly associated with youth. It thrives on ignorance, inexperience, and firstness; its enemies are knowledge, memory, and repetition" (95). And it is in the unpredictability of our reading, of surprise arising from a state of expectancy, that the experience of wonder emerges—an experience in which we feel certainties dissolve, a sense of things as they ought to be shifted into some other order, of words unfolding and turning against themselves. While Longenbach considers only poetry, the experience might as easily be extended to prose: "We want to feel poetry turning against itself again and again—not only because we need to interrogate our best ideas but because we want to experience the sensation, the sound, of words leaping just beyond our capacity to know them certainly. We live in unexpected detours of syntax, the exfoliating connotations of metaphor" (108). Prose narrative may not as readily elicit such encomiums to the unexpected, but Barthes's testament to narrative bliss matches Longenbach's praise of poetry, in the dislocations performed by unheralded, often astonishing verbal maneuvers. Of course, wonder itself begins as stupefaction coupled with admiration for something we barely understand, and ends with renewed fascination in figuring out the terms of our puzzlement. That process brings us back to reasons why slow, surface reading is so essential to our most valued literary experiences.

III. Missteps of Close Reading

While the call for close reading this past decade has led to the rise among literary critics of what they term the "new formalism," most proponents have focused attention on poetry or drama, the English Renaissance or the Romantics. At the same time, nearly every "new formalist" has been careful to distinguish him- or herself from the earlier New Critics exemplified by Cleanth Brooks's *The Well Wrought Urn* (1947), not simply because of his alleged resistance to social contexts but because of his belief in a unified text whose structure led to a self-consistent interpretation. The deconstructive efforts of Jacques Derrida and Paul de Man in the 1970s exposed that assumption as woefully inadequate to the very poems Brooks read as self-contained, in their revelations of self-contradictory valences of diction and syntax. Yet it is worth acknowledging how fully their insights were indebted to Brooks's own concentration on texts themselves, rather than historical contexts or simple paraphrases. And even the advent of New Historicism, heralded by Stephen Greenblatt's *Renaissance Self-Fashioning* (1980), succeeded in displacing deconstruction by offering close readings more engaging than ever (even if later acolytes were hardly as attentive to the verbal nuances of the texts they studied).[10]

For those focused on prose narrative, no close readings were more influential than Erich Auerbach's *Mimesis: The Representation of Reality in Western Literature* (1953). Auerbach offered a model of attention by concentrating on single passages that revealed not only entire texts but entire cultures, as if synechdochally. His opening chapter on "Odysseus' Scar" famously contrasts Homer's descriptions with the Elohist depiction of Abraham's sacrifice of Isaac, reading Homer's externalized rendition as evidence of a singular strand through all Western literature: "the syntactical connection between part and part is perfectly clear, no contour is blurred. There is also room and time for orderly, perfectly well-articulated, uniformly illuminated descriptions of implements, ministrations, and gestures" (Auerbach 3). The alternative strand is represented by the Genesis story, which:

unrolls with no episodes in a few independent sentences whose syntactical connection is of the most rudimentary sort. In this atmosphere it is unthinkable that an implement, a landscape through which the travelers passed, the serving-men, or the ass, should be described, that their origin or descent or material or appearance or usefulness should be set forth in terms of praise; they do not even admit an adjective.

Auerbach 9

And from this contrast of two passages—one physical, the other psychological—Auerbach builds an interpretation that weaves through nearly twenty major masterpieces over as many centuries, assessing their cultural moments in terms of stylistic idiosyncrasies.[11] This forms at once an inspiring *tour de force* and a tendentious reading (or readings) based on minimal evidence, often appearing to counter his initial claim for realist style by working backwards from ideological presumptions to aesthetic criteria that support his case. As Alan Dale notes in another context, this form of criticism tends tautologically to assume a synechdochal relationship between text and culture, reading the text as evidence of ideology by "eliminating aesthetics as a discipline" (173).[12] Making the text a rough-edged tool of endorsement, it obviates the need for any more fine-grained prod to further reflection.

For all Auerbach's brilliance as a reader, he ignored a principle central to close reading, exemplified in Paul de Man's recollection of Reuben Brower's Harvard HUM 6 course in the 1960s:

Students, as they began to write on the writings of others, were not to say anything that was not derived from the text they were considering. They were not to make any statements that they could not support by a specific use of language that actually occurred in the text. They were asked, in other words, to begin by reading texts closely as texts and not to move at once into the general context of human experience or history. Much more humbly or modestly, they were to start out from the bafflement that such singular turns of tone, phrase, and figure were bound to produce in readers attentive enough to notice them and honest enough not to hide their non-understanding behind the screen of received ideas that often passes, in literary instruction, for humanisitic knowledge.

de Man 23

As de Man, a graduate "section man" in that course, then added: "This very simple rule, surprisingly enough, had far-reaching didactic consequences. I have never known a course by which students were so transformed" (23). Brower perfected "reading in slow motion" (Brower 4) as a defense against the then common practice of reading for social, cultural, or biographical significance.[13] And this focused technique cultivated, as Jonathan Culler has observed:

> a respect for the stubbornness of texts, which resist easy comprehension or description in terms of expected themes and motifs. The close reader needs to be willing to take seriously the difficulties of singular, unexpected turns of phrase, juxtapositions, and opacity. Close reading teaches an interest in the strangeness or distinctiveness of individual works and parts of works. . . . In fact, the work of close reading is not primarily to resolve difficulties but above all to describe them, to elucidate their source and implications.
>
> "Closeness" 22

The simple act of description becomes immediately less than simple, since the "source and implications" of difficulties thrown up by a text hardly reveal themselves without some sort of imputation from the reader.

Making the process even more tenuous is that tensions structuring complex texts rarely resolve the difficulties they evoke, something long suspected by those unpersuaded by the New Critics' holistic vision. This premise was powerfully broached by the philosopher Isaiah Berlin, contending against those who would resolve incompatible values or who otherwise tried negotiating a happy medium. His thesis of "value pluralism" argued that no single cultural truth be regarded as absolute or dominant over others, and that therefore incommensurate ideals are always in competition. "Not all good things are compatible," he asserts, and "To admit that the fulfilment of some of our ideals may in principle make the fulfilment of others impossible is to say that the notion of total human fulfilment is a formal contradiction, a metaphysical chimera" (Berlin 213). At profound levels, no universal truth prevails, at least without severely diminishing a more general humanity. And that experience is true in local contexts, defined textually as more multifarious than any "final solution" allows. To accept Berlin's thesis (as John Gray observes) is to agree "that fundamental human values are many, that they are often in conflict and rarely, if ever, *necessarily* harmonious, and that some at least of these conflicts are among incommensurables—conflicts among values for which there is no single, common standard of measurement or arbitration" (Gray 6).[14]

The very condition of principled irresolution is inherent in our condition and the only escape from moral dilemmas lies in denying them outright.

Of course, so obtuse a response is what the category of "literature" aspires to avoid in its plot-driven resistance to resolutions of our most troubling contradictions. Even more deeply, literature embraces instability at the very level of language, of words that invariably mean more (or sometimes less) than they appear to claim. Walter Benjamin intuitively made this point in asserting that: "To write a novel means to carry the incommensurable to extremes in the representation of human life. In the midst of life's fullness, and through the representation of this fullness, the novel gives evidence of the profound perplexity of living" (87). That "perplexity" corresponds to the contradictory, irreconcilable aspect Berlin observes as part of all ethical ideals in their cultural setting. Thus readers who tend to extract workable morals from elaborate texts do so by misreading, often with little attention to passages themselves. In the effort to cope with ostensible scenes lurking behind diction and syntax, they ignore contradictory rhythms inherent in the text itself.

Yet before too readily dismissing ethical readings in favor of blissful, or wondrous, or sheer verbal responses, it is well to recall how fully complex literary texts keep turning us to nuanced appraisals of action and choice. The plastic arts (painting, photography, architecture) rarely induce such a response, certainly not with the same force or terrible detail. Instrumental music rarely poses dilemmas or solicits moral judgment, which is largely the province of philosophy or history or law, each of which engages considerations of what humans might do, or should have done. The only arts that consistently bridge the divide between human form and human choice (in the process inciting a schizophrenic response) are literary. Even works that try deliberately to avoid ethical scrutiny—Dreiser's *Sister Carrie*, say, or Beckett's *Waiting for Godot*—force us to reconsider why their fictional characters should *not* be questioned about what we persist in assuming are "their" choices. Ethics keeps blundering in, an unavoidable encounter. That is not to agree with either John Gardner or William Bennett in requiring novels to provide simple moral reassurance. After all, works that most capture our attention seem to do the opposite, arousing formal admiration even as they unsettle us with questions about our ethical categories. And it may now be worth turning to this irresistible nature of narrative, which for all its verbal allure never fails to generate moral considerations on behalf of fictional characters, textual events, imagined actions. Does close reading lead to something more than sheer pleasure or bliss, or are the quandaries enacted in narrative simply part of our aesthetic wonder, without some more constructive (or instructive) role?

IV. An Ethics of Reading

Perhaps the most severe skeptic of an ethics of reading is George Steiner, who argued nearly a half-century ago that it was a bankrupt idea, a will-o'-the-wisp for intellectuals, long before Matthew Arnold had made a case for "the best that has been thought and said." Refuting Arnold, Steiner contended that the Holocaust discredited any assumption of literature's capacity to humanize. "The simple yet appalling fact," he wrote, "is that we have very little solid evidence that literary studies do very much to enrich or stabilize moral perception, that they *humanize*. We have little proof that a tradition of literary studies in fact makes a man more humane. What is worse—a certain body of evidence points the other way" (Steiner 60–61). By which he meant the notorious example of cultivated Gestapo officers reading Rilke in concentration camps. Yet Steiner's point is more troubling than the suspicion that literature does little to cultivate true moral feeling. For him, the specter looms that literature may be actively *un*ethical and *im*moral, inuring us to outrage, easing our revulsion from horror in the phenomenal world, allowing us simply to wallow in the pleasures of a text. And unnerving as it is to take Steiner seriously, he strikes at the heart of what it is we do in teaching a novel, poem, or play. "Unlike Matthew Arnold and unlike Dr. Leavis," Steiner observes:

> I find myself unable to assert confidently that the humanities humanize. Indeed, I would go further: it is at least conceivable that the focusing of consciousness on a written text which is the substance of our training and pursuit diminishes the sharpness and readiness of our actual moral response. Because we are trained to give psychological and moral credence to the imaginary, to the character in a play or a novel, to the condition of spirit we gather from a poem, we may find it more difficult to identify with the real world, to take the world of actual experience to heart.
>
> 61

As he adds in an image at once unthinkable and eerily persuasive, "thus the cry in the poem may come to sound louder, more urgent, more real than the cry in the street outside. The death in the novel may move us more potently than the death in the next room. Thus there may be a covert, betraying link between the cultivation of aesthetic response and the potential of personal inhumanity. What then are we doing when we study and teach literature?" (Steiner 61). The question is meant to haunt us, as Steiner himself is haunted by the Holocaust and the lack of restraints felt by cultured, book-loving men and women bent on genocide.

In the end, perhaps no response to Steiner is adequate, except to acknowledge warily that art cannot innoculate against immorality. The more troubling intimation that art actively cultivates immorality—by encouraging fuller responsiveness to imagined ills than real ones, or by providing a *hortus conclusis* to which we can retreat—is less convincing. Or rather, Steiner's insinuation can just as readily be turned on its head: that literature represents not fewer possibilities but far more for a life than we might otherwise imagine. After all, normally our accounts of ourselves are flat, uninflected, straightforward (as in the casual excuses we offer, or the legal pleas we contrive, or the philosophical examples we formulate), without the resonances we expect from fiction or poetry. Someone cuts in front of us on the street, or ignores a promise, or bothers us for a favor, or fails to live up to their evaluation: in these and dozens of other daily instances, we mostly respond through dismissive narratives. And what opens us up to implications in our own and others' behavior are the nuanced or unexpected emotions, the responses explored in fiction, drama, and poetry—the possibilities, in short, that we regularly overlook or shortchange. The philosopher Bernard Williams expressed this view succinctly. "In seeking a reflective understanding of ethical life," he observed, philosophy "quite often takes examples from literature. Why not take examples from life? It is a perfectly good question, and it has a short answer: what philosophers will lay before themselves and their readers as an alternative to literature will not be life, but bad literature" (Williams 12–13). This does not deny how repugnant it is when the cry in the poem becomes "more urgent" than "the cry in the street outside." But poetic anguish does not inevitably create this response. We simply do not know what effect a refined appreciation of literature may have on conduct, for good or for ill. We cannot tell whether a thoughtful reading of Henry James's *The Golden Bowl*, say, or Edith Wharton's *The House of Mirth* will alter how a reader copes with a flawed marriage or face-losing social decline, much less the larger issues that prompt Steiner's dismay.

Which leaves those of us still interested in ethical inquiry stripped of global absolutes, or of the need to answer questions like: Do works of art foster or impair possibilities for moral behavior? Can we gain reliable knowledge on how best to live? Instead, what we are left with is a second nuance, a reduction in scale, involving immediate queries about the relative strength of different *kinds* of ethical reading. Limiting the field this way hardly simplifies the case, however, or eases discussion, if only because critics committed to ethical readings of literature begin with different notions of what such a reading might involve, which itself becomes a thermometer for measuring moral fervor. Steiner, for instance, who looks to literature for self-transformation, values novels that directly assault one's deepest assumptions. "What we must have," he says, citing Kafka, "are those books which come upon us like ill-fortune, and distress us deeply, like the death of one we love better than ourselves, like suicide. A book must be an ice-axe to break the sea frozen inside us" (Steiner 67). Michael Levenson, on the other hand, in an incisive account of modernism, argues the contrary—for disinterestedness as a moral good—and invokes the example of Conrad's Marlow and James's Strether to underscore his point. And from a third perspective, Martha Nussbaum prizes the condition of being "finely aware and richly responsible" (borrowing her phrase from James), looking to characters like Maggie Verver as a model for our lives. In short, the ethical precepts with which readers begin often dictate the novels they read, and how they then interpret them. Being transformed in the process is not really an issue.

Curiously, this is a question that few pause to contemplate: whether we are predisposed to texts that offer answers we already know and prize. And the converse question then would be whether some literature evades certain ethical considerations more readily than others. Is there something about a recondite style or a convoluted narrative structure that makes general ethical analysis more or less promising? Consider this mixed pair of questions as three major critics of American literature have, each of whom proclaims a distinct theoretical agenda. Eric Sundquist's study of "race in the making of American literature," the subtitle of his magisterial *To Wake the Nations* (1993), brings together convincing readings of African-American authors with analyses of canonical white authors, thus re-integrating the American canon. What is salutary about his approach is the response to the opening question he asks himself: "what makes a piece of literature worthy of sustained attention"? And his answer is that "the value of a work of literature— what defines it as literature, for that matter—derives from its contribution to articulating and sustaining the values of a given culture, whether or not that culture is national or 'racial' in scope. Justice and value therefore must be recognized to be aesthetic as well as philosophical terms" (Sundquist 18). Or as he goes on to contend, "The power of these works ...must be measured...within the new conception of American culture that they are able to bring forth" (Sundquist 19). The readings that follow are performed in these terms, engaging texts in a refreshingly thick historical context so as to define a cultural dialogue over our most central dilemma: race.

Yet nothing could be further from Sundquist's double imperative of justice and cultural value (they "must be recognized"; they "must be measured") than Elaine Scarry's approach. Her claim in fact is that Sundquist's social concerns have summarily trumped aesthetics in recent readings: "The banishing of beauty from the humanities in the last two decades has been carried out by a set of political complaints against it" (Scarry 57). And the burden of her argument in *On Beauty and Being Just* (1999) is to demonstrate "that beauty really is allied with truth. This is not to say that what is beautiful is also true [but that beauty] ignites the desire for truth by giving us ... the experience of conviction and the experience, as well, of error" (Scarry 52). Like Sundquist, who resurrects an older form of literary historicism, Scarry reverts to an earlier aesthetic philosophy (with Schiller as her model) to describe "the radical decentering we undergo in the presence of the beautiful" (112). And though beauty may be hard to define, it ever consists in local details, specific touches, particular nuances: "Beauty always takes place in the particular, and if there are no particulars, the chances of seeing it go down" (Scarry 18). More to the point, beauty leads ineluctably to truth: "beautiful things give rise to the notion of distribution, to a lifesaving reciprocity, to fairness" as symmetry, which in turn enables the possibility of justice and cultural value (Scarry 95). It is as if Scarry had inverted Sundquist, who founded his aesthetic not on beauty abstractly considered, but on a text's articulation of "justice and value."

Martha Nussbaum is less enthralled by beauty than by "truth"—though she is just as attuned to specific criteria in her aesthetic premises, selecting novels only if "written in a style that gives sufficient attention to particularity and emotion, and so long as they involve their readers in relevant activities of searching and feeling" (*Love's Knowledge* 46). For Nussbaum, the central concern with "how should a human being live" focuses her canonical list of novels, each of which addresses "the ethical and social questions that give literature its high importance in our lives" (*Love's Knowledge* 168). This sounds perhaps more like Sundquist than Scarry, though Nussbaum argues in *Love's Knowledge* (1990) and *Poetic*

Justice (1995) for a distinctly trans-cultural knowledge, gained from novels that test characters in order to give readers the experience "of ethical reasoning that is context-specific without being relativistic" (*Poetic Justice* 8). Aesthetics becomes an issue not of formal features but of imagined consciousness, of developing a sensitivity to fine discriminations and subtle emotions.

For all their divergences, what unites these critics is dismay at directions criticism has taken, coupled with a renewed interest in defending literature's importance by redirecting readers toward specific agendas: in Sundquist's case, of the informing "values of a given culture"; in Scarry's, of the possibility of beauty universally considered; and in Nussbaum's, of Aristotelian notions of how best to live. Individually considered, the agendas are plausible, even laudable, though brief reflection gives pause at the differences among them. Those differences reveal how fully the approach each takes dictates the novels each reads, in a tautology that binds together prescribed goals and textual revelations. Readers have always pressed special agendas for reading, long before Arnold sounded the call. Yet the figure who interestingly stands apart in this is Henry James, who occasionally paused to summarize his ideas about what literature should be. Early on, he joined those with agendas in embracing an ethical bias to reading: "Every out-and-out realist ... is a moralist," he wrote in 1876. "They sow the seeds of virtue ... Excellence in this matter consists in the tale and the moral hanging well together, and this they are certainly more likely to do when there has been a definite intention—that intention of which artists who cultivate 'art for art' are usually so extremely mistrustful" (James, *LC* 169–70). Yet with time, James grew to doubt this early moral enthusiasm—indeed, to hesitate before any functionalist reading of literature—and to become less precise about what the novel should do.

What finally settled his thinking was Walter Besant's lecture on "The Art of Fiction" (1884), which prompted James to articulate a position that abjures agendas altogether. "The only reason for the existence of a novel," he wrote, "is that it does attempt to represent life. When it relinquishes this attempt ... it will have arrived at a very strange pass" (James, *LC* 46). The freedom of view and technique that James goes on to allow the novel is due to its allegedly deep connection with "life," which never follows fixed rules. To be sure, James sympathized with Besant (and by extension with more recent critics who enforce aesthetic rules), even as he declared the enterprise futile:

As I shall take the liberty of making but a single criticism of Mr. Besant, whose tone is so full of the love of his art, I may as well have done with it at once. He seems to me to mistake in attempting to say so definitely beforehand what sort of an affair the good novel will be. To indicate the danger of such an error as that has been the purpose of these few pages; to suggest that certain traditions on the subject, applied *a priori*, have already had much to answer for, and that the good health of an art which undertakes so immediately to reproduce life must demand that it be perfectly free. It lives upon exercise, and the very meaning of exercise is freedom. The only obligation to which in advance we may hold a novel, without incurring the accusation of being arbitrary, is that it be interesting. That general responsibility rests upon it, but it is the only one I can think of.

James, *LC* 49

James, in other words, agrees with much Besant recommends, but not as fixed dogma or exclusionary law:

For the value of these different injunctions—so beautiful and so vague—is wholly in the meaning one attaches to them. The characters, the situation, which strike one as real will be those that touch and interest one most, but the measure of reality is very difficult to fix. The reality of Don Quixote or of Mr. Micawber is a very delicate shade.

James, *LC* 51

In short, claims for morality, or culture, or beauty all become either so expansive as to seem either feeble and indeterminate, or so restrictive as to seem simply inadequate and misinformed. "May not people differ infinitely," James inquired, "as to what constitutes life—what constitutes representation?" For after all, "nothing will ever take the place of the good old fashion of 'liking' a work of art or not liking it: the most improved criticism will not abolish that primitive, that ultimate test" (James, *LC* 57).

Since those firm words, more than a century of contentious tilting back and forth has ensued, between those who would establish restrictions on literature and those simply willing to let it roam free. D. H. Lawrence made vitalist claims for the novel as "the book of life" (105) while Nabokov cantankerously argued that "literature consists ... not of general ideas but of particular revelations, not of schools of thought but of individuals of genius. Literature is not about something:

it is the thing itself, the quiddity" (*Lectures* 116). E. M. Forster, who argued for all sorts of specious rules in *Aspects of the Novel* (1927), finally seems to side with Nabokov in regretting that a novel should even tell a story: "That is the highest factor common to all novels, and I wish that it was not so, that it could be something different—melody, or perception of the truth, not this low atavistic form" (26). In general, the division falls between those eager for literature to beguile and those who think it should educate—with both sides fierce in denouncing the other (the Foreword and Afterword of Nabokov's *Lolita* stand as caricatures of this standoff). As William Gass observes, taking even Nabokov to an extreme: "when a character of mine looks out through a window, or occasionally peeks in through one, it is the word 'window' he is really looking through; it's the word pane that preoccupies; it's the idea of 'glass'" (*Finding* 33). So postmodern a stress on textuality may be one reason for finding interest in a novel or poem, though hardly a reason that will satisfy every reader.

In fact, this view of literary delight that reaches no further than lyrical tones in the ear has had a generally beleaguered experience. And in an increasingly politicized environment, it seems a view less and less worth defending. Gass's brother-in-arms, Roland Barthes, once complained about the cultural resistance to his own exclusively aesthetic agenda: "No sooner has a word been said, somewhere, about the pleasure of the text, than two policemen are ready to jump on you: the political policeman and the psychoanalytic policeman: futility and/or guilt, pleasure is either idle or vain, a class notion or an illusion." As he elaborated, disconsolately, "pleasure is continually disappointed, reduced, deflated, in favor of strong, noble values: Truth, Death, Progress, Struggle, Joy, etc." (Barthes, *Pleasure* 57). One might demur that Barthes's pleasure could easily be another's tedium, but from his perspective, Sundquist's "justice" and "value," or Nussbaum's "ethical reasoning," or even Scarry's "beauty" and "truth" seem overblown abstractions, akin to police words. Literature as a category has been converted into "cultural work," a phrase intended to justify fiction's role in a bourgeois realm where play is presumed to be mere self-indulgence.

The point is not to side for or against such readings so much as to recognize that we read for many different kinds of reasons, sometimes ethically, sometimes aesthetically, sometimes simply for escape. As Wai-Chee Dimock observes, "the literary text ... is not a perfectly working unit, not a feat of engineering, but something less efficient, less goal oriented, less instrumentally assignable, and because of that perhaps also less exhausted by its rational purpose, its strategic end"

(169). Which is to say that persuasive readers tell controvertible stories even about truths they discover in the novels and poems they study. Literature *as* literature perpetually defies resolution, making any firm decision about our criteria insecure.

A better way to understand the reasons for that uncertainty is to think more carefully about what reading actually requires in transforming words into characters, sentences into scenes, paragraphs into events. Consider two very different kinds of texts, James's *The Ambassadors* (1903) and Maurice Sendak's *Where the Wild Things Are* (1963), each of which engages us on both aesthetic and ethical levels. Still, it's not at all clear that Sendak, whose book consists of a mere twenty-one lucid sentences ("so he was sent to bed without eating anything") is any more transparent ethically than James. As much to the point, Chad Newsome's abandonment of Mme. de Vionnet and Max's rejection of his mother are, when stripped to bare essentials, strikingly similar actions. Yet if each author represents these scenes of abandonment differently, neither one reduces that action to something "merely wrong," however large ethical considerations loom in each. We respond to these characters with varying degrees of approbation or disapproval, as we do in what James called "life." We mull over fictional decisions and actions, we scrutinize invented intentions and fanciful consequences, once again as we do in life.

The difference is that literature, unlike life, is already so thoroughly *textualized* that two things occur: first, decisions and actions are mitigated by the forms in which they are represented, making them less straightforward, thus open to contested interpretations. And second, those verbal forms themselves begin to dazzle the eye more fully than the worlds they supposedly represent. In short, the more complex a story (the less flat it is as sheer account), the more our attention shifts from what used to be called "story" to "discourse," from signified to signifier—or from Joe Friday's "Just the facts, ma'am" to the text's elaborate imagery and characterization, to its narrative plotting and descriptive power: to Max in the book's illustrations, not Max the admonishment of bad character. It is hardly the case that we forget moral rules, but rather that we become lost in wonder at the artistry involved in making words (and images) move so brilliantly. After all, only a moral simpleton or the most tone-deaf reader would want to ban, say, Humbert Humbert from literature simply because his reprehensible activities are appropriately banned in life.

In fact, Humbert's plangent voice (like so many other memorable characters in fiction) induces emotional extremes independent of the scenes it describes, reminding us of what literature demands at both its ethical *and* aesthetic poles. One might even claim that awe before the words of a text—the attention we pay to the written forms in which characters emerge—constitutes the single ethical position all art requires.[15] Elaine Scarry argues this point (with due deference to Steiner): that attentiveness *is* translatable to the real world and our actions in it. We are more likely to notice and become suitably engaged because we are schooled in noticing. Careful reading becomes a good in itself, in the attention spent on recalcitrant details, the lingering over verbal nuance, the inventing of generous but scrupulous readings, all on behalf of treating texts as individuals with their own distinctive requirements. From this point of view, a reader's negligence of words on the page registers an ethical flaw, just as much as any flat-footed projections onto the text. A narrow interpretation of the ethics of reading, in other words, would be simply to become as sympathetic a reader of texts as we are of each other, responsive to idiosyncrasies, resistant to imposing our views, flexible in the face of contradiction, and so on.

V. *Problems of Paraphrase*

To value how things hold together in complex forms is to come closer to understanding the convergence of aesthetics and ethics. Yet at the same time, it alerts us to the problems involved in any interpretation, in transforming a particular constellation of words and events into a formulation that makes sense of our experience of reading narrative indirections and verbal peculiarities. That is the ever-present burden of paraphrase, restating in different words what is at stake in a narrative. For only by offering an account, giving a synopsis, can we understand what it is we've experienced. By that token, one might claim that all thought is paraphrase, converting a concept into words, an event into a memory, even people we meet into our impressions of those people. At more extreme levels, racism or sexism or homophobia are also forms of paraphrase, in that stereotypes always convert unique encounters into something familiar and already understood. But this only dramatizes what happens in less volatile situations, whether historians give a version of past events or anthropologists explain strange peoples, or scientists demonstrate a theory—each offering an explanation by selecting and excluding, reducing a whole and erasing the noise in order to clarify essential meanings.

Cleanth Brooks notoriously challenged "the heresy of paraphrase" precisely because he thought it unnecessarily reduced poetry to a supposed "message," forcing the critic "to judge the poem by its political or scientific or philosophical truth," despite "the resistance which any good poem sets up against all attempts to paraphrase it" (180). Paraphrase becomes simply the "lowest common denominator" (Brooks 184) of a poem, whose power rests like other temporal arts (ballet, music) on "a pattern of resolutions and balances and harmonizations, developed through a temporal scheme" (Brooks 186). For Brooks, poetry defies efforts to reduce it to a plain message since its "apparent irrelevancies [of] metrical pattern and metaphor" (191) alter any discursive statement it might otherwise seem to make. Of course, it is worth noting that Brooks's theoretical argument comes as the concluding chapter of a series of persuasive practical essays each of which offers an interpretation of poems he admires. In short, Brooks quarrels with paraphrase only in its simple-minded practice, since his own restatements of what poems do in their complex structures form themselves a version of very persuasive paraphrase.

More recently, Lionel Gossman has questioned a different aspect of paraphrase, in assessing how to teach eighteenth-century literature, far removed from the social and literary conventions that produced it. This complicates Brooks's effort, since history itself (with all the changes introduced in interpretive understanding) further erodes the possibility of any adequate paraphrase. Contextualizing poems or plays may make them more accessible to us today but also tends to domesticate them, undercutting their peculiar power. As Gossman poses the question: "Is my aim (or should it be) to defamiliarize texts and try to restore their potentially challenging and disturbing otherness, to make them as hard as possible, maybe even impossible, to 'understand,' or is it to appropriate them to my own and my students' time by discovering 'meaning' in them (and how can meaning not be modern meaning?) and so ensuring their continued 'relevance'?" (61). The very exhilaration once elicited by a work of literature seems at odds with the rational interpretive process of placing it historically: "I have to admit that I occasionally wonder what our critical and interpretative activities have to do with the extraordinary, exhilarating, overwhelming experience that reading a work of literature sometimes *can* be" (Gossman 78).

Yet Gossman is finally committed, albeit circumspectly, to a model of cultural transmission that hazards the loss of a certain ecstatic energy in favor of mutual understanding. The alternative, as he acknowledges, is that "the literature of the past may well be saved from appropriation by the present, but it is also placed beyond common discourse and public function" (Gossman 74). Herein he admits, more straightforwardly than Brooks, that the paradox of paraphrase cannot be resolved. And the historian Martin Jay agrees, in offering (only, but at least) "two cheers for paraphrase," which he concedes as well forms a strategy of domestication. Synopsis for Jay functions much the same as Foucault's view of the totalizing panoptic gaze in Jeremy Bentham's model prison, and that recognition makes him want the text to speak for itself—in his case, texts of intellectual history. Such radical restraint is only a theoretical hope, however, since he also realizes that "*any* reception must inevitably entail a certain amount of domestication and familiarization on the part of his readers" (Jay 61). There always exists a tension between the ideal of "perfect communicability" (Jay 60) on the one hand and, on the other, the unique revelation a text proffers. Paraphrase is thus never enough, as Jay believes, but like Gossman he is committed to a mode of "communicative rationality." As he concludes, "In the past few years, we have become increasingly sensitive to the ways in which language erodes meaning, disperses intentionality, and frustrates understanding. It is perhaps time to be equally open to those aspects of it that preserve hope for a very different kind of human solidarity" (Jay 63).

If paraphrase is always problematic in its inherently subjective, necessarily slanted distillation of content out of form, Gossman and Jay nonetheless resist retreating from the larger social prospect of mutual exchange and discursive communication. It *is* possible to convey to another something of an opera, or a poem, or a painting in terms less elaborate than the complete work. As well, the "complete work" is never the same in its supposed completeness for each of us, or even for any one of us at different moments in time. We paraphrase experiences even to ourselves, attending to some details, ignoring others, in the process of making meaning out of chaotic experience. Still, Robert Frost's misattributed claim that "poetry is what gets lost in translation" is an apt reminder that synopsis is always rough and troubled. Whenever we translate (or paraphrase), we want to explicate our immediate felt version of the artistic experience in an activity that is eminently sociable and culturally enriching.

Yet keep in mind that the strangeness of a work of art and the commensurate wonder it inspires flow from its unique weave of materials that cannot be translated into another form. Great art, as Gossman argues, has an uncanniness that makes it unlike anything else we know, offering us a sense of personal transformation. Paraphrasing that into understandable terms can only unduly reduce and unfairly domesticate the very strangeness that moved us in the first place. How can we explain a text without stripping its alien power away, altering it to conform to our interests, our perspectives, our values—the very values brought into question by the work itself? To make Shakespeare "our contemporary" is to risk ignoring his plays' power, converting them into conventional categories rather than allowing those categories to be unsettled. Of course, the alternative is to risk mystification, inexpressibility, even silence itself, leaving the strange to remain simply strange. The question finally is not whether or not we paraphrase—as intelligent social beings we do so willy-nilly, all the time—but rather how well we accomplish the task, ever aware of how removed we are from the original experience untranslated, thus ever unable to achieve a final truth of the matter. And that is another way in which reading aesthetically and reading ethically become the same, since paying attention to formal details becomes inseparable from maintaining a certain deliberate tentativeness in our interpretations.

VI. Getting It Wrong

The problem of paraphrase is the problem of interpretation, which is always inherently flawed, irreducible to settled rules or predictable methods. Any presumption that one can achieve a final say interpretatively is misconceived, though that limitation should hardly forestall us. As Hilary Putnam argues (borrowing a phrase from John Austin): "Still, *enough is enough, enough isn't everything.* We *have* practices of interpretation. Those practices may be context-sensitive and interest-relative, but there is, given enough context—given, as Wittgenstein says, the language in place—such a thing as *getting it right* or *getting it wrong.* There may be some indeterminacy of translation, but it isn't a case of 'anything goes'" (231). Putnam's warning against a vain "craving for absolutes" (239), his encouragement to recognize acceptable limits to interpretation, is salutary, giving us pause in the very basic terms he introduces: of "*getting it right* or *getting it wrong.*" For even to think of interpretation that way already weights the challenge ethically.

Nathan Zuckerman contemplates this in Philip Roth's *American Pastoral* (1997) when he tries to imagine the inconceivable life of his high school hero, Swede Levov. For even as he begins, Zuckerman regrets how little can actually be known, given our conventional biases and expectations:

[It's] an astonishing farce of misperception. And yet what are we to do about this terribly significant business of *other people*, . . . so ill-equipped are we all to envision one another's interior workings and invisible aims? Is everyone to go off and lock the door and sit secluded like the lonely writers do, in a soundproof cell, summoning people out of words and then proposing that these word people are closer to the real thing than the real people that we mangle with our ignorance every day?

Roth 35

The answer, of course, is no, that "getting people wrong" is key to any redemptively humane effort. Or as Zuckerman concludes, "That's how we know we're alive: we're wrong" (Roth 35). What's intriguing about this moment is its refraction against itself in the counter-example of characters invented by lonely writers in soundproof cells, characters supposedly less real than the speaker himself. The heightening of a "reality effect" begins here, in Zuckerman's suggestion that he and the Swede are more "real" than fictional characters because they share inscrutable personalities. But of course, both he and the Swede are themselves fictional, and any distinction between misinterpreting actual people and doing the same with fictional characters slowly disintegrates.

"Getting people wrong," in short, is what happens in both fiction and in life, though only as we develop a willingness to entertain our own fallibility do the implications of *mis*interpretation become clear as at once an ethically informed and aesthetically challenging ideal. Zuckerman's insight seems to be that getting people "right" once and for all is less a path toward true understanding than a mere reinforcement of conventional expectations, closing the box, confirming us in prior assumptions about each other and about art. Admitting to "getting them wrong," by contrast, suggests an imaginative capaciousness about others (lying beyond our fixed assessments, ready to surprise us) as well as an awareness of the intractable nature of art (which delights in its crafted defiance of the predictable). The dilatory, digressive, wandering tone of narrative itself suggests that error and serendipitous insight trump *a priori* claims every time.

Consider one of the canonical texts of the Western tradition: Ariosto's *Orlando Furioso*, which takes error as its central conceit, not only in the knights' false wanderings but in the deviant narrative that defies all expectations. As Patricia Parker observes of the poem in tones strangely akin to Zuckerman's (and in the process, characterizing the genre of romance), "the suggestion seems to be that fiction by its very nature feeds upon frustration, that the real interest begins only when things go wrong" (33). Ariosto's successor, Spenser, was likewise obsessed by such misperception, prompting Maureen Quilligan to assert that the entire plot of *The Faerie Queen* "unfolds as Spenser's investigation into the meaning of one particular word: error" (33). In fact, the birth of actual error in Spenser's poem (as Jeff Dolven asserts) occurs with the idea that the serpent Error *could* be killed, and that this allegorical treatment of error points to the failure of allegory itself in a poem so unflinchingly structured *as* an allegory. Or consider the centrality of *felix culpa* in Milton's *Paradise Lost*, whose Book 4 famously invokes its poetic predecessors, where "mazy error led." The power of "getting it wrong" has a long literary pedigree, largely because these classic texts—romance, allegory, epic—were conceived within religious culture in which a single sacred truth held sway. Error was our earthly condition (ethically, aesthetically) since we still saw in Pauline terms "as through a glass darkly," not yet "face to face." The only remedy was the revelation represented by heaven, at least until a secularization of cultural norms diminished its prominence as both social idea and literary topos.

Yet the prominence of error, for readers as for characters, made a striking reappearance in the modernist period, anticipated most self-consciously by Henry James in novels that question their own interpretive matrices—presenting not only characters who dramatically and persistently misread each other, but narrators who abjure responsibility for their own narrative roles. Consider *Portrait of a Lady*, whose tragedy lies in Isabel Archer as a figure largely misjudged by others, who in turn misreads them. To have her be any different, more adept at "getting it right," would be to have someone other than Isabel—less independent, less naive, less filled with the brash exuberance that makes her worthy of our attention in the first place. Her misinterpretations, moreover, match everyone else's in this novel of failed marriages, and is given best expression by Ralph Touchett, explaining Henrietta Stackpole's unlikely affair with Mr. Bantling: "There's no more usual basis of union than a mutual misunderstanding" (James, *Portrait* 198). The narrator shares in this interpretive dynamic, regularly admitting ignorance of matters normally taken to be his fictive responsibility. The process becomes more enlivening in later novels, beginning with *The Ambassadors*, where Strether misreads Paris at every turn with a responsiveness that elicits only further misreadings, exciting at the same time a more nuanced, more sympathetic comprehension. His "too interpretative innocence" (James, *Ambassadors* 472) of Chad's affair with Mme. de Vionnet may not be matched by us, but our reading *is* akin to Strether's because he continues to surprise *us* throughout. Misconceptions—ours, Strether's—are imposed, then withdrawn only to have others imposed instead. The Jamesian aesthetic of narrative indirection intertwines with an ethic of withheld judgment, of listening projectively yet tentatively in a stance that always remains unstable.

This emphasis on the subjective isolation in which we exist, constrained by our subjectivity—"ill-equipped," as Zuckerman says, "to envision one another's interior workings and invisible aims"—increases in James's other late novels, which offer a kaleidoscopic view of relations among characters who fumble at knowing each other, losing even a sense of their own motives and impulses. *The Wings of the Dove* opens with Kate Croy's irritation at her father's delay, and when he "at last appeared she became, as usual, instantly aware of the futility of any effort to hold him to anything" (James 57). The scene anticipates the rest of the novel, of Kate's resilient suspension of interpretive judgment with Aunt Maud, Lord Mark, and Milly Theale, as well as her willingness to allow herself to be misread by others. Later, *The Golden Bowl* presents us with everyone's view of everyone else, though Maggie Verver's triumph rests on her faculty for suspending just that view. Imagining others' relations with her in terms both vertiginously elliptical and highly metaphorical, she allows interpretive possibilities to cascade counter-intuitively in sequences that become for her (and us) that much more fully revelatory.

James's attraction to the interpretive possibilities of "getting it wrong," both thematically and narratively, confirms a growing skepticism about any effort to register "another's interior workings and invisible aims." Contrary to classical texts where true revelation is proffered as the desirable end, James's late novels testify to the partial, self-interested cast of all but our most banal perceptions. That may not preclude our "getting people right," but it does clarify how fully his fiction shifted interest from accuracy of judgment to a more complex array of imaginative possibilities—possibilities for aesthetic elaboration as well as ethical mishandling. In fact, the most salient ethical aspect to "getting it wrong" is as the actual *point* of reading, generating an irritating awareness that the fictional world is in part invisible to the reading eye, escaping our interpretive conceptions, existing independently, consisting of characters as capable of transforming us as we do them. What emerges from this perspective is an appreciation of narrative as consisting not just of irreconcilable readings, but as outside of reading itself. This is typified in the alleged "round" vs. "flat" (78) constitution (in

E. M. Forster's notorious contrast) that we grant to our most vivid characters—characters who, perhaps especially in modernist texts, deliberately escape our assessments. Roth's Swede Levov represents only a more recent instance in an Americanist line extending back well beyond Isabel Archer: each a character effectively evading narratives that take from them their reason for being. That such figures loom larger than their representations—that they define themselves outside their verbal structures, resist being conflated with texts—forms both an aesthetic *and* an ethical injunction, whose power can be measured by the contrast with those one-sided readings available in formulaic narratives and generic accounts.

In late James "getting it wrong" often leads to contested readings; indeed, so contested that simply trying to adjudicate between those who have praised or condemned his style, or those who have celebrated or demonized characters (Kate Croy, Maggie Verver, Charlotte Stant all leap to mind), has become a large critical enterprise. Contested readings like these perfectly embody James's vision of character as capacious, never quite reducible to a single interpretive grid, even if our different ways of "getting it wrong" themselves do not doom the novels to a simple relativism. It is hardly irrelevant that James once claimed "the reader does quite half the labour," and that the failure of characters in his novels adequately to read each other is regularly reflected in the reader's own repeated failures, on repeated readings.[16]

The reason so much modernist literature takes error as its ethical and aesthetic crux may have to do with the self-reflexiveness imbedded in modernism, ever alerting the reader to his own activity. Of course, error has had a strong pedigree in narrative from the beginning, as a birthright we have never quite escaped. But what the past century has taught is the virtue of getting it wrong, not right, in the process helping us learn: first, to appreciate narrative forms that make us labor more intensely than our pleasure initially accepts; and second, to value the half-knowledge that keeps us ever in uncertainty about others even as we know we must create narratives of them, in life and in novels. That creation, in its flexible responsiveness, becomes an ethical act. The alternative is summed up by that expert aesthete, Humbert Humbert, who peremptorily states—in a judgment directly at odds with Nathan Zuckerman—that:

> we expect our friends to follow this or that logical and conventional pattern we have fixed for them. Thus X will never compose the immortal music that would clash with the second-rate symphonies

he has accustomed us to. Y will never commit murder. Under no circumstances can Z ever betray us. We have it all arranged in our minds, and the less often we see a particular person the more satisfying it is to check how obediently he conforms to our notion of him every time he hear of him. Any deviation in the fates we have ordained would strike us as not only anomalous but unethical. We would prefer not to have known at all our neighbor, the retired hot-dog stand operator, if it turns out he has just produced the greatest book of poetry his age has seen.

Lolita 265

In fact, Humbert is ironically wrong here in his preening aplomb (forming another sign of his ethical deficiency), and the more alert of his modernist fictional colleagues testify to that misjudgment. What they understand is that the most intriguing of our valued narratives (*Lolita* very much included) deliberately mislead and misdirect, compelling us into productive, readerly errors that take us out of ourselves, defying our narrow prescriptions, showing us once again how wrong we can be.

VII. Clash of Values

What has been taken as the salient failure of paraphrase, in other words—its inability to capture the experience that prompts its interpretive energies—might rather be seen as a more cautionary aid, slowing us down in our translation of complicated images into more conventional categories. To the extent that enduring literature defies those categories more than we readily imagine, its test lies in the capacity to get us to accede at least momentarily, if only imaginatively, to reversals in our ways of thinking. Necessary as paraphrase is to interpretation, then, part of what literary achievement means is resistance to such co-optation, to such absorption by the reader, whether into simply reductive forms or into another domain altogether, of philosophy, say, or history, or politics. Great art achieves its status by compelling our attention, even inspiring us with admiration for characters, scenes, motives, and achievements that in more normal waking moments we would never countenance. As Wendy Steiner remarks: "What art *can* do, and do very well, is show us the relation between what we respond to and what we are, between our pleasure and our principles. As a result, it inevitably relates us to other people whose pleasures and principles either do or do not coincide with our own" (59). This is one important aspect of reading as an ethical activity: to compel us to slow down, to pay attention, to foster an attitude of respect, at least, for people, places, things, attitudes, emotions, actions off the radar screen of our daily lives.

To return to Isaiah Berlin, this is why literature does have ethical value, if only because our values do clash, with no overarching ideal aligning them or redeeming one at the cost of another. Becoming more vividly aware of choices among contested values, between irreconcilable goals, makes us appreciate how any choice may well involve irreparable loss. All we can do, Berlin observed, is to "engage in what are called trade-offs—rules, values, principles must yield to each other in varying degrees in specific situations" (17). And they must yield not to the abstract and general, but to the specific and local. Or as he cogently states, "The concrete situation is almost everything. There is no escape: we must decide as we decide; moral risk cannot, at times, be avoided" (Berlin 18). In short, a comprehensive harmony exists no more in ethical contexts than in literary ones, with no common standard of measurement allowing us to adjudicate a *summum bonum*. Human life (as John Gray notes) "is something invented, and perpetually reinvented, through choice, and it is plural and diverse, not common or universal" (23). This is a far cry from Kant's conception of a categorical imperative, which defines a single moral standard to be applied in all situations. In fact, no such standard *could* apply, any more than Esperanto could displace our different languages, and that is as we would have it. "We determine our fate in the end," Jeff Stout observes, "not . . . by finding the right general principle of acceptability, but by drawing the line here or there in countless particular cases, given our sense of the daily detail" (242).

This focus on the local and particular informs a strong strand of recent moral philosophy, which rejects those who would reduce ethics to blanket virtues and in the process refutes those who would erode competing notions of what constitutes human well-being. As Bernard Williams pointed out, in a comment that extends well beyond philosophy: "Theory looks characteristically for considerations that are very general and have as little distinctive content as possible, because it is trying to systematize and because it wants to represent as many reasons as possible as applications of other reasons" (116). He goes on to argue, however, that the opposing need to make one's rules seem feasible requires examples, examples that are necessarily realistic, and the more detail one adds to make such realism convincing, the more the example *as* example tends to dissolve. This tug-of-war between theory and practice never ends, of course, though to credit too fully their irreconcilability is to be reduced to all-embracing moral platitude on the one hand or to the incoherence of vivid detail on the other.

The point of this excursion is to show that at least some moral philosophers themselves are hesitant before the sweeping ethical claims made by literary critics. My earlier description of the "ethical" readings offered by Levenson, Nussbaum, and Steiner suggests that even better critics fall into a trap of offering up normative views of idiosyncratic episodes. And it would be easy to cite other examples on both sides of the aisle, not only of those committed to salutary readings of literature but of those indignant at the thought, unwilling to have their pleasures marred by any moral considerations at all. Of course, an exclusive devotion to reading as mere unadulterated bliss can quickly come to seem as partial and misguided as readings bound by ethical or other agendas. For though there is much to agree with in Stanley Fish's description of the delight he takes in Milton's mighty line, it seems odd to hear someone talk so narrowly about exclusive aesthetic pleasure in the case of one of the more morally rigorous of our canonical writers. It is as if Fish deliberately held back from the obvious pressures Milton applies, a Milton he himself had read early in his career as willing to surprise the reader into sin. This is, if not a barren, at least a bad-faith gesture, resulting from the kind of absolutism expressed earlier by George Steiner: that since great literature did not prevent the Holocaust, it cannot reliably frame ethical sensitivity. Katha Pollit has rightly chided this kind of reductive thinking: "Books do not shape character in any simple way, if indeed they do so at all, or the most literate would be the most virtuous instead of just the ordinary run of humanity with larger vocabularies" (210). In short, it is a mistake to argue that literary sophistication is at one with propriety, or to ask of literature that it take a larger role in forging character than we grant to other cultural forces. Especially given the complicated tensions shaping each of us, it is hard to know what counts as ethical suasion in a poem or a novel, or what the connection between a text and our given behavior might be. This extends from sermons to self-help manuals, from parental injunctions to national narratives, from laundry lists to lectures.

In this regard, Martha Nussbaum most flagrantly continues a practice she admittedly borrows from F. R. Leavis in his broad claims for literature's ethical role, as well as his willingness regularly to paraphrase complex formulations into simple plot summaries.[17] Though she gestures to a tenet of close reading in repeatedly declaring that "any style makes, itself, a statement about what is important" (Nussbaum, *Love's Knowledge* 7), in fact her readings of James's late novels rarely inquire into verbal features, instead offering occasional quotes simply as philosophical set-pieces. Holding up scenes as transparent, she views them tendentiously *through* his occluded prose rather than *in* it, as if free from the figurative indeterminacies that register its subject kaleidoscopically, refracting understanding in multiple forms. As Geoffrey Galt Harpham dryly observes: "In Nussbaum, the specificity of literature as a discourse, an object of professional study, is almost altogether erased and replaced by a conception that treats it bluntly as moral philosophy" (59).[18] And Harpham further shows that moral philosophy itself is severely weakened by her willingness to identify so fully with characters essentially extracted from their textual environment, from the stylistic constraints that create and produce them. By that accounting, a character from Pynchon's postmodern California is little different from one in Faulkner's baroque Yoknapatawpha County or in Raymond Carver's stripped-down Northwest—each plucked from his or her own stylistic constructedness to be reimagined by the critic in her own mental formulation as an off-the-rack, perfectly-identifiable, generic human being.

That indifference to style rightly troubles the "new formalists" as a form of deep and desperate misreading, but something like the converse can be even more unsettling: an attention to style that simply dismisses it as ever particularly suasive, revealing, or otherwise singular. According to David Smit, James's late style has no effect, differing only marginally from other authors, registering transformations of neither perspective nor understanding. A "reading of style for its own plot" (in Garrett Stewart's expression) is simply a non-starter. In fact, Smit assumes that style itself is all but tautological, best conceived "not as a set of formal features in a text, but as the result of a reader-critic's perception of the text, as those features in a text that provide the evidence for the critic's attitude or argument" (4–5). For him, stylistic analysis is invariably based not on close- or open-minded examination of verbal features but on an imposed interpretive grid dictating features that subsequently warrant our interest—a practice like Auerbach's, but according to Smit true not just of those with large theoretical ambitions but of anyone who makes an effort at interpretive judgment based on supposedly singular dispositions of words, syntax, or grammar.[19] Even a stylist as distinctive as James, however idiosyncratic in his late fiction, is not creating a specific or particularly evocative strain: "he may use longer and more complicated sentences than other writers, but it does not follow that when we read James's prose 'our minds are made to move' in a qualitatively different way from the way we read any prose" (Smit 34).

For Smit, "James's style is what we make of it, what we notice for reasons of our own, what we use to document our critical judgments. James's style is a function of our own interests and our own critical procedures" (51). And in a conclusion that corresponds to arguments by Stanley Fish and Barbara Herrnstein Smith, "there is no necessary correlation between a given stylistic feature and what it is supposed to imitate" (Smit 81).

That assertion may or may not be true, given how hard it is to prove a negative. And in the case of James, each of whose novels differ demonstrably in style, one from another—as if deliberately evoking psychological states through singular and conducive verbal choices— the question that remains involves the interpretive reasons for such differences, for stylistic gestures so appropriate to distinctive thematic strains. But more generally, it is clear that James shares little with, say, Dreiser or Twain or Howells. Like the characteristic modes adopted by Impressionist painters in contrast to French Academy practitioners (Monet, say, versus Bouguereau), or musical styles contrasting classical symphonies with jazz improvisations (Stravinsky, say, versus Ellington), the contrast between James's stylistic preferences and those of his notable contemporaries produce very different effects entirely independent of our chosen "critical procedures." And the effects they have necessarily help construct the meanings we inhabit, in another instance of style producing plot.

VIII. Late Modernism

This book is an effort to avoid these somewhat paradoxically-linked twin poles: on the one hand, touting a distinctive style only to quickly bypass its formal features in favor of a fixed interpretive grid; on the other, rejecting the notion of distinctive styles altogether, failing to see them *as* a productive interpretive tool. The premise I begin with, already obvious in the preceding, is that distinctive styles matter deeply, generating the meaning of texts. And part of the obviously arbitrary quality of the following selection is intended to prove how fully various styles produce divergent narratives. My intention is clearly not to identify a single theme or motif threading through modernist American novels, which might lead one to presume nothing connects so disparate a series of chapters. On the contrary, the very distinctiveness of texts in the following chapters is meant to reveal how authors command their styles differently, altering plots and in the process defying shared

patterns. Effectively, this book defies thematically-oriented studies that
see persistent strains of identity, or event, or cultural ideal, or even
narrative proclivities beneath the different tones and sounds of the
prose that produces them. The examples are all exclusively American,
drawn from the past century, though the iconoclasm of this selection of
texts has more to do with an American legacy extending from a century
earlier than from any shared modernist or late modernist agenda.[20] That
legacy has been vibrantly compounded, with each of the following
novels distinguished by a calculated, even flamboyantly idiosyncratic
verbal strain, as if these American writers were pressing language in
peculiar ways as a means of effecting a new understanding of what
narrative might accomplish.

It may be appropriate here to briefly address the issue of late
modernism, especially as distinguished from conventional assessments
of postmodernism in the twentieth century.[21] The fiction of John Barth,
Donald Barthelme, William Gass, and Thomas Pynchon, among others,
established postmodernism as a defiance of modernist distinctions
between character and behavior, essence and its representation, offering
instead narratives based on the premise that discourse *constructs* reality,
and thereby engaging the reader in refusing to distinguish between
rhetorical form and narrative content. Skepticism and irony define the
relatively short-lived era of postmodern American literature, which
largely dismisses the notion of human authenticity as little more than a
simulated version of itself.[22] Successors to postmodernism have not so
much rejected its techniques as turned them against its own premises,
willingly accepting the contingency of human action and choice, even
the constructed nature of meaning, but moving beyond parodic
assumptions to the more settled claims of mimetic realism. Or as
Irmtraud Huber admits: "It appears that what comes beyond
postmodernism turns towards a revival of authenticity, an authenticity
that is often anchored in the subject of the author" (27). Reclaiming that
high modernist premise while at the same time drawing on distinctly
postmodern techniques (such as metareferentiality), the late modernists
(otherwise known as "neo-realists" or "post-postmodernists") have
reasserted the ethical claims of genuine human subjects and shared
community values.[23] "Rather than a return to realist aesthetics," Huber
concludes, "I would suggest it is just such a profession of faith in the
ultimate possibility of communication, established in intersubjective
relations and based on a shared awareness of its own conventions and
limitations, that seems to inform recent literature more generally and
that can be seen as a decisive move beyond postmodernist disillusion"

(28). Whether this view risks a too enthusiastic embrace of liberal humanism is left up for grabs. But the fact that prominent critics of late modernism should so often turn to David Foster Wallace and Dave Eggers while ignoring Junot Díaz, say, or Cormac McCarthy, raises more specific questions about late modernist innovation itself. For both of these authors, like those preceding them in this study, confront the capacity of words themselves, sometimes at the level of phonemic echoes, to tantalize us with a vertiginous feeling of unearned possibility, inducing a sense of both mystery and wonder at mutually exclusive yet somehow congenial verbal possibilities.

The most trenchant admirer of this characteristic strain in American literature was Tony Tanner, who identified "a continuous interest in 'wonder' and the naive vision" (*Reign* 10) structuring a tradition that extends from Emerson to J. D. Salinger. Canonical writers, so Tanner argued, focus their narratives repeatedly through a "wondering eye" (278) that envisions "the world as seen for the first time" (125), even if the tradition finally subsides into a more skeptical mode. Whitman "does not simply *see*—he tries to *become* what he sees" (80), while Twain's Huck Finn "wonders at the usual and in so doing makes the usual wonderful" (125). Tanner's argument illuminates a host of other figures, ranging from Emerson and Thoreau's first-person personas, to James's Maisie Farange, to Sherwood Anderson's and Hemingway's male narrators, and the present book might well be understood as extending his insights into the twenty-first century. Indeed, the rationale for beginning each of the chapters that follow with epigraphs drawn from or about earlier American authors (Emerson, Poe, Thoreau, Melville, Whitman, Sherwood Anderson, Faulkner) is to affirm something like an unbroken tradition, a link between them and both modernist and late modernist authors, in a shared devotion to "the naive vision" that instills a continuing sense of wonder. Tanner's focus, however, lay in broad imagistic patterns and large thematic sequences, if with occasional nods to James's "syntactical complexity" (268) or Stein's repetitions (201) or Hemingway's "registered particular[s]" (230). By contrast, I want to turn more closely to the stylistic suasions of particular passages, focusing more fully than he on the transformations such passages perform on readers even more than on characters. Tanner's revelation of the reign of wonder *in* nineteenth-century texts, it might be said, has set the stage for us to value how fully that reign extends to the reader *of* late modernist novels.

As critics since Aristotle have already been seen to observe, a sense of wonder is the feeling associated more often with poetry than prose, if only because poetry seems a more compressed idiom, flaunting its gaps and silences, seemingly more self-attuned to slippages of meaning. Yet literary prose offers as well a certain self-consciousness about the effect of dispositions of words—performing much as poetry does—which at its most acute may constitute a feature characteristic of modernism. After all, modernism frequently draws attention to the supposed schism between experience and verbal representation, between its representation of physical behavior and the words invoked to depict and enact it. Faulkner had Addie Bundren famously complain at how "words go straight up in a thin line, quick and harmless, and how terribly doing goes along the earth" (*As I Lay Dying* 173). And that insight into the arbitrariness of symbolic constructs, shared by assorted modernist novelists, coincided with a distrust of straightforward narrative sequence itself.[24] Veering away from predictably crafted plots and pivoting instead on strained verbal structures and strange expressive modes, these authors increasingly defied conventional expectations in order more fully to engage the reader—not simply to do "quite half the labour" (as James notoriously claimed), but to experience the wonder of literary revelation that does not occur sequentially, or as a simple narrative progression.

Appositely, Peter Brooks has acknowledged that "lyric poetry ... strives toward an ideal simultaneity of meaning, encouraging us to read backward as well as forward (through rhyme and repetition, for instance), to grasp the whole in one visual and auditory image" (20). Instead of this description offering a distinct contrast to modernist novels, however, it seems to embody their inherent aspirations as well, in slowing down reading poetically to enforce a non-narrative consideration of multiple tensions at work. Brooks, in fact, appears to buy into an experience of reading that seems more akin to Cleanth Brooks than Paul de Man, by assuming a unified text as prerequisite to determinate meaning, and by contrasting the "simultaneity of meaning" of poetry with "the necessary retrospectivity of narrative" (22). As he goes on to explain, "only the end can finally determine meaning, close the sentence as a signifying totality" in a novel, modernist or otherwise. This evaluative contrast fails, however, to account for the recollective, backward-looking aspect of lyric poetry as well, which likewise rests on the "strange logic" of an "*anticipation of retrospection*" (23) that Brooks assumes singularly characteristic of prose narrative. It is not simply reading for plot that dictates an anticipatory look back, but reading for sense at all, especially in verbal settings where multiple possibilities emerge simultaneously.

IX. A Disruptive Reading

Perhaps this destabilizing process can be clarified by a glance at Hemingway's early story "Up in Michigan" (1922), which captures the dizzying effect of narrative compression and stylistic allusiveness that more generally distinguishes all the novels in this study. The story involves the sexual initiation of Liz Coates, and the uncertainty of her (and the reader's) response. The whole opens with a flat introduction to the dull life led by a blacksmith, Jim Gilmore, with whom Liz has a puppy-love infatuation, as they go on to eye each other speculatively in the small-town world of Hortons Bay. Suddenly, midway through the story, late in an evening in which he has been drinking heavily, in which she has been waiting for him, he starts to paw her unexpectedly:

> She was thinking about him hard and then Jim came out. His eyes were shining and his hair was a little rumpled. Liz looked down at her book. Jim came over back of her chair and stood there and she could feel him breathing and then he put his arms around her. Her breasts felt plump and firm and the nipples were erect under his hands. Liz was terribly frightened, no one had ever touched her.
>
> Hemingway 84

Jim's size, his intoxication, his calm assumption of her availability: all are apparent, with even her own body seeming to betray her in its tumescent responsiveness. Clearly, Liz is at once fearful and unable to resist: "She held herself stiff because she was so frightened and did not know anything else to do and then Jim held her tight against the chair and kissed her. It was such a sharp, aching, hurting feeling that she thought she couldn't stand it" (Hemingway 84). The description is disquieting in the sexual brutality Jim represents, and that Hemingway reveals in Liz's own responses. Yet, for reasons not readily apparent, she nonetheless joins him—if out of uncertainty, or innocence, or sheer sexual desire—on a walk in the night where things become steamier:

> They sat down in the shelter of the warehouse and Jim pulled Liz close to him. She was frightened. One of Jim's hands went inside her dress and stroked over her breast and the other hand was in her lap. She was very frightened and didn't know how he was going to go about things but she snuggled close to him. Then the hand that felt so big in her lap went away and was on her leg and started to move up

it. 'Don't, Jim,' Liz said. Jim slid the hand further up. 'You mustn't, Jim. You mustn't.' Neither Jim nor Jim's big hand paid any attention to her.
Hemingway 85

She protests, she resists, she denies they have to "do it," until finally: "No we haven't, Jim. We ain't got to. Oh, it isn't right. Oh, it's so big and it hurts so. You can't. Oh, Jim. Jim. Oh." The moment of thrusting intercourse occurs in Liz's four exclaimed "Oh"s, as groans that suggest some combination of responsiveness and resistance, in her failure to stop him. In particular, the chiasmus here at the end of her protest produces an odd effect, offering something like a sonically responsive closure to the scene, introducing (paradoxically) an uncertain but nonetheless possible acquiescence to a scene she had started by resisting.

The story moves quickly, elliptically, with little physical description and a narrative suturing of broken moments that derails confident interpretation. Are we meant to commiserate with Liz's painful distress? To censure Jim for his heedlessness, his callous behavior? And what do we make of the sustained focus on Liz's psychology, as Jim's drunken sensibility drops out early? The central moment erupts into the story unexpectedly, yet leading to neither regret nor anger. What seemed, in short, a bleak account of a young woman's violation, with Jim simply falling into an alcoholic stupor at the end—an account favored by some critics—reveals to the contrary a subtler, and more complicated series of events and emotions.

Hemingway's understated style should not be underestimated, or otherwise occluded by the usual confident interpretive assumptions. That realization emerged for me in a surprising class on the story a decade ago, reminding me how literature achieves its status most obviously in its ability to arouse conflicting, mutually exclusive but also jointly sustaining responses. Despite Jim's having fondled her rudely, for instance, she still continues to desire him: "Liz was terribly frightened, no one had ever touched her, but she thought, 'He's come to me finally. He's really come'" (Hemingway 84). And soon after, "she couldn't stand it and then something clicked inside of her and the feeling was warmer and softer. Jim held her tight hard against the chair and she wanted it now." That seems the reason she accompanies him on their walk, and shares kisses; they "stopped and pressed against each other" (Hemingway 84), and later they snuggle, both willingly. Even at the moment immediately prior to penetration, we are told once again: "She was frightened but she wanted it. She had to have it but it frightened her." At a minimum, things are moderately confused, even confusing, as students in that long-ago session readily understood.

It began with Emily Weigel engaging us in a Blackboard post before class, apologizing for quoting the sexually explicit passage cited above ("you mustn't Jim"). As she wrote in a description that brought to the fore considerations otherwise hidden in the story:

> In some ways, the very words of the text leading up to the rape-but-not-really scene enclose Liz in their building momentum and preclude any escape. A cadence of sexually charged puns and overly relevant vocabulary propel us into the scene itself: 'She was thinking about him hard,' 'She thought "he's come to me finally. He's really come,"' and 'Jim held her tight hard.' The short, paratactic sentences seem breathless, and Liz is sexualized through both her (inadvertent) punning and Hemingway's frequent variations on 'she wanted it now.'

Focusing on Hemingway's syntax as fully as on his diction, Emily continued in a way that troubled her classmates' initial interpretations as well as a host of published judgments—even suggesting a slippery contradiction between syntax and diction in evoking what was itself a paradoxical experience:

> The crisis builds in tandem with this sexual energy—indeed, perhaps part of the crisis itself is that the situation produces sexual desire in its apparent victim. But only perhaps. Hemingway profoundly problematizes Liz's complicitness in the event that takes place. The fateful sort of pre-punning before the event that makes it seem inevitable ('hard,' 'coming' and so on) is contradicted by the polysyndetic repetition, especially of 'and' throughout that makes the sequence of events—tragic as it is—seem somewhat spontaneous: 'She was very frightened *and* didn't know how he was going to go about things *but* she snuggled close to him. Then the hand that felt so big in her lap went away *and* was on her leg *and* started to move up it.' The explicit disjunction of the hand (meaning Jim, obviously) from its owner—always referred to not as 'Jim's hand,' but as 'the hand'—seems to displace blame, or at least suggest that Liz does not fault Jim for her discomfort, which perhaps intimates that . . . the human bodies involved in it have 'minds,' if you will, of their own. That is—Liz seems to withhold judgment on the basis that Jim's body is doing this to her, not Jim himself.

By focusing on Hemingway's actual words themselves, unlike many critics who resort to simple paraphrase, this reading reveals the ambiguous, precarious emotional tension underlying events. Simply by listening to Hemingway's urgent rhythms, Emily hears Liz in a way other readers have not, with the resonance of punning verbs lending to Liz a sexuality that might not seem at first obvious. Moreover, the syntactic polysyndeton (the urgent "and … and … and") plus that disjointed, all but independent hand, come to explain Liz's psychology in an evocative fashion that hardly exculpates Jim, but nonetheless lends to Liz an agency she had not had before. Of course, in the way of most seminars, Emily's explanation predictably failed to convince everyone, and some of the better disagreements came from those who had read just as closely.

For the only means of controverting Emily's reading was to turn back to the story, to look more inquiringly at its wording, and to realize that though Liz midway through tells Jim "You mustn't," the narrator nonetheless informs us from her perspective that "She was frightened but she wanted it. She had to have it but it frightened her" (Hemingway 85). Again, the chiasmus here is striking, affirming at once Liz's sexual longing *and* her anxiety. As one student observed, her narrated mental state (aroused, aware, partially desiring sexual union) is no more fundamental than her expressed dissent (frightened, uncertain, seemingly overpowered); the two exist in an emotional standoff that nicely captures the complicated feelings many of us have had about experiences far from immediately sexual. Somewhat muddling the experience, as another student pointed out, is Liz's inability to know yet what "it" is, given her virginal state. How could she offer full and free consent to an experience she had never had, nor necessarily imagined. Legally, we do this all the time, regularly consenting to new experiences for which we are rightly held culpable. But fictionally, in the drama of a frenzied moment, culpability seems (however wrongly) somehow diminished, especially for experiences never experienced. We tend to be more sympathetic to those who assent without quite knowing to what. Moreover, as Nikhil Gupta (a math major) nicely claimed, Liz offers resistance as only a woman in 1922 could, in the only language available. For her to have responded differently (in words as opposed to feelings) would be for her to have been or become the kind of woman she was not. That is, the prospect of welcoming her feelings, and admitting to herself and Jim that she did indeed want sex, was simply not a part of the available cultural vocabulary at the time. In short, we need to read the story in historical terms, not as a contemporary today might in a culture where no means no.

This interpretation prompted Michael Juel-Larsen, heading off to Teach for America, to argue sharply to the contrary, claiming the scene clearly corresponded to "date rape" scenarios that college deans had so often warned against as incoming freshmen. How else could it be read? Which, given the rhythm of back-and-forth seminar discussion, then elicited a more moderate, less categorical response: that Hemingway disrupts such politically correct judgments, since the story so deeply muddies our understanding of motives and feelings. After all, as future law student Sarah Paige argued, Liz does resist Jim but she resists more the collapse of her own conventional vision of love than the actual scene as it then ensues. Moreover, Liz does not *feel* violated, as the student continued; instead, the story simply (or rather, not so simply) speaks to what she described as "the messy quality of sex, of who initiates and who desires." That makes it hard for those of us raised in an age of no means no—indeed, where actively asserted "affirmative consent" is now more frequently required—to give Liz's experience a clear-cut label. None of Sarah's interpretive gestures were meant to diminish the trauma of sexual assault, but as she said, the story roams around the borders of something less unwelcome, less traumatic, less marginal.

The entire plot unfolds as a series of fragile, conflicted responses leading up to, falling off from, a central emotional outburst, allowing no decisive ruling on what has happened (beyond the rude, even brutal, physical act itself). In the process, the reader is compelled back into a responsive stance, alert to nuances in the situation through the suasions of Hemingway's prose, read slowly and in patient attentiveness to its troubling, unsettling oscillations. We are left stymied by the poignancy of the story's conclusion, no more certain of where we are or should be than at the beginning, with judgment withheld, making it hard to know whether the reader should jump in with a judgment. After all that has happened, we are left as "Liz took off her coat and leaned over and covered him with it. She tucked it around him neatly and carefully. Then she walked across the dock and up the steep sandy road to go to bed. A cold mist was coming up through the woods from the bay" (Hemingway 86). Clearly, without being said directly, Liz's silent disappointment emerges in the coincidence between the cooling night scene and what we presume to be her emotional aftermath. But the forward-moving, inclined pressure of syntax itself also captures something of her resilience, evoked by the broken paratactic rhythm of the two final sentences. Building on a series of prepositional clauses—linking "across" to "and up," then "to go to" with "coming up through," finally turning "from the bay"—the sentences quietly suggest disillusionment yet persistence, fortitude yet discouragement. Even so, this registers a scene distinctly far from the psychological devastation that a rape victim would otherwise feel. We end with a feeling William Gass has wisely observed about such occasions: "Immersed in a context, wedded to a single run of words . . ., [when] fiction tries to undo the very formulas its narrative is made of" (*Tests* 13). The story offers a disturbing evocation of sexual desire, of sexual oppression, of sexual excitement and victimization—but not only that latter.

X. *Medley of Styles*

Each of the following novels aspires to this condition of being read, slowing us down to preclude instant judgments or easy readings of character and event. Sometimes that braking is achieved through gaps and silences, at others through sounds, rhythms, repetitions, and rhymes. But in every case, the novels at those moments take on a heightened poetic status, even as the pressures of plot that otherwise push us ineluctably forward tend to fade away. Narrative regularly pauses, often yielding to description, for reasons not always clear at first, though in every instance the effect is similar to that achieved in poetry— to inspire a keenly responsive sense of awe, mystery, wonder. That is the effect Fitzgerald creates in his lyric transformations, and if *The Great Gatsby* is notably absent from the following chapters (much as it lies behind so much that emerges in the modern American novel), it is only because his novel has already been so thoroughly assessed for a highly poetic style that induces to a species of enchantment analogous to that created by the authors in this book. Indeed, his novel flamboyantly displays Nick Carraway's transmutation of James Gatz's puerile narrative into an account that defies straightforward temporal progression, and defies as well any simple reading via the figurations that leave the reader "with something commensurate to his capacity for wonder" (Fitzgerald 189). Fitzgerald's legacy over the past century has been confirmed in the eclectic set of novels I have chosen, novels that share very little save their resistance to transparent readings. The selection represents a kaleidoscope of narrative and stylistic possibilities, in part to confirm one of the premises of close reading: that no single strategy is appropriate for every text, and that the very surprise sprung by innovations at a formal level requires an *ad hoc* response from the reader intent on understanding. A second premise ensues from the first: that the kinds of sustained and singular methods that so often go into symptomatic readings will also not be appropriate. Just as Evelyn Woods's patented method of patterned hand movements proves a painfully reductive reading habit, so too are more sophisticated but arbitrary interpretive schemes when applied across the board to different texts, whether it is an Empsonian concentration on ambiguity, or a New Critical valuing of paradox and irony, or a structuralist focus on shared narrative tensions, or a neo-Marxist exposure of institutional causality, or a psychoanalytic attention to the tropes of a text's "unconscious," or a deconstructive alertness to verbal reversals and oppositions. Each of these efforts imposes a critical regime before having begun, before simply listening to test the choices a novel makes, in words, rhythms, sonorities, and narrative disjunctions.

The sequence below—from Willa Cather to Vladimir Nabokov, then from Marilynne Robinson to Cormac McCarthy and Junot Díaz—is admittedly arbitrary, dictated primarily by the wondrous possibilities each novel presents to those willing to slow their reading down. Apart from each one's clear claim to literary status, collectively they offer dramatically different responses to the problem of reinventing the novel in the modernist and late modernist period. Breaking from conventional expectations for what a novel should be and do, they each confound readers in very different ways. And though other selections might have been made (especially from the likes of Faulkner and Ellison, Pynchon, Morrison, and Roth), each choice below quintessentially "brings to a crisis [our] relationship with language," doing so in formal ways that break unexpectedly from earlier novels, sometimes by the same author. Their sequence reveals how complex and entangled our ongoing relationship with words is, happily never fully settled nor quite fully disrupted. In short, the following discussions are not intended to exhaust or even define a particular tradition, in part because that would defy a third premise of this study: that paying close attention to a literary work results in unexpected revelations, unanticipated insights, even in texts we thought we knew. Instead of a clear line of canonical narratives, chosen for certain consistent themes, features, or structures, what the following interpretations would like to suggest is that novels depend on their readers as much as their authors, and that the canon is open as long as close readings can reveal wondrous possibilities we had otherwise overlooked.

The first chapter turns to Cather's *The Professor's House* (1925), which from its opening words defies traditional ways of reading narrative and in the process begins immediately to teach us how to read it by ignoring the causal, action-oriented aspects of narration in favor of a more temporally dislocated, radically associational mode. Focusing on description at the expense of narration, the novel appears to celebrate a series of wondrous moments. And as readers, we come to feel a sense of wonder analogous to Tom Outland's experience on the Blue Mesa, released from causality, suspended in time, no longer intent on the pleasures of narrative closure. Yet no matter how resolutely time seems slowed in the presence of evocations both immediate and ideal, the very rhythm of our reading jump-starts this lyric pause, ushering in patterns of sequence and story that reintroduce probable motives, likely assumptions about lives lived, temporal progressions rather than visionary exemptions from time. The transcending claims of wonder, fleetingly revealed by Cather's novel, cannot withstand the more pedestrian pulse of reading on which her novel also relies, since readers immediately invent sequences of motive and consequence, of past and future, from any given scene. Cather's visionary conception only *seems* to be anti-narrative, then; but since that cannot succeed, she wants to open possibilities through a minimalist, allusive, synechdochal style that evokes a moment where "the mood is the thing" and all else has been expunged. One achieves visionary insight only by giving up narrative, abandoning plots of intention, motive, and closure. Yet novels by necessity inspire a process of narrative in us willy-nilly, defying those moments of epiphany they allude to, establishing in the process the paradox of their own reading. Of course, Cather was perfectly aware of this paradox, and in playing out its implications revealed her own delight in the conflict between our most basic novelistic gestures: description and narration.

The next chapter seizes on *Lolita* (1955/1958) as a rather more notorious text of "bliss," a word first invoked by Nabokov to speak of the experience of reading, and that may well have inspired Barthes to consider the way our "relationship with language" is always transformed by the slippery verbal realm of brilliant literary texts, texts that become at once referential and self-enclosed. Nabokov builds on Cather and other modernists in his lapidary novel, which more than any other is at once scabrous ethically and delightful aesthetically, deliberately so in exploiting each of two supposedly exclusive modes of reading—swaying us into sympathy with characters *in* the text even as that text glitters and glows, an impersonal artifact. The novel, in fact, delights in the slippage between these two realms: between a verbal figure defined by narrative rules, and an actual person capable ever of surprising us. Strict narrative probability tilts perpetually against looser actual possibilities. Humbert Humbert's invocation of Lolita oscillates between lyric exultation and dismissive contempt, much as his account oscillates between words as realistic representation and as sheer sound, raising serious questions about how any novel is to be judged. Indeed, the larger split experienced by readers between an oppressive reality and a redemptive if obsessive lyric voice is captured in Humbert's own admitted concession to "the gap between the little given and the great promised" (Nabokov, *Lolita* 264). That gap occurs as an oscillation between straightforwardly readerly interpretation and a countering sense of emotional, psychological loss, which makes this novel as ambitious as any in addressing more than moral issues—indeed, in unsettling the reader in profoundly ethical ways. The confusion is reflected in our unstable sense of character itself, with Nabokov leaving us in doubt of the extent to which authors are ever ethically liable for the fictive acts they perform on their characters. And among the novel's troubling questions is: What are the ethics not of actually acting towards others in such and such a way, but of writing them into imagined plots that end with their equally imagined demise? In this regard, the novel seems to veer from important aesthetic questions only to plunge right back into those very questions again, albeit in a different tone. The ethical and the aesthetic intersect like a Möbius strip, much as Humbert and Quilty roll about together. Cather's paradox of narrative emerging ineluctably from description finds its analogue in this, the first major American novel to verge into postmodern textual strategies without finally succumbing.

Marilynne Robinson's *Housekeeping* (1980) implicitly elaborates on Nabokov's inquiry into literal and figurative styles, pressing the implications of its title in a novel not only so regularly flooded that ordinary household management fails, but flooded with rhetorical forms of housekeeping that seem to offer more promising solvents for life's disorders. "Housekeeping" itself connotes both strict household maintenance and a more generous notion of hospitality, in a tension that structures Ruth Stone's efforts to assuage her feelings of abandonment, imagining the lost voices of her grandfather, grandmother, mother and sister as she plucks from memory the shards of a past that might help configure an acceptable future. For Ruth chooses a mixed mode stylistically and narratively, defined by the twin poles of housekeeping, as she grants the guests and strangers of her fragmented life a hospitable hearing, even as she structures her account to ensure a suitable order. Yet even this mixed mode is unavailing in a novel that denies prescriptive responses to vocation, to trauma, to psychology itself. Robinson's narrative of housekeeping begins literally as physical accommodation in creating household order, and ends figuratively by revising and revisioning one's sensibility. Moreover, in this species of literary housekeeping, Robinson at once revises and responds to a long (largely male) tradition of American canonical texts. What first appears a cluttered style (describing a species of failed housekeeping) emerges as a more comprehensive if also more flexible means for grasping one's past and one's self, even as past and self ever continue to elude that grasp.

The fourth chapter turns to McCarthy's *Blood Meridian* (1985), a novel that seems nearly the opposite of Cather's or Robinson's in both subject matter and style. Yet like Cather in her fictionalization of the actual history of Richard Wetherill's discovery of the Cliff Palace at Mesa Verde on December 18, 1888, McCarthy transposed the gruesome marauding of John Joel Glanton and his gang along the Texas border in 1849–50. McCarthy also resembles Robinson and Nabokov in his alertness to how fully literature is built on predecessors, or as he acerbically remarks: "The ugly fact is that books are made out of books" (Woodward 30). That legacy is clear in *Blood Meridian,* perhaps particularly in its representations of violence that trace a heritage backwards through Hemingway, Crane, and Melville. As with them, the grim subject matter of the novel is burnished by its wrenching style, the abrupt shift among discursive registers (from lyrical to archaic to barely literate), assaulting the reader as fully as any character, and doing so as a means of making our experience at once strange and new. In short, as with Cather, Nabokov, and Robinson, the triumph of McCarthy's novel emerges from its formal maneuvers, its strained similes and unstable visionary mode, in the tension sustained by prose whose shape-shifting construction alerts us to its self-transforming capacities. Taking the debased facts of history and redeeming them through a narrative eye that selects, disposes, excludes, embellishes, McCarthy's novel registers a rhetorical violence everywhere contesting the barbarism so variously depicted, and thereby enhances ethical and aesthetic possibilities that otherwise seem flattened out. In short, the dissociative style of *Blood Meridian* defies accommodation to conventional assumptions. And that's the point, in making the world once again new, free of readerly accommodations, no longer bled "of its strangeness" (McCarthy, *BM* 245).

The next chapter perversely continues with McCarthy in his very different novel, *The Road* (2006), if only because it seems so curious and radically revisionist a gesture, written in a style completely at odds with *Blood Meridian* and justified aesthetically not as an arbitrary feature of his prose but as expressive of its own distinctive perceptual realm.[25]

Looking back through his earlier novels and those that preceded him, McCarthy offers a fable in which language itself, rather than some behavior or belief or cultural purview, becomes a necessary if hardly sufficient stay against dissolution. The novel's strangely dissociated structure emerges unobtrusively as a series of crucial rhythms, beginning with a thematic alternation of threat and escape from danger that is echoed narratively in a temporal ebb and flow, of flashbacks, dreams, and present consciousness. This rhythm corresponds to stylistic swings amid prose registers, so that gradually, what had seemed a fable of survival becomes a complex meditation on the relation of past and present, of language and experience. Yet it is the father's efforts to get his son to sustain a dialogue that points to the novel's central concern, in his valuing the power of words to recast the "long forgotten" (31) into living possibilities. *The Road* echoes that invocation, in full appreciation of its belated status as narrative in a tradition now exhausted, seemingly irrelevant. Ending on a hum "of mystery" (287), the novel reminds us how enigmatic the survival of language itself has been. Who has in fact told this story of the death of possibility in a fable that at once invokes and rejects literary tradition? McCarthy's version of wasteland, a common trope of modernism from the beginning, abandons conventional modernist techniques by drawing instead on a pastiche of parable, epic, and prose poem, returning us in the process to the long-standing resources of language as a means of recovering our ethical moorings.

The final chapter turns to Junot Díaz's *The Brief Wondrous Life of Oscar Wao* (2007), which imitates earlier authors by not only building out of familiar canonical texts but also by likewise defying precursors in its tumultuous revision of that canon. It is hard to imagine a novel less like McCarthy's stripped-down fable than this explosive, frenzied, thoroughly unpredictable tour de force that regularly interrupts itself, muddying the distinctions between text and context, incorporating marginal materials and intertextual comments as if to shatter any desire for coherence or conventional logic. Footnotes compete with charged references to anime, fairy tales, science fiction, canonical novels, and comic books that incrementally chip away at any consistent mood; professions of anxiety about literary influence erupt occasionally throughout; and pointed historical judgments punctuate a novel that never deigns to confirm its authenticity. It is as if Díaz were discovering in its very writing how to create a novel in the late modernist period. Many have commented productively on this fictional account of diaspora, engaging the cultural and historical aspects of Dominican-Americans represented by this highly touted novel. Less studied, however, have been the formal, meta-textual aspects of Díaz's effort, and few have tried to answer the question of why he turns so persistently to the twisting margins as displacement for a narrative line, as if he were turning the novel inside out by transfiguring these otherwise peripheral features into a central structural role. Formal gymnastics succeed by transgressing boundaries presumed crucial to fiction's suspension of disbelief, which becomes Díaz's means of giving voice to both Oscar and Yunior de Las Casas (as well as to Oscar's sister, Lola, and their mother, Beli Cabral). Upending the novel form itself, Díaz reveals fresh possibilities among the diminished prospects available to late modernism, as narrative becomes a series of hiccuping, hyphenated, unruly but finally exhilarating interruptions. Like his predecessors above, he at once acknowledges an anxiety of influence and revises the literary map, unsettling readers in the process of revealing how fully formal dislocations can allow us to hear voices otherwise silenced.

XI. *"Mere" Reading*

The premise of these chapters—each devoted to close, slow-motion, even recursive readings of a disparate range of modern American novels—is that literature occurs in a verbal woof of words, sounds, rhythms, patterns of syntax, figures of speech, even marginal asides and casual interruptions. Or from a different figurative angle, it emerges in the interstices, in odd formal patterns and disruptive sequences as words are invoked imaginatively, often fancifully and misshapenly, askew from their sometimes more obvious meanings and in constructions that draw our eyes away from straightforward plots to more disruptive cadences, our ears away from sense to sound (which is, of course, always another kind of sense). Claiming this is hardly to deny the historical and ethical (and thereby largely thematic) aspects of novels, nor is it to shortchange their ideological underpinnings and resonances, nor to ignore the structural significance of scenes, characters, gestures, expressions. But it is meant to return us to Paul de Man's encouragement that "literature, instead of being taught only as a historical and humanistic subject, should be taught as a rhetoric and a poetics prior to being taught as a hermeneutics and history" (25). Two decades later, for all his differences with de Man, Denis Donoghue declaimed in similar terms against persistent trends: "the teaching of English, the vernacular subject for many though not for all of our students, is represented as a cafeteria in which the food on offer is soft sociology, soft history, and soft psychology. The question of the language of literature is regularly set aside" (13). Ironically, Donoghue then went on to castigate de Man's rejection of the more local aspects of poetry, in his supposedly larger concern with rhetorical strategies rather than diction and sound. The point is that even those in favor of close reading are hardly united in their response, with each feeling a certain proprietary concern over ways of practicing that approach. More recently, Jane Gallop has made a call in similar tones for a responsiveness to literature that Cleanth Brooks celebrated long ago, and that Reuben Brower encouraged as a defense against too easy conventionality, too ready acceptance of ideological premises far from obvious at first glance. As she admits:

> It is precisely my opposition to timeless universals that makes me value close reading. I would argue that close reading poses an ongoing threat to easy, reductive generalization, that it is a method for resisting and calling into question our inevitable tendency to bring things together in smug, overarching conclusions. I would argue that close reading may in fact be the best antidote we have to the timeless and the universal.
>
> Gallop, "Historicization" 185

And this call for a return to older practice is echoed in Cecily Devereux's timely reminder that the teaching of literature in recent years has lost students because it has lost its way: "What has been lost is a shared sense of literature: what it is and why it matters" (223). As she warns, "if literature is not to be differentiated from any other kind of cultural production, the point of a discipline whose purpose is the study of literature becomes unclear" (Devereux 224).

The recurrent theme underlying these adjurations is that the return to "mere reading" is a gesture meant to honor the unadulterated intractability of literary texts, their persistent irresolution, indeed the way in which "literary" status itself rests squarely on the fragile play of irreconcilables that emerges from the verbal tensions we find ourselves first wondering at, then delighting in. Literature only confirms assumptions when it becomes propaganda, or generic, or somehow fully stable and correct, which is to say when it is no longer recognizable as literature. The true test lies in its destabilizing, defamiliarizing perspectives, which always leave us less certain than we were when we began, and more in a state of bewilderment and awe. Keep in mind that the wonder we feel in the face of our own incomprehension is akin to a magic performance, with its testing the powers of understanding, which is (in Adam Gopnik's words) "the dramatization of explanation more than it is the engineering of effects" (66). The very resistance to closure, to perfect understanding and final determination, is what generates the compelling magic of the shortest lyric as of a long novel, neither of which can effectively be reduced to a straightforward paraphrase, a tightly cohesive conclusion. Certainly New Historicists, feminists, Marxists and those of other ideological stripes will presume that their symptomatic readings transcribe the essential meanings of a text, and in doing so will frequently help us understand its silent resonances. But what these transcriptions so often neglect or discount is the text's discrepancies and indeterminacies, resulting from the contradictory tensions of language itself, the verbal patterns that beguile us into the pleasures of re-reading. The perversity of those texts we call literature is in their regularly seducing us into efforts at comprehension, only to evade our grasp before we resolve the dilemmas that attracted us to begin with. And if it is true that any close reading always moves toward an interpretation that necessarily paraphrases, the best of such assessments recognize that this occurs only in contestable ways, leaving open alternative close readings, divergent interpretations. As Gopnik concludes of "the Too Perfect theory," it "explains the force of the off-slant scene in a film, the power of elliptical dialogue in the theatre, the constant artistic need to turn away from apparent perfection toward the laconic or unfixed. Illusion affects us only when it is incomplete" (67). And that incompleteness is part of the lure of reading, in corresponding to Isaiah Berlin's notion of plural values ever in tension with each other, and to deconstructionists' notion of contested readings for single texts, even single words (of interpretations dictating facts fully as much as facts dictate interpretations). "In the final analysis," Barbara Johnson observes, "it is perhaps precisely as an apprenticeship in the repeated and inescapable oscillation between humanism and deconstruction that literature works its most rigorous and inexhaustible seductions" (148). It is those multiple, variable "seductions" that the following chapters are meant to query and contemplate.[26]

Notes

1   A number of studies have recently appeared declaiming the influence of the Internet in terms curiously akin to those I bring forward against speed reading (see Birkerts; Piper). Perhaps most incisively, Nicholas Carr offers a

detailed, well-researched account of the ways in which reading has changed since the advent of the World Wide Web, with studies suggesting that people no longer "necessarily read a page from left to right and from top to bottom. They might instead skip around, scanning for pertinent information of interest" (9). Tracing the advent of printing presses, maps, clocks, typewriters, and other major inventions, he reveals the ways thinking is transformed. As he observes: "The oral world of our distant ancestors may well have had emotional and intuitive depths that we can no longer appreciate. [Marshall] McLuhan believed that preliterate peoples must have enjoyed a particularly intense 'sensuous involvement' with the world. When we learned to read, he argued, we suffered a 'considerable detachment from the feelings or emotional involvement that a nonliterate man or society would experience'" (Carr 56–57). But if that distant experience is only hypothetical, more recent changes can be scientifically measured, and the conclusion is that the reading experience we have known since the fifteenth century is changing, with more skimming, "power-browsing," and "out-sourcing' of memory": "Even though the World Wide Web has made hypertext commonplace, indeed ubiquitous, research continues to show that people who read linear text comprehend more, remember more, and learn more than those who read text peppered with links" (Carr 127). Our powers of concentration deteriorate in a multi-tasking environment that is just the opposite of what close and slow reading encourage.

2   It seems oddly coincidental that both Vladimir Nabokov and Barthes invoke the state of "bliss" to describe the experience of reading. Nabokov claims that "aesthetic bliss" alone is a measure of artistic and literary success in his Afterward to *Lolita* (1955/1958); Barthes, nearly two decades later, invokes the state for a species of literary text. Could Barthes have been aware of Nabokov's usage?

3   Stewart's more recent book, *The Deed of Reading*, came to my attention after completing this manuscript, but it powerfully extends my case for slow reading. Acknowledging "the deflated status of verbal alertness" (12) in current studies, he elegantly reminds us that "Strong literature has a way of weaning us anew from the edge of gibberish into emergent sense, as well as from routine discourse into a more telling strain of phrase. Literary force may often seem to be not the putting away of childish things but a building directly on them. It marks, in its very marks, the growing out of babble into aptitude, of sound into meaning, of linguistic blur into pertinence, of thickness into intricacy, of the merely weighted into the layered, sometimes of sheer chaos into the potently inchoate" (37).

4   Of course, the original "Abracadabra" is the opening of the Gospel according to John: "In the beginning was the Word, and the Word was with God, and the Word was God."

5   As he states later in the lecture: "I believe that aesthetically and symbolically magic ultimately is about the very nature of mystery. Magic

reminds us that things are not always as they seem, that life is full of the unexpected, the unpredictable, and even the unexplainable. Magic says, metaphorically, on a symbolic level, that that which has been destroyed perhaps can be restored, that that which has disappeared can perhaps be made to reappear. And so magic says, that with imagination and creativity, we can face the challenges of our lives, we can even overcome the tragedies of our lives. And this is where magic lives and breathes. . . . Finally, though I've avoided the word, magic has something to do with wonder. Now I don't mean childlike wonder that we hear so much about. I think wonder is an adult, mature experience and emotion. . . . When you stand on that threshold of knowledge and mystery, that's where you experience real wonder. And that's where magic lives."

6   Dubois later adds a comment about such interpretation that dovetails with Fish and Altieri's rationales: "This, for many of us, is a reason to enjoy criticism: not only because it explains to us or helps us better understand a particular text, but also because loving to read ourselves, we enjoy watching other people read. Criticism, seen in this light, implies a community of readers . . ." (14).

7   It should be clear that I find this form of critical imposition misguided, even in the hands of so brilliant a reader as Jameson. As Best and Marcus continue, in describing such critics as Eve Sedgwick and Toni Morrison, they read a text's "silences . . . as symptoms of the queerness or race absent only apparently from its pages" (6). One should, from a close-reader's perspective, well be wary of such top-down readings. For a different take on description itself as a form of demystifying close reading, see Heather Love, who argues: "by refusing the role of privileged messenger prescribed by hermeneutics and emphasizing instead the minimalist but painstaking work of description, this approach undermines the ethical charisma of the critic" (387).

8   For a fuller investigation of the flattening effect of paraphrase, see Mitchell (86–7).

9   But as they observe, citing Marjorie Levinson's claim for a "new formalist" alternative: "In this essentially modernist view of art as a locus of critical autonomy, reading becomes what Levinson calls 'learned submission', which is not as submissive as it sounds, because in submitting to the artwork, we come to share its freedom, by experiencing 'the deep challenge that the artwork poses to ideology, or to the flattening, routinizing, absorptive effects associated with ideological regimes' (560). Immersion in texts frees us from the apathy and instrumentality of capitalism by allowing us to bathe in the artwork's disinterested purposelessness" (14).

10 Mark David Rasmussen has observed that, "Simply put, Greenblatt's readings often seemed to do a better job of explaining what was going on within these works than previous, mainly New Critical, accounts had managed to do, and so supplanted the authority of those accounts . . . but both Greenblatt's subsequent work and that of his followers has set aside

such explication as its goal, in favor of the mining of literature for evidence of cultural practices" (2).

11 As Auerbach concludes: "The two styles, in their opposition, represent basic types: on the one hand fully externalized description, uniform illumination, uninterrupted connection, free expression, all events in the foreground, displaying unmistakable meanings, few elements of historical development and of psychological perspective; on the other, certain parts brought into high relief, others left obscure, abruptness, suggestive influence of the unexpressed, 'background' quality, multiplicity of meanings and the need for interpretation, universal-historical claims, development of the concept of the historically becoming, and preoccupation with the problematic" (23). David Damrosch offers the best assessment of Auerbach's own informing premises: "Throughout *Mimesis*, in many guises, there appears a conflict between two sets of values that Auerbach sets sharply against one another, but both of which he himself holds: classical (Greek) harmony, balance, free play, and presence . . . all in opposition to modernist (Jewish) fragmentation, psychological complexity, and exile or absence." As he adds, however, in a severe irony, Jewish fragmentation and "modernist retreat from system and chronology itself paved the way for the rise of fascism" (Damrosch 113).

12 Dale is discussing the reception of Ang Lee's film, *Brokeback Mountain*, and the opposition between readers who, despite their severe disagreement, cannot argue convincingly because they work "backward from ideological statements about homosexuality to a justification of the movie couched in aesthetic terms. But this kind of criticism comes close to eliminating aesthetics as a discipline" (173).

13 Brower quotes Coleridge's recollection of his own teacher, that "'severe master, the Reverend James Bowyer' . . . I learned from him, that poetry, even that of the loftiest and, seemingly, that of the wildest odes, had a logic of its own, as severe as that of science; and more difficult, because more subtle, more complex, and dependent on more and more fugitive causes. In the truly great poets, he would say, there is a reason assignable not only for every word, but for the position of every word; and I well remember that, availing himself of the synonymes to the Homer of Didymus, he made us attempt to show, with regard to each, why it would not have answered the same purpose; and wherein consisted the peculiar fitness of the word in the original text" (7). As Brower adds, "The Reverend James Bowyer and not Coleridge, it appears, was the original New Criticism, which is to say that much New Criticism is old criticism writ large" (7).

As Brower noted in 1962, in anticipation of a situation that would recur three decades later: "Surely those who now call for a 'return to literary history' cannot be thinking that history is a 'thing' that we can study without first helping to construct it" (viii). As with Cleanth Brooks before him, and "new formalists" more recently, he shared a strong belief in historical contextualization: "Words, literature, the forms of expression in any given age, it need hardly be said, are implicated in a historical context, and in a context of literary tradition" (Brower ix). Brower's "section men" included a number of important close readers who would emerge in decades to come: Paul Alpers, Thomas Edwards, Ann Davidson Ferry, Neil H. Hertz, Stephen Orgel, Richard Poirier, William H. Pritchard, William Taylor, and Thomas Whitbread.

14 As John Gray adds, Berlin's central idea is of "value pluralism, that ultimate human values are objective but irreducibly diverse, that they are conflicting and often uncombinable, and that sometimes when they come into conflict with one another they are incommensurable; that is, they are not comparable by any rational measure" (1).

15 W. H. Auden has notably claimed: "Whatever its actual content and overt interest, every poem is rooted in imaginative awe. Poetry can do a hundred and one things—delight, sadden, amuse, instruct—it may express every possible shade of emotion, and describe every conceivable kind of event, but there is only one thing that all poetry must do; it must praise all it can for being and for happening" (60).

16 The phrase occurs in James's lament that George Eliot concluded *Adam Bede* by directly informing her readers of Adam's marriage to Dinah Morris: "The assurance of this possibility is what I should have desired the author to place the sympathetic reader at a standpoint to deduce for himself. . . . In every novel the work is divided between the writer and the reader; but the writer makes the reader very much as he makes his characters. When he makes him ill, that is, makes him indifferent, he does no work; the writer does all. When he makes him well, that is, makes him interested, then the reader does quite half the labour. In making such a deduction as I have just indicated, the reader would be doing but his share of the task, the grand point is to get him to make it" ("Novels of George Eliot" 321).

17 For her indebtedness to Leavis, see *Love's Knowledge* 12. And for her odd resistance to close reading, see her brazen claim in support of a paraphrase: "I presuppose, then, the quotation of Book Fifth, Chapter III of *The Golden Bowl*. Indeed, honoring its 'chains of relation and responsibility,' I presuppose the quotation of the entire novel" (*LK* 149).

18 Harpham asserts "her work is full of what seem to many to be unjustified claims or inferences, plain misreadings, or simple failures to think through her own arguments" (54).

19 As Smit states: "Sooner or later, all critics of style, if they want to avoid being trivial, must stop randomly describing a text and start providing a rationale for the features they discover or speculate about the affective impact of those features. And that rationale, that speculation, is an interpretation" (24).

20 Clearly, the stylistic deviations of American literature can be traced in a lineage from Hawthorne and Melville through Twain and James, Dreiser and Cather, and so on in sharply dissimilar sequences. By contrast, the notable continuity from Dickens and Trollope through Hardy, Lawrence,

even Woolf, offers a clearer, more self-consistent line of transition. That this should have led to a significant edge for American modernism (Stein, Pound, Eliot) over the British variety (Conrad, Joyce) is, of course, not at all obvious.

21 Throughout this book, I invoke the term "late modernism," which I take to be at once historical (literature post WWII, well after the "high modernism" of the 1920s) and thematic (novels that sustain a humanist understanding of character and event, written in varying but largely non-ironic styles). By contrast, literary postmodernism (historically situated in the 1970s and 1980s) sustains a vision of character that is purely textual, and a largely ironic presentation of events. As Leonard Wilcox observes: "images, signs, and codes engulf objective reality; signs become more real than reality and stand in for the world they erase" (346–47). Linda Hutcheon asserts that postmodernism "takes the form of self-conscious, self-contradictory, self-undermining statement. It is rather like saying something whilst at the same time putting inverted commas around what is being said" (1). And she adds, the mode "foreground[s] above all the textuality of its representations" (92). Fredric Jameson confirms this view of postmodernism, observing of its features: "The first and most evident is the emergence of a new kind of flatness or depthlessness, a new kind of superficiality in the most literal sense, perhaps the supreme formal feature of all the postmodernisms to which we will have occasion to return . . ." (*Postmodernism* 9). John McGowfan likewise proclaims: "Postmodernism is thus distinguished from modernism by the belief that artistic autonomy is neither possible nor desirable. Postmodernism questions the efficacy of strategies of transformation associated with autonomy, declaring that modernism inexorably reaches a dead end. The modernist hope and belief that intellectuals can occupy a space outside capitalist society is not only illusionary but also artistically and politically sterile" (25).

By contrast, David Holloway has claimed that late modernism is "a kind of writing that embodies aspects of the postmodern so as to map a route through and beyond the condition it describes. A writing that seizes upon the postmodern so as to use it against itself and negate it dialectically from within. But a kind of writing that also remains self-consciously mired in what it strives to go beyond" (4). More generally, late modernism recovers a notion of subjectivity that is deliberately excluded in the thoroughly textualized realm of postmodernism. For two standard examinations that agree on modernism as "the unstable name of a period," see Levenson (*Cambridge* 1) and Lewis (xvii). Levenson elaborates on the persistence of modernist techniques in novels written today: "Within the historical revision there can still be found certain common devices and general preoccupations: the recurrent act of fragmenting unities (unities of character or plot or pictorial space or lyric form), the use of mythic paradigms, the refusal of norms of beauty, the willingness to make radical linguistic experiment, all inspired by the resolve (in Eliot's phrase) to startle and disturb the public" (3).

22 Wolfgang Funk nicely distinguishes between postmodernism and late modernism in terms of a return to authenticity, which paradoxically "can *only* be appreciated as an aesthetic phenomenon" (17). He further acknowledges: "As Baudrillard's simulacrum, Derrida's *différance* and Jameson's critique of postmodern superficiality attest, art and theory in postmodernism have effectively put an end to any meaningful distinction between inner and outer personality, surface and deep structure, essence and representation. Does this now mean the end of authenticity?" (28). Only postmodernism offers "the 'impossible' knowledge fictional characters appear to have of their being mere characters" (96).

23 As Irmtraud Huber claims: "If all narrative acts are contingent, the choice of mimetic realism at the end of the day is just as valid as an anti-illusionist metafictional disruption; it's just a different kind of game to play" (26). Wolfgang Funk invokes the term "reconstruction" for current fiction's renewed concern with "autonomy and solipsism" (3). As he states of the technique adopted by many late modernists (Wallace, Eggers, Foer, Diáz), "metareference constitutes the most appropriate aesthetic device for evoking, enacting or at least investigating authenticity" (64). For the best early review of "the Chinese-box world" of postmodern assumptions, see Brian McHale (125). More generally, McHale provides a particularly useful and exhaustive survey of postmodern techniques.

24 As Peter Brooks observes, "with the advent of Modernism came an era of suspicion toward plot, engendered perhaps by an overelaboration of and over-dependence on plots in the nineteenth century" (7).

25 In this, I am refuting David Smit's argument that style is simply random or arbitrary, as he claims for Henry James but by extension for any writer: "In many ways, the late style cannot be justified aesthetically; it is simply the way James wrote" (93).

26 Samuel Otter has recently observed "a sense that there has been a loss of recalcitrance, idiosyncrasy, and surprise in textual analysis. Critics move too quickly through text to context or from ideology to text, without conceding the 'slowness of the perception' that the Russian formalist Victor Shklovsky described as characteristically produced by verbal art. We might label such responses as nostalgic or reactionary, but this would be too easy a diagnosis. Something is going on in the profession of literary studies, and the evidence indicates that we may not be as finished with questions of literary value as we thought we were, even if such questions must now be pursued in relation to the poststructuralist, historicist, and political developments in literary criticism over the past thirty years" (117).

Chapter 1

POSSESSION IN *THE PROFESSOR'S HOUSE* (1925)

Ah, the pickerel of Walden!.... They are not green like the pines,
nor gray like the stones, nor blue like the sky; but they have, to my
eyes, if possible, yet rarer colors, like flowers and precious stones,
as if they were the pearls, the animalized nuclei or crystals of the
Walden water. They, of course, are Walden all over and all through;
are themselves small Waldens in the animal kingdom, Waldenses.
It is surprising that they are caught here—that in this deep and
capacious spring, far beneath the rattling teams and chaises
and tinkling sleighs that travel the Walden road, this great gold
and emerald fish swims.

> —Henry David Thoreau *Walden* (549)

Why tell us? They don't trip on the sidewalk or make love on its
rough surface; it is just that as the author's eye goes over the scene it
includes many of the surrounding facts. There is no apparent
principle of selection and omission at work. Minor characters
suddenly receive a moment of unrelated scrutiny.... No one detail
is more or less important than another: all merit attention. The eye
is deliberately *not* informed by any selective modes of thinking. It
sees without thinking, or perhaps we could fairly say, 'it sees without
looking.'

> —Tony Tanner (*Reign* 208) on Sherwood
> Anderson describing a sidewalk

From first publication, Willa Cather's *The Professor's House* has stymied
readers, eluding analysis sometimes at the most basic descriptive level.
Recently, those efforts have grown more ingenious, interpreting the
novel as misogynist exercise, as homosocial romance, as nation-building
fantasy. But first readers were simply bewildered. I. A. Richards, in the
midst of formulating his influential ideas on literary reception, offered a

telling insight: "She has very little sense of action, and action and invention go together. Such observation, perspective, and balance as hers are rare, but all her work is strangely static" (O'Connor 276–77).[1] And Richards was hardly alone. Another reviewer claimed, with a touch of delight, that "the point of the book lies in the fact that she leaves it perfectly pointless"; and he concluded with a similarly paradoxical assessment:

> in the end nothing happens. Unless a truer statement is that in the end everything has happened. These are all very vivid human beings … but there are no heroes or heroines, no particular beginnings and no conclusions. Miss Cather is not interested in their passions but simply in their lives; and about life she finds it possible to say only that one lives it, and that when it is over it is over.
>
> O'Connor 264

Curiously, what first sounds like dismissive critique becomes muted celebration of Cather's technique. Yet if admiration has only grown in the decades since, it has not been for her "strangely static" style but for conclusions based on symptomatic readings of what we know of her convictions (racial, sexual), or of stances shared by her contemporaries (political, cultural).[2] And while those readings have illuminated various strands of the novel, they nonetheless have avoided confronting its perplexing formal disruptions, the dramatic alternations it induces between feeling that "nothing happens" and "everything happens."

It is time to return again to that alternation, and more generally to the odd elusiveness of *The Professor's House*—indeed to so many other novels equally elusive—by first resisting the impulse to firm up tremulous constructions into sturdy thematic readings. For by ignoring the quandary so vividly felt by its first readers (and still felt by subsequent first readers), we fail to realize how little the novel sounds *like* a novel in its curious silences, its "strangely static" rhythm. And that might caution us against speaking for texts that so often seem to speak both ways (that is, when they speak at all). To reiterate: before explaining *what* goes on beneath the surface of uncanny novels, we should look again at *how* they are put together, since their structures so regularly disrupt our historical and cultural expectations. And in the case of Cather, that disruption ensues most often from her apparent preference for description over narration or exposition, for her willingness to suspend action and events, motives and means, in order to simply linger over the colorful display of surfaces.[3] The conventional imperative of the

novel to "tell a story" subsides regularly in Cather's delight in letting
action and character go in order to let the eye wander over local
details, as if all but timelessly.[4] Yet much as she values this seemingly
atemporal state of description revered, the state itself is all but impossible
to sustain for long, if only because readers transmute it back into a logic
of cause and effect, of gazing intention and felt aftermath that once
again constitutes part of the ongoing plot. In this, Cather confronts a
paradox engaged by other modernist authors committed to altering the
novel, in discovering how persistently the linguistic and emotional
complexity of their texts at once emerges from and undercuts their
formal structure. The effort to get outside the text, in the variously
different gestures made by each author in this study, is heroic and
partially successful but always necessarily brings us back into a familiar
readerly realm.

Cather's reason for turning so often to description in *The Professor's
House* seems linked to the novel's emphasis on the condition of wonder
as a thematic strain, which Tony Tanner has described as "the distrust of
judgement and analysis, the conviction of the need for a renewed sense
of wonder and admiration, a new stress on 'the passive susceptibilities', a
longing to feel the wholeness of the universe rather than merely
understand it" (*Reign* 7). As described in the introduction above, Tanner
claims this constitutes American literature's most significant strain,
which helps explain why narrative sequence so often seems to peter out
in canonical texts. Tanner observes of Whitman:

> In his desire to vivify the common facts of life, to illuminate them
> with a new kind of reverence, to bathe them in wonder, he sometimes
> lets the naive eye move from one thing to another so fast and so
> unrestrictedly that the excess of particulars starts to blur and we lose
> the sense of any logic as his ecstatic gaze sweeps on. . . . Of course his
> whole strategy of enumeration is related to Emerson's idea that things
> sing themselves and Thoreau's contention that the clearly stated fact
> will appear fabulous. Such theories on their own provide no hints for
> the ordering of the fabulous facts, for the orchestration of the singing
> things.
>
> *Reign* 79

Throughout his study, Tanner reminds us how often characters
(frequently children) pause wide-eyed in admiring, often reverential,
stances. As he claims of Gertrude Stein, whose efforts match those
of an entire literature: "Stein is against narrative which fosters a

causal time sense, which forces us to ask of the material in front of us—
what is happening and why? Better, she would maintain, to develop
an art which makes us ponder what is existing, now and for itself"
(Tanner 195).

Notably, however, Tanner ignores the writer most thoroughly
engaged in just this effort, who insists that readers as well as characters
suspend temporal considerations. In the decade from *My Ántonia*
(1918) to *Death Comes for the Archbishop* (1927), Willa Cather reversed
and revised herself, experimenting with style largely out of a shared
fascination with contemporaries like Hemingway, Fitzgerald, and Eliot
for objects simply seen, transcribed into prose description untethered
from fictional, made to stand unalloyed, free of the constraints of
continuity or plot.[5] And frequently she succeeds in this modernist
venture at narrative dislocation, making her readers read again, forcing
them to pause over scenes not seen, or at least not seen exactly
enough. The success is revealed paradoxically in the interpretations she
inspires, in the confidence with which critics impose their own
contradictory judgments, leaving Lionel Trilling sounding oddly akin
to Eve Sedgwick, at least in the confidence of his analytic tones. Trilling's
dismissal of Cather's "mystical concern with pots and pans ... [as not]
very far from the gaudy domesticity of bourgeois accumulation glorified
in the *Woman's Home Companion*" (*Review* 154–55) forms a telling
contrast to Sedgwick's celebration of "the gorgeous homosocial romance
of two men on a mesa in New Mexico" (68). Yet both share a desire
to paraphrase ineluctable passages into ready-made categories, re-
possessing the novel interpretively (misogynistically, homosocially) in
terms eroded by the novel's own dissociative stylistic pressures.

Among Cather's novels, the most dramatic experiment occurs in *The
Professor's House*, which persistently seems to favor description over
narrative sequence, lingering over physical details that rarely appear
quite relevant to the story at hand. And if paraphrase of the novel often
undervalues its "strangely static" power, that may have to do with
Cather's resistance to the tenets of traditional plot exposition.[6] After
all, the novel foregoes questions of motivation and intent in favor of
Tom Outland's revelation on the Blue Mesa, when he "wakened with the
feeling that I had found everything, instead of having lost everything"
(PH 227). That superlative feeling is recapitulated in Godfrey St. Peter's
recollection of Tom, echoed in turn by Cather herself in the process
of writing. The novel exemplifies her abiding effort to suspend the
causal, action-oriented aspects of plot in favor of a more temporally
dislocated, fundamentally transcendent mode, which largely succeeds

by embodying its thematic celebration of the state of wonder in a style that is insistently descriptive, not narrative. It is hardly coincidental that Professor St. Peter achieves his fame as a historian with his eight-volume *Spanish Adventurers in North America*, anticipating Cather's own experimental efforts: "Nobody saw that he was trying to do something quite different" (Cather, *PH* 22). As importantly, Cather seems here to be pointing to the venerable pedigree wonder has in America, as "the decisive emotional and intellectual experience" among Europeans first confronted with the New World (*PH* 14). Stephen Greenblatt follows Tanner, extending historically back much further, in claiming that the experience of wonder has from the first encounter with native soil always been "elusive and ambiguous" (19), neither quite cause nor fully effect because it "depends upon a suspension or failure of categories and is a kind of paralysis, a stilling of the normal associative restlessness of the mind" (20). If such "associative restlessness" constitutes our normal compositional mode, moments of wonder disrupt that mode before desire reasserts itself, in an alternation between stunned admiration and ongoing accounts of appropriation, between momentary self-dispossession and the continuing urge for intellectual control. That alternation produces a paradox inhering in countless travel accounts of the New World from Cortés to Díaz, of wonder "at war with itself." Or as Greenblatt sums up, "This is the utopian moment of travel: when you realize that what seems most unattainably marvelous, most desirable, is what you almost already have, what you could have—if you could only strip away the banality and corruption of the everyday—at home" (25).

Stripping such banality away lies at the center of *The Professor's House*, as Cather focuses on the "intense pleasure of looking" (77) that Greenblatt cites as characteristic of Columbus's journals but that Tanner reveals is true of every other genuinely "American" writer. While she wants to regenerate the novel in a distinctly modernist mode, it is a mode that ironically hearkens back to an all-too-familiar travel convention. And the Cliff City lyrically described in the central sequence of "Tom Outland's Story" is meant to sustain a particularly focused kind of clarity, not only in the immediate present but ever after in retrospect—a process of vision that is allowed only fleetingly elsewhere in the novel. Of course, the "paradox of wonder at war with itself" cannot finally be avoided, which means that Cather's turn from sequence to visionary stasis can be only momentary, a pause in our reading, since the engine of narrativizing itself is irrepressible, part of what we automatically do as we read. In Peter Brooks' formulation, we read incessantly for plot itself, and in its absence we create plots to accommodate our reading. So that no matter how vigorously Cather wanted to reshape the novel into moments of stopped time, of lyrical evocations both immediate and ideal, the very rhythm of reading which she defied still presses on, invariably ushering in patterns of sequence and story that reintroduce probable motives, likely assumptions about lives lived, temporal processions rather than visionary exemptions from time. The transcendent claims of wonder, fleetingly revealed by her novel, simply cannot withstand the more pedestrian rhythms of reading, on which her novel also relies.

I. Unnerving Descriptions, Wondrous Visions

Readers of *The Professor's House* have felt from the beginning that "in the end nothing happens," even though they have also felt compelled to understand why. The opening page introduces Godfrey St. Peter still working in a "dismantled house" that is "ugly," inconvenient, broken-down. If he speculates about what has brought him to this present pass, so do we, though he lingers not on formative causes but on present effects. Rather than focusing on the sequence of events that brought him here, and that *as* sequence might drive a story forward, he focuses on local scenes, beginning with his unsightly house, then with a glance shifting to his French garden:

> it was a tidy half-acre of glistening gravel and glistening shrubs and bright flowers. There were trees, of course; a spreading horse-chestnut, a row of slender Lombardy poplars at the back, along the white wall, and in the middle two symmetrical, round-topped linden-trees. Masses of green-brier grew in the corners, the prickly stems interwoven and clipped until they were like great bushes. There was a bed for salad herbs. Salmon-pink geraniums dripped over the wall. The French marigolds and dahlias were just now at their best—such dahlias as no one else in Hamilton could grow.
>
> Cather, *PH* 6

This description is exemplary in a novel that so often compels us to figure out why we are being given descriptions at all. A garden is depicted with a landscape architect's precision, but its overall significance is hardly apparent. St. Peter does take invidious pride in it, we understand, treating it as sanctuary from a family we've yet to meet and from his own fretful discontent with circumstances. And these do help reveal his perspective, even his character, one supposes, though it is hard to know how much to read into such nominal preferences. As well, the scene will offer the first initial reference to Tom Outland, muted and unexplained. But mostly, the passage commands attention to a setting never seen again and objects whose importance is less than obvious. We pause to admire the alliteratively "glistening gravel and glistening shrubs," the green-briar, geraniums, and French marigolds, as does he, but with little understanding of what drives this enforced pause. In short, dramatic action seems eclipsed, with ecstatic description allowed to register the entirety of St. Peter's mental state.

Gérard Genette has pointed out how Proust's "lavish descriptions" have the effect of "slowing down the narrative" (*Narrative* 99), even though "Proustian narrative never comes to a standstill at an object or a sight unless that halt corresponds to a contemplative pause by the hero himself . . . and thus the descriptive piece never evades the temporality of the story" (100). Perhaps so in Proust, though not quite in Cather, where description remains unattached, unascribed to the eye of a character. She sometimes comes close, as revealed above and compounded by other, equally free-floating scenes:

> But the great fact in life, the always possible escape from dullness, was the lake. The sun rose out of it, the day began there; it was like an open door that nobody could shut. The land and all its dreariness could never close in on you. You had only to look at the lake, and you knew you would soon be free . . . it ran through the days like the weather, not a thing thought about, but a part of consciousness itself.
>
> Cather, PH 20–21

Here, description bursts on St. Peter as he sits in his room, vaguely if enthusiastically recalling his past. Strikingly, the brilliance of the scene is disproportionate to the present setting, as a memory from forty years before that intrudes with a power to transfigure him. The image of the lake is at once denied ("not a thing thought about") yet foundational ("a part of consciousness itself"), embodying long after the fact a Wordsworthian poetic of powerful "emotion recollected in tranquility." As much to the point, the passage epitomizes a novel whose driving force is sheer pictures themselves, disconnected, undesired, automatic.

It may go without saying that Cather is an intensely visual novelist who shares a desire famously expressed by Conrad as "by the power of the written word to make you hear, to make you feel—it is, before all, to make you *see*" (4). Yet she strips out what in Conrad's descriptions (or Proust's) occurs as silently informing apparatus to explain the meaning of a scene in terms of character. As Genette observes, "Proustian 'description' is less a depiction of an object contemplated than it is a narrative and analysis of the perceptual activity of the character contemplating: of his perspective, errors and corrections, enthusiasms or disappointments" (*Narrative* 102).[7] And this might equally well be said of Conrad or even Woolf; consider the scene of Clarissa Dalloway entering a flower shop: "There were flowers: delphiniums, sweet peas, bunches of lilac; and carnations, masses of carnations. There were roses; there were irises. Ah yes—so she breathed in the earthy garden sweet smell as she stood talking to Miss Pym who owed her help, and thought her kind" (Woolf 17–18). The floral moment is lyrical if brief, and characteristically Woolf ties these impressions firmly into Clarissa's consciousness, with the startled anaphora ("there were … there were …") coupled with exclamatory pauses ("Ah yes") that evoke her breathless excitement as the primary meaning of the flowers she sees.

By contrast, what readers (at least, initial readers) seem to find so often unnerving in Cather is the apparent lack of motive *in* her character's seeing—the failure to register a distinctive response or otherwise to elicit meaning out of the energies displayed by scenic description. All we get is a tepid sense of St. Peter's general happiness, explained almost impersonally, even automatically ("They had made pictures in him when he was unwilling and unconscious, when his eyes were merely open wide."). That disconnection between evocative description and uninflected narration seems to lie behind Joseph Wood Krutch's quietly incisive remark, in his 1925 review of the novel, that "there is nothing that indicates more clearly the nature of Miss Willa Cather's peculiar excellence than the fact that the intention of her works generally defies any such attempt at restatement" (O'Connor 251). More recently, Jo Ann Middleton has similarly observed of Cather's effort to "leave out" material in her novels: "Perhaps the most intriguing and perplexing aspect of Willa Cather's work is the effect on the reader of what he or she cannot find on the written page" (51). In this, Cather resembles Hemingway, whose verbal style appears initially quite different and yet achieves a similar effect.

Hemingway's inaugural effort, *In Our Time* (1925), coincided with the appearance of *The Professor's House*, and registered his own commitment to a so-called iceberg principle in which a story's structure should lie, as he said, "seven-eighths under water for every part that shows" (192). Cather's manifesto, "The Novel Démeublé" (1922), uncannily affirms a similar view that accentuates the "pervasive quality of reserve" (Janis Stout 67) many have noted in her fiction:

> Whatever is felt upon the page without being specifically named there—that, one might say, is created. It is the inexplicable presence of the thing not named, of the overtone divined by the ear but not heard by it, the verbal mood, the emotional aura of the fact or the thing or the deed, that gives high quality to the novel or the drama, as well as to poetry itself.... A novel crowded with physical sensations is no less a catalogue than one crowded with furniture.
>
> OW 41

Various critics inspired by Sharon O'Brien have focused on that "thing not named," a phrase echoing Oscar Wilde's "love that dare not speak its name," suggesting an aesthetic of disavowal ("don't ask, don't tell") perfectly suited for a lesbian writer speaking indirectly.[8] Yet the larger concern of this passage lies with silence itself, in Cather's meticulous avoidance of things, overtones, sensations—all the descriptive materials that might help shape a conventional narrative. Whatever the larger thematic ramifications for *The Professor's House*, we are well advised to acknowledge first how much Cather's style hearkens back to a symbolist mode of *au-délà*, with latent meanings achieved through poetic compression.

Cather vividly wanted to turn the novel in a new direction. She never forgot her birthright as an American novelist committed to a species of wonder, but was also inspired by innovations generated by literary modernism. Yet other modernists seemed to her more or less conventional (confirmed in her essay's critique of Lawrence's *The Rainbow*). Having declared her radical bona fides, she concludes with the hope that her own novelistic descriptions will whittle the traditional novel back from comprehensive metonymic arrays to achieve a more concentrated, even transfiguring effect akin to epiphany:

> How wonderful it would be if we could throw all the furniture out of the window; and along with it, all the meaningless reiterations concerning physical sensations, all the tiresome old patterns, and leave the room as bare as the stage of a Greek theatre, or as that house into which the glory of Pentecost descended; leave the scene bare for the play of emotions, great and little—for the nursery tale, no less

than the tragedy, is killed by tasteless amplitude. The elder Dumas enunciated a great principle when he said that to make a drama, a man needed one passion, and four walls.

OW 41–42

One hardly expects an aesthetics of understatement from the author of *Three Musketeers*, but the lesson Cather takes from the aphorism—the embrace of a bare, neutralized space—becomes the ground where "nothing happens" and yet "everything has happened." Her antipathy for "tasteless amplitude" rests on its presumed inarticulateness, its inability to speak of anything but its own excess. In this, moreover, she may well aspire to the style of early Spanish accounts, at least as Greenblatt describes them, which were meant to be tractable, humble, unobtrusive, as a means of establishing the status of a naked truth (147).

One more example helps clarify Cather's descriptive practice in *The Professor's House*, especially in the apt contrast it offers to Clarissa Dalloway's entrance into the flower shop. St. Peter returns home only to pause outside his drawing-room, admiring it:

> full of autumn flowers, dahlias and wild asters and goldenrod. The red-gold sunlight lay in bright puddles on the thick blue carpet, made hazy aureoles about the stuffed blue chairs. There was, in the room, as he looked through the window, a rich, intense effect of autumn, something that presented October much more sharply and sweetly to him than the coloured maples and the aster-bordered paths by which he had come home. It struck him that the seasons sometimes gain by being brought into the house, just as they gain by being brought into painting, and into poetry. The hand, fastidious and bold, which selected and placed—it was that which made the difference. In Nature there is no selection.

Cather, PH 61

The view is clearly St. Peter's, and yet nothing suggests that the perceptions are somehow distinctively his, in that the description calls up nothing from his past nor indicates much about his present emotional state. By contrast with Woolf's scene, the syntax here is sedate, measured, almost discursive. The passage's sole self-reflexive trick occurs in the observation that "the seasons sometimes gain by being brought into the house," just as they gain by being brought into novels. Yet that is hardly possible, in a paradox captured by Mary Ann O'Farrell: "The call for a novel démeublé can *only* succeed (every novel is démeublé) if we understand writing in the way it sometimes has been understood: as the very site of thinglessness, a space without spatiality, in which—because there can be no rooms—all rooms are unfurnished" (212). The point is that Cather's metaphorical "hand, fastidious and bold," has arranged the room simply so that we *see* it, recognizing a "selection" that Nature cannot do. It needs to be said once again that "description, of necessity, generates narrative", as Mieke Bal asserts of our readerly propensity to project and interpret (593). We simply cannot evade our own preternatural impulse to derive consequence from sequence, to find plots ensuing from assorted details; but Cather here comes as close to quashing that propensity as possible, leaving us little more informed of characters or plot than we were before the scene occurred.[9]

Elsewhere in the novel, this emphasis on the reader's calm observation is reinforced whenever descriptions are circumscribed, made to mean less (as it were) than they otherwise seem. Given how fully the long novelistic tradition depends on a species of metonymy, any descriptions of place or person automatically generate meanings: this is the status quo, the basis for Genette's and Bal's aptly commanding claims. Yet while Cather strives to inoculate her descriptions against this metonymic default, her studied care about it in *The Professor's House* is clear not only in its descriptive language, but in anxieties expressed by characters, for whom appearances matter so much that common expressions take on weighted meaning. Professor Crane laments that "appearances are against me" (Cather, *PH* 128), in turn prompting St. Peter to realize he had "never seen his colleague in such an unbecoming light before" (*PH* 130). Tom Outland becomes contemptuous of Washington bureaucrats who "spent their lives trying to keep up appearances" (*PH* 209) of what they are not. This recurrent motif underscores the novel's alternative descriptive mode, which everywhere denies that appearances should cause distress—indeed, that they should matter at all. Instead of description leading seamlessly to narrative denouements, narrative time itself seems to collapse into moments of sheer vision. Minutiae is reviewed and calibrated but nothing is finally added up, and instead is left to simply stand for itself, left untransformed by any calculus of meaning into something other than itself.

This is one of the reasons Cather so admired Stephen Crane, for his ability to focus description without elaborating a setting—that is, without the setting becoming an obvious plot engine, primed to speak for what occurs, rather than remaining more or less self-contained, as if resisting exposition:

He simply knew from the beginning how to handle detail. He estimated it at its true worth—made it serve his purpose and felt no further responsibility about it. I doubt whether he ever spent a laborious half-hour in doing his duty by detail—in enumerating, like an honest, grubby auctioneer. If he saw one thing that engaged him in a room, he mentioned it ... but he never tried to make a faithful report of everything else within his field of vision.

OW 69

The paradox seemed to be, for Crane as for herself, to make description more intensely itself by narrowing its scope, by refusing to become a "grubby auctioneer" of objects, by concentrating on specific moments of vision enthralled rather than accumulating details that tend toward flat explication. Or as she observed of Crane, once again driven to paradox to explicate her own anti-narrative agenda: "He is rather the best of our writers in what is called 'description' because he is the least describing" (Cather, *OW* 69). To make such a claim about so vividly impressionistic a writer is to reveal once again how little details are meant to accumulate in her (or his) verbal vision.

One clear revelation of how fully Cather wanted to dramatize the distinction between narration and description occurs in her placement of "Tom Outland's Story" squarely in the middle of a novel that up to now has seemed to move simply from one aimless description to another, in a desultory review of St. Peter's relations with family, of teaching obligations, of summer days spent alone. Immediately, we are made aware of an energy involved in narrative exposition: "The thing that side-tracked me and made me so late coming to college was a somewhat unusual accident, or string of accidents. It began with a poker game, when I was a call boy in Pardee, New Mexico" (Cather, *PH* 159). And as the second sentence continues this forward drive ("One cold, clear night in the fall I started out to hunt up a freight crew that was to go out soon after midnight."), the reader is swept up into a story of Tom's developing friendship with Roddy Blake, their work as cowboys, all in a thinly veiled fictionalization of Richard Wetherill and Charlie Mason's actual 1888 discovery of the Cliff Palace at Mesa Verde. Clearly, Cather is an accomplished narrator of dramatic action, and yet it is as if the ensuing chapters were nonetheless intended to offer a distinct contrast with the visionary descriptions of the Blue Mesa, to reveal all but self-consciously the contrast between polished narrative at its most effective and descriptions that trump even such sequences in their consummate ability to stop time itself, to achieve something like a visionary status.

II. Defying Sequence

Cather positions herself directly against novelists like Proust and Woolf, where description tends to form a connective tissue to energize narratives, offering its indirect insights about the way central figures see. Yet because Cather intentionally does less with plot sequence, less even with description itself—all as a means of focusing the reader's vision— she needs another principle of novelistic organization; and she finds it (again, as Hemingway would) in juxtaposition. Already by 1921 she understood the importance of this technique, as she admitted in an interview: "I'm trying to cut out all analysis, observation, description, even the picture-making quality, in order to make things and people tell their own story simply by juxtaposition, without any persuasion or explanation on my part." She then continued, more specifically:

> Just as if I put here on the table a green vase, and beside it a yellow orange. Now, those two things affect each other. Side by side, they produce a reaction which neither of them will produce alone. Why should I try to say anything clever, or by any colorful rhetoric detract attention from those two objects, the relation they have to each other and the effect they have upon each other? I want the reader to see the orange and the vase—beyond that, *I* am out of it.
>
> Cather, *Interviews* 24

The example again recalls a symbolist aesthetic, best exemplified in Maeterlinck's plays where "objects" (situations, phrases) are inexplicably brought together to resonate for the reader. A green vase, a yellow orange: the contrast explains itself, as Patrick McGuiness observes, in a "discontinuous melodrama of strange juxtapositions [that] leaves meanings to the spectator" (127). More provocatively, Michael Leddy argues that Cather's comment "points toward an idea of the novel not as narrative but as image, as if placing objects against one another in space were indeed a way to tell a (temporal) story" (183). Images resonate without becoming part of a causal or psychological sequence, forming tableaux that resemble the favorite technique of Hawthorne and Faulkner. Yet Cather complicated that technique, as Eudora Welty affirmed: "she worked out some of her most significant effects by bringing widely separated lives, times, experiences together—placing them side by side or one within the other, opening out of it almost like a vision—like Tom Outland's story from *The Professor's House*—or existing along with it, waiting in its path, like the mirage" (47).

Even those dismissive of the novel attest to this effect by assuming "incompleteness" is a liability. "It is really not possible to take this work seriously as a whole," thundered an anonymous reviewer: "As you look back over the first book you have a recurring sense of gaps and vacancies, incompleteness in the story—as if parts had been hastily cut out of the manuscript and the ends not joined up" (O'Connor 237). *Mutatis mutandi*, these qualities are what Adorno would identify as the failure of "style" in modernism (308–09). Of course, that was precisely Cather's intent in her later novels, breaking up narrative as a means of breaking free from authorial tyranny, fracturing the limiting perspective of traditional novels, defying sanctioned notions of story and conventional understandings of time. Juxtaposition, moreover, was meant to serve as much a thematic as a stylistic end, disrupting a causal logic to events that Cather viewed more haphazardly. As she said in an interview following the novel's appearance:

> I also wanted to show that most of the really important events in our lives come to us through some entirely accidental contact. St. Peter, by the mere chance of Tom Outland's arrival, had in his life a series of circumstances started which inevitably eventuated in his realization ... that he simply was not the same man, and in a sense, a very deep sense, he was more Tom Outland than he was himself. ... That's what I want to do—the kind of thing that gets the design of life, not just the picture.
>
> O'Connor 238

This stress on "accidental" qualities of life that paradoxically make us not quite ourselves, or that otherwise seem to displace us from a comforting conception of our own character, is captured in St. Peter's own closing presumption that his life had been "accidental and ordered from the outside ... not his life at all, but a chain of events which had happened to him" (Cather, *PH* 240). Of course, that idealized surmise speaks more to his present dissociated perspective than to his "life," reminding us again how description itself opens up contradictory narratives. Yet Cather's stress on "the design of life, not just the picture" confirms her aversion to the misshapen pleasures of simple sequence, and her preference for keeping accidental delights unaccounted for. The very imperative to subordinate detail to a larger logic is what she wants to avoid, resisting an ineluctable impulse to read for plot where no plot exists. The wonder of Tom's life lies, therefore, in its chance events—meeting Roddy Blake, finding the Blue Mesa, discovering intellectual excitement in the Latin classics, and in engagement with St. Peter. Instead of a prefigured sequence reminiscent of Zane Grey (as Cather dismissively notes), she wants to celebrate a more aleatory, more haphazard, non-linear process that (at least, so she believes) approximates the rhythm of our lives—a rhythm that, as Peter Brooks observes, informs the modernist "suspicion toward plot" (7).

In fact, Cather hopes through juxtaposition and dislocation to achieve a transformed vision in the reader even more than in St. Peter himself. Hermione Lee observes something similar in *Death Comes for the Archbishop*, which likewise reveals the method of *The Professor's House* in wanting "everything [to be] seen and understood at once— as though God were telling the story." Lee then continues, "this redistributed narrative makes its centre a conception of time, not as linear accumulation, but as a conjunction of 'timeless moments'. To this end, a sustained chronology is carefully subverted" (270). The novel deliberately subverts a plot sequence that leads from introductory to concluding events—a sequence that can only be imposed after the fact, thus distorting the immediacy of initial impressions. As Lee adds, "If history in the eye of God (or the archbishop) is a series of pictures all seen, in stasis, at the same time, the narrative has to make its meaning not out of slowly developing psychological states or complex political entanglements, but out of gesture, appearance, colour and light" (272).

Even more than that later novel, *The Professor's House* fulfills this goal by organizing its "pictures" through a curious tripartite structure built on juxtaposition, on the arbitrary dislocation generated by a cognitive switch between dissimilar scenes. Sequence is abandoned as a familiar generator of meaning, and instead a different kind of significance emerges in abrupt disconnections. At first, each section seems simply unrelated to the one before, though the imagistic alternation produces a cumulative emotional effect. That was Cather's intention, revealed in her reasons for placing the novel's lyrical center against the mundane opening and closing segments in order, as she said, to achieve a calculated painterly effect:

Just before I began the book I had seen, in Paris, an exhibition of old and modern Dutch paintings. In many of them the scene presented was a living-room warmly furnished, or a kitchen full of food and coppers. But in most of the interiors, whether drawing-room or kitchen, there was a square window, open, through which one saw the

masts of ships, or a stretch of grey sea. The feeling of the sea that one
got through those square windows was remarkable . . . I tried to make
Professor St. Peter's house rather overcrowded and stuffy with new
things; American proprieties, clothes, furs, petty ambitions, quivering
jealousies—until one got rather stifled. Then I wanted to open the
square window and let in the fresh air that blew off the Blue Mesa,
and the fine disregard of trivialities which was in Tom Outland's face
and in his behavior.

OW 31–32

This offers a strange authorial analogy, transforming narrative into
something pictorial and temporally static, contradicting Cather's
heartfelt claims for description—of avoiding details, resisting physical
elaboration. Yet the effect remains, and the anti-narrative logic prevails,
with no other juxtaposition in Cather's fiction as abrupt or intense as
the interjection of the long flashback, "Tom Outland's Story," into the
dreary quotidian account of St. Peter's latter-day Hamilton. Still, even to
agree that she achieves a "fine disregard of trivialities" through this
sudden structural dislocation does not explain what helps bind *The
Professor's House* together.

Accident, after all, frequently fractures lives, though memory works
by piecing together a sequence to heal the wounds, thereby organizing
events into a pattern—a pattern that may be misleading, even inaccurate,
but that serves a purpose nonetheless. In short, mishaps become
incorporated into the design of a new narrative. Underscoring this
tension, the novel offers St. Peter's recollection of Tom's story thrust into
the haphazard midst of his present circumstances, and thus presents
a sequential arrangement as tentative stay against the confusion of
otherwise disconnected events. Hermione Lee notes "how much
fracture and dislocation there is throughout the novel. The attempt to
make a coherent, harmonized shape through memory is constantly
straining against processes of separation and substitution" (233). In
short, a novel so much more devoted to descriptive possibilities than
narrative sequence requires *other* centripetal forces to help contain its
energies. Other kinds of design—dramatic, rhythmic, painterly—make
the parts into a whole.

The novel's dramatic elements include the traditional, Aristotelian
"unities" that bind together the outer frame story—and specifically, the
opening and closing chapters. The time span consists of exactly one
academic year, extending from September through to the following
September on days when classes have already begun. Likewise, the place

is precisely the same, as are the characters. The cycle of events has run full circle without anything being displaced or disrupted, while the flashback middle section is told to St. Peter on a late summer evening in 1910, as he rewrites it from memory on another summer evening a decade later. The novel's rhythm is apparent in the duration of sections, each of which is less than half as long as the preceding. In fact, Cather herself pointed out, "This story is built like a piece of music, the theme of St. Peter, then the theme of Tom Outland, and the last part of the book the mingling of the two themes" (O'Connor 237). Even more effectively, this "rhythmic" strategy serves to propel the reader along, making us converge on the climax with increasing urgency, with a sense of acceleration, a more intense beat. Lastly, a painterly design emerges in colors and images shared by the college town of Hamilton and the Cliff City in the Southwest—linking the two frames, outer and inner, together. The Blue Mesa is implicitly contrasted with the exquisite blue of Lake Michigan, as well as the blue Mediterranean that St. Peter recalls having sailed in his youth. And that repetition of blue evokes a set of different impulses, whether an "escape from dullness" (*PH* 20) in the lake, or the depressed "blue" (153) feeling Tom experiences in the government bureaucracy of Washington D.C. Yet overall, blue has positive implications, reflecting the generous spirit Tom represents in the semiprecious stones he gives St. Peter's daughters, or the turquoise bracelet he gives to Rosamond. Most of all, it suggests the cerulean skies on the Blue Mesa, as Tom later recalls his summer alone there: "Happiness is something one can't explain. You must take my word for it. Troubles enough came afterward, but there was that summer, high and blue, a life in itself" (228).[10]

A painterly use of color throughout, the gentle pressure of musical and dramatic structures—and yet, the novel does not suddenly become structurally integrated, if only because novels are *not* paintings, or plays, or music. What these analogies do instead is make us aware in the absence of conventional plot structures how fully Cather is reassessing what novels generally do: i.e., tell a story.[11] Repeatedly, *The Professor's House* pauses at moments of vision, as if sight itself were meant to lead to insight, ocular evidence all but directly pointing to some sort of larger significance—whether of personalities, or places, or things. Of course, metonymy generally works this way, establishing our knowledge via associations generated by a character's selections and appurtenances. Yet Cather's description of the house in which St. Peter dwells—as well as all the other houses in the novel, pretentious, cheap, fashionable, naïve, urban—strives to give a different account from the customary realist novel. Part of this has to do with the intensity and starkness of these descriptions, which point more to a wide-ranging depiction of cultural directions than to individual character choices.

Architectural sites, instead of reflecting or revealing, more pointedly offer an imagined overview of cultural devolution from integral, organic form to crass commercialism. They are meant as pictorial statements, all but sufficient each to itself. And from this perspective, Tom's discovery of the Cliff City serves as the novel's indisputable highpoint, in its emphasis on the sheer act of description, of seeing "a little city of stone, asleep ... with flat roofs, narrow windows, straight walls, and in the middle of the group, a round tower." As he adds:

> It was beautifully proportioned, that tower, swelling out to a larger girth a little above the base, then growing slender again. There was something symmetrical and powerful about the swell of the masonry. The tower was the fine thing that held all the jumble of houses together and made them mean something. It was red in colour, even on that grey day. In sunlight it was the colour of winter oak-leaves. A fringe of cedars grew along the edge of the cavern, like a garden. They were the only living things. Such silence and stillness and repose— immortal repose. That village sat looking down into the canyon with the calmness of eternity.
>
> PH 179–80

As if in elaboration of Cather's aspiration for the novel, everything has been narrowed down to ekphrasis. Simple sentences supposedly represent what it is Tom sees, exactly as he sees it. Granted, neither the reader nor St. Peter (as he recalls Tom's description) can avoid the implicit contrast it offers with his own shabby house, his petty town. But the account of Tom's discovery, now part of the story of that long-ago, long-lost summer, is meant to register nothing more than a quiet vision, as the scene becomes a perfect instance of *ut pictura poesis.* In fact, the lyric suspension in this vision of the Cliff City offers a moment apparently outside time, beyond progression or telos, of sculptural and architectural poise that speaks to a supposedly perfect psychological balance. The plain diction, measured repetitions, and intense concentration all elaborate a Keatsian vision of "silence and slow time" in a narrative pause that aspires to the condition of stillness it represents. The scene's "immortal repose" seems Cather's effort to "tease us out of thought" by quietly seducing us from explanations of cause and effect. Whether or not it succeeds, it surely aspires as invocation to leave us unquestioning of any befores or afters, as much in awe of the scene represented as Tom himself.

III. Selfless Wonder, Yet Possession Persists

Repeatedly, passages in *The Professor's House* concentrate on sheer description itself, regularly failing to advance a plot and in the process rattling a reader's impression of what actually counts as important. Still, a larger design does eventually emerge in those lyric scenes that punctuate Tom Outland's account, as they slowly sum up and even seem to explain the similar, less intense moments scattered through the outer frame section, otherwise isolated and unintegrated. Simply the act of calm scrutiny links the vivid scenes experienced by an older St. Peter, of "autumn flowers, dahlias and wild asters," to the inner Outland section—as if "silence and stillness and repose" were not merely part of the depicted scene but prescribed for characters and readers as well. Of course, novels conventionally depend on the opposite, as Peter Brooks argues in his claim for the centrality of desire in a reader's experience: "The ambitious hero thus stands as a figure of the reader's efforts to construct meanings in ever-larger wholes, to totalize his experience of human existence in time, to grasp past, present, and future in a significant shape" (39). Yet Cather seems to want to celebrate observation for itself, in a process whose self-contained delights are elaborated in Tom Outland's mental reflections: "That cluster of buildings, in its arch, with the dizzy drop into empty air from its doorways and the wall of cliff above, was as clear in my mind as a picture. By closing my eyes I could see it against the dark, like a magic-lantern slide" (182). Description, sheer and unadulterated, once again trumps plot progression.

In fact, at moments on the mesa, an extreme hyperattentiveness sets in just as Cather slows narrative down, as if all that were required was absolutely rigorous and stringent physical description. In the frame section, of course, depictions of characters proliferate as fully as of settings and structures, but the Cliff City itself is so resonant a scene that, interestingly, the few characters in "Tom Outland's Story" are *not* actually pictured, giving the impression that all observational energies have been absorbed by the Blue Mesa. We never see Roddy Blake or Henry Atkins as physical beings, unlike the excessively self-conscious figures in the frame story. Another way to measure Cather's presentation of the mesa's supernal beauty is that it exists unexplained and unaccounted for. We are left merely with questions that instead are meant paradoxically to promote narrative, without an ensuing account itself about the initial cliff-dwellers: Who were they? What were they like? When did they leave? How did it get built? The mystery of their existence serves at once as a defiance of plot and its instigator: an unknown and unknowable story that still remains an ostensible provocation *to* plot, to account for those who transformed the Blue Mesa into an architectural wonder. Description, after all, always induces narrative *in* us (as Genette and Bal confirm), rendering Cather's modernist effort at unadulterated description a futile exercise.

Yet her depiction of Cliff Dweller ruins is salutary nonetheless, in registering *in* narrative the partial failure *of* narrative—that is, in its erasure of static wonder, its willful avoidance of mystery sustained, its need to find an answer that will nullify the amazement first drawing us in. This is admittedly a romantic vision to which Cather was clearly drawn, of becoming like Keats's Shakespeare in that state of Negative Capability, "of being in uncertainties, Mysteries, doubts without any irritable reaching after fact & reason" (Keats 277). Certainly, St. Peter's scholarly investment in writing a history of Spanish explorers itself offers a contrary vision, though the point seems to be that his deep spiritual and emotional anomie results at least in part from his resolutely historicist, conventionally narrative practice. It may be as well that St. Peter has come to realize the disjunction between the accounts Spanish explorers wrote and their actions, or as Stephen Greenblatt observes: "Words in the New World seem always to be trailing after events that pursue a terrible logic quite other than the fragile meanings that they construct" (63). And this would help explain something of St. Peter's own history, in the "paralysis" that Greenblatt observes was a quality of early explorers' reports, now become an aspect of his mid-life crisis as he absorbs the full significance of his own scholarship. Cather's reversion to a romantic idealism, however, could just as easily be paying homage to a stereotypically native American vision— the very vision occluded from *The Professor's House* in the absence of native Americans themselves—in Tom's identification with the Blue Mesa.

Cather's attraction to this posture is evident throughout her career, and becomes especially marked in her novels of the 1920s. In fact, her comments on writing *Death Comes for the Archbishop*—in wanting "something without accent, with none of the artificial elements of composition"—are again instructive for understanding her efforts in *The Professor's House*:

The essence of such writing is not to hold the note, not to use an incident for all there is in it—but to touch and pass on. I felt that such writing would be a kind of discipline in these days when the 'situation' is made to count for so much in writing . . . In this kind of writing the mood is the thing—all the little figures and stories are mere improvisations that come out of it.

OW 5, 9–10

This starts with a curious claim for a writer, that things (churches) can tell "their own story," before she turns to frescoes in romanticizing their supposed lack of convention ("with none of the artificial elements of composition"). It is almost as if Cather were acknowledging here the very psychological imperative of reading that her practice seems intent to deny: that description must *always* lead necessarily to narrative, since readers immediately and irrepressibly invent sequences of motive and consequence, of past and future, from any given scene. Description can never stand simply for itself, despite Cather's gestures intended to slow down the causal interpretive impulse that always kicks in.

Her agenda only *seems* to be anti-narrative, but since that cannot succeed, she wants to open possibilities through a minimalist, allusive, synechdochal style that evokes a moment where "the mood is the thing" and all else has been expunged. Such purity of expression lies beyond the realm of language, as Cather implicitly realizes by invoking Tom Outland's diary, which can only be alluded to, not given first-hand. No actual verbal record could live up to the extreme linguistic claims St. Peter makes for Tom's "plain account":

The adjectives were purely descriptive, relating to form and colour, and were used to present the objects under consideration, not the young explorer's emotions. Yet through this austerity one felt the kindling imagination, and ardour and excitement of the boy, like the vibration in a voice when the speaker strives to conceal his emotion by using only conventional phrases.

PH 238

Here is Cather's own ostensible idiom abstracted, with description defined as the bare evocation of whatever sits before the eye, prior to any interpretive gesture, which also helps explain her admiration for Stephen Crane.

It is as if Tom's description corresponded in another key with the Cliff City architecture it is meant to represent. The "austerity" of his account itself is taken to signal a "kindling imagination," represented in a curious simile of "the vibration" in a distinctive *voice* that emerges despite its "conventional phrases." Yet the interesting aspect of Tom's voice, apart from its stripped-down style itself, is that it emerges from a distant double remove, as little more than disembodied memory, in St. Peter's recollection of the evening nearly a decade before when Tom finally explained himself and his past. The voice, in other words, exists only as a trace of something no longer possessed, though the memory itself seems to reproduce its effects in those who treasure it. What has become clear is that Cather's central theme—to explore "possession" as a narrative vehicle—has been all along her *stylistic* means as well. The novel is filled with possessions, as Cather later admitted (intending to make it "overcrowded and stuffy"); and most of the actions that occur throughout have to do with sacrificing them, or acquiring replacements, or envying those who have even more. Yet the alternative vision in the novel is revealed when, after Roddy Blake has sold the cliff-dweller artifacts, Tom buries his disappointment in the recognition of another response: "Something had happened in me that made it possible for me to co-ordinate and simplify, and that process, going on in my mind, brought with it great happiness. It was possession" (*PH* 227). As he adds about the "religious emotion" he discovered, "I wakened with the feeling that I had found everything, instead of having lost everything . . . I didn't want to go back and unravel things step by step. Perhaps I was afraid that I would lose the whole in the parts" (227–28). Critics have observed that the entire novel is pitched toward this moment, in offering a visionary euphoria that displaces narrative sequence itself ("no longer an adventure, but a religious emotion"), as Tom finds each day repeating itself in exaltation. And his wariness about lingering over separate details forms a gesture comparable to Cather's own stylistic constraints.[12] As he expresses it, any mourning of individual possessions would cause him to lose "the whole in the parts."

The commitment to that synechdochal vision is expressed in Tom's gifts of the artifacts he discovered that summer (to Kitty, to Rosamond, to Mrs. St. Peter) paying tribute at once to Cliff-dweller ideals as well as to the value of renunciation that defines his transformation. Some have questioned Tom's appropriation of artifacts not his to give, and point to the larger issue of possessing native objects themselves.[13] Still, Cather may be more historical than her critics by stressing a context in which archaeology was coming of age, with amateurs like Tom and Roddy investing their savings to excavate the site, traveling to Washington to ensure its preservation—all, only to be rebuffed by government officials. Moreover, Tom's outrage at Roddy's "stupidity and presumption" (*PH* 216) in selling the relics is meant to repudiate a crass commercial logic: "There never was any question of money with me, where this mesa and its people were concerned" (*PH* 220). St. Peter later echoes that statement in rebuffing Louie's offer of assistance—"there can be no question of money between me and Tom Outland" (*PH* 50)—as if underwriting a larger immunity to commercialism. Yet just as description stimulates narrative, despite Cather's idealist efforts, so the novel confirms how commerce always circulates, despite efforts at denying its currency. St. Peter, after all and despite his protest, has benefitted immensely from Tom's discoveries just as Tom himself profits from Roddy Blake's paternal efforts. In short, Tom's reverence for the mesa, like his outrage at Roddy, confirms an idealizing perspective that is regularly challenged by the novel.

IV. Lives Suspended

Tom's epiphany is often cited as a transitional moment in *The Professor's House*, even if it is rarely invoked by those who focus on Cather's larger deployment of modernist means to thematic ends.[14] That is, those who concentrate on her juxtapositions, uninflected descriptions, and structural dislocations tend simply to accept the novel's investigation of dispossession, physically and emotionally. But the two actively reinforce each other, perhaps most clearly near the novel's conclusion when St. Peter wonders about the course his life has taken, the values he has embodied. And what he presumes is that his past has been shaped not by personal choices and family dramas but by a series of accidents that appear irrelevant to the conception he has had of himself all along. The figure he imaginatively confronts at the end is the static image of himself as a young boy, as he was before his marriage created another account of himself, of the striving intellectual, academic, husband, bread-winner. One-sided as this idealizing view may seem, it confirms an emptying out of desire, a studied acquisition of indifference, that represents quite a different vision from, say, the novels of Theodore Dreiser. St. Peter struggles toward a reading of his life that resembles a portrait, not a narrative, since sustainable narratives depend on a desire for more, for further developments, that he has come to find odious. Yet odious or not, the desire for more has been revealed throughout as life-enhancing, since his recovery and loss is itself a narrative.

Just as he thinks of Tom's experience as an ideal, suspended in amber, he begins to think of his own life that way, enshrining himself as well as others. The need to take other ambitious actions, to live with a vision of one's life as a kind of striving, is what St. Peter finds deplorable about the move from his old house. In contrast, what opens him up again to the idea of his authentic self is an access in memory to objects untouched, not actions achieved or pursuits completed. It is in contemplating towers or lakes that Cather's descriptive mode comes to the fore, and in which St. Peter in turn feels most himself. These form the high moments in life, unavailable to nearly everyone else in the novel—moments when the self falls into the "blue." As Peter Balaam has written, "The blue is the saving loss of narrative (narrative being that which always misplaces and misreads objects, sells them short, or sells them out). Even St. Peter's award-winning history somehow inevitably abstracts and takes improper possession through narrative" (private correspondence). This sense of gaining everything by abandoning a desire for possession—whether of things themselves or of their accounts—resonates up until the closing pages of the novel, despite the novel's persistent revelation that a desire for possession can never be assuaged.

Yet precisely at the novel's conclusion, we realize at once how satisfying yet ultimately (and admittedly) futile Cather's agenda has been: satisfying, because her visionary scenes truly do dislodge the narrative logic of conventional novels; and ultimately futile, because narrative keeps reasserting itself, as Cather knew all too well, even despite claims for its demise. The "life of another person" that St. Peter at last finds his own life to be, to which "he was indifferent" (*PH* 243), has nonetheless structured the novel we have read and enjoyed, just as Tom Outland's epiphany "*on the mesa*, in a world above the world" (217) occurs only after a summer in which he has scrupulously tried to reconstruct with Father Duchene the history of the cliff dwellers ("'I see them here, isolated, cut off from other tribes'" [198]). Tom's joy in the recovery of native artifacts is, as Walter Benn Michaels has argued, part of his feeling of possession, as the grafting of a white national history onto native materials: "The 'happiness unalloyed' that Tom experiences on the Blue Mesa is thus the recovery of Indian culture, which is to say, of the very idea of culture" (36). And this helps explain Tom's outburst at Roddy Blake, along with his subsequent summer spent on the mesa. But that explanation is countered at the same time by Tom's final resistance to recovering native experience, leaving his journal untouched and buried, his account abandoned when he leaves for Hamilton College. And one might claim Tom's joy finally has less to do with anything specifically cultural, white or native, than with an emotional release that results from his own psychological transformation, expressed as the renunciation of an idea of recovery itself, or of possession.

In short, the novel seems to have things two ways, in part due to the fundamental paradox in Cather's modernism itself. After all, wonder is always "a prelude to appropriation" (136), as Stephen Greenblatt observes, no less so in Cather's novel than in the travel accounts of early Spanish explorers, reminding us that one cannot stay in a perpetual state of wonder, of visionary stasis. Like other exceptional states, they remain exceptional precisely by being exceptional, a break from the present, a turn away from familiar procedures. The effort to evade narrative—whether Tom's on the mesa, or St. Peter's in his final concession, or Cather's in the novel itself—always returns us *to* narrative, if only as the temporal stage within which wondrous epiphanies, having occurred, now subside. Wonder may be the state we experience in the face of a continent unexplored, which has been the experience of those on this continent since the beginning; but ever since, of course, it is no longer so unexplored, and wonder diminishes with the passing of time.

Part of Cather's triumph in the novel is to engage readers in the oscillation between "everything happens" and "nothing happens," which roughly corresponds to a tension between narrative and description. Yet an equal part of the novel's taut balance between enacted temporal sequence and timeless quiescence, registered in St. Peter's obscure concessions at the end, has to do with its unattainable visionary aspirations. Tom's realization that he has "found everything" just when he had assumed all was lost seems the contrary of his mentor's final realization that he must now "live without delight ... without joy, without passionate griefs" (*PH* 257). Yet that vision is also presented in the same semi-religious terms that Tom had first articulated, in the need to lose a desire for possession in order to gain true wisdom. And this conclusion offers a thematic comment on the novel's descriptive technique: "He had let something go—and it was gone: something very precious, that he could not consciously have relinquished" (*PH* 258). One achieves visionary insight only by giving up narrative, abandoning plots of intention, motive, and closure. Yet novels by necessity inspire a process of narrative in us willy-nilly, defying those moments of epiphany they allude to, establishing in the process the dilemma of their own reading. Cather fully appreciated this paradox, and in *The Professor's House* became among the most prominent American modernists to turn the novel inside out, getting readers to understand what reading for plot (and reading to ignore it, in a state of wonderment) might actually mean.

Notes

1   Richards had already published *The Principles of Literary Criticism* (1924), and was formulating studies that would lead to *Practical Criticism* (1929), which pioneered a technique of close reading that inspired the New Criticism. A few months later, Joseph Wood Krutch expanded on Richards' observation in an intriguing observation that anticipates aspects of my argument: "Even when Miss Cather strives most consciously to give to her books a narrative movement there is likely to be something static or picture-like about her best effects, and when she falters it is usually in the effort to carry the reader from one to the other of the moments which rise like memories before her. In the present instance she has nothing that could properly be called a plot, but she is wisely content to accept the fact and to depend upon the continuous presence of beauty rather than upon any movement to hold the interest of the reader. When things are recalled in the mood of elegy there is no suspense and they do not take place one after the other because, all things being merely past, there is no time but one" (337).

2   It should be noted that thematic readings of the novel have altered drastically in the eighty years since its appearance. In particular, a recent celebration of Cather's lesbian identity has led to intriguing readings of the relationships between Tom Outland, Roddy Blake, and Godfrey St. Peter. See Sharon O'Brien's influential essay, as well as Eve Sedgwick and John Anders. But see also Deborah Carlin, who argues: "Reading Cather's fiction as sexually coded is prevalent among current scholarship ... [W]hat distinguishes these readings is the implicit assumption that the fiction masks, submerges, and even distorts the lesbianism that resides, albeit coded, in the texts. The critical task then becomes one of decoding, uncovering, and recovering what has been unwritten, unmentionable, and unnamed. Yet it also involves a mode of interpretation that reads between and beyond what is literally inscribed on the page, basing its interpretive burden of proof on the life rather than the text" (20). As Carlin goes on to state, in terms that inform any thematic reading: "One way then to reclaim the later novels as 'women's texts' is to acknowledge just how frustratingly feminist and potentially antifeminist they are simultaneously. Cather, one is forced to accept, will always demand to have her texts read both ways, and at once" (24).

3   On behalf of surface reading, Heather Love has recently observed: "Description has had a mostly poor reputation in literary studies, where it

has been seen as inferior to narration. In neoclassical aesthetics, description as a feature of literary texts was often seen as either an extraneous ornament or a dangerous indulgence. In Marxist aesthetics, it was seen as a capitulation to a reified world. As a feature of criticism itself, description has been discredited through its associations with empiricism and seen as necessarily subordinate to the key activity of interpretation. However, recent questioning of depth hermeneutics across the field has meant a partial recuperation of description" (381–82).

4   Carlota Smith offers a linguistic distinction between narrative mode, report mode, description mode, information mode, and argument mode, all of which are affective by temporal markers (19–20). I have collapsed her information mode as part of what I mean by description, but it is clear that her narrative mode always includes participants involved in a "causal relationship . . . The key to narrative advancement is the dynamism of events. Recall that dynamism involves successive stages of time" (Smith 26). By contrast, in descriptive passages "Time is static or suspended. There are no significant changes or advancements. . . . Descriptive passages progress spatially through a scene" (Smith 28).

5   As Cather commented self-deflatingly about her early novel, *O Pioneers!* (1913), "I did not in the least expect that other people would see anything in a slow-moving story, without 'action,' without 'humour,' without a 'hero'; a story concerned entirely with heavy farming people, with cornfields and pasture lands and pig yards—set in Nebraska, of all places!" (*On Writing*, 94). Deborah Carlin states that one "reason why Cather's late fiction eludes easy classification is that she was self-consciously experimenting with both narrative structure and technique after 1922" (22).

6   Those tenets consist (according to Marie-Laure Ryan) in lining up events in order to find answers, "asking in what order did the represented events occur; what changes did they cause in the depicted world; what do the events (and their results) mean for the characters; what motivates actions and how does the outcome of these actions compare to the intent of the agent. If a text confronts us with such questions, and if we are able to answer them, we read the text as a story, or rather, we read the story told by the text, whether or not we are aware of what we are doing" (33).

7   To which he adds "that description, in Proust, becomes absorbed into narration . . . for the obvious reason that with him description is everything *except* a pause in the narrative" (Genette 105).

8   O'Brien cautioned against reducing a possible resonance to a formal agenda, or otherwise reading for the supposedly authentic text beneath the novel's gaps and fissures. As she concludes, "we need to examine the dialectic between what is named and what is not, rather than assuming that what is not named is the 'real' text, the one Cather would have written in a different social environment" (O'Brien 598). Deborah Carlin concurs: "Reading Cather's fiction as sexually coded is prevalent among current scholarship . . . what distinguishes these readings is the implicit assumption

that the fiction masks, submerges, and even distorts the lesbianism that resides, albeit coded, in the texts. The critical task then becomes one of decoding, uncovering, and recovering what has been unwritten, unmentionable, and unnamed. Yet it also involves a mode of interpretation that reads between and beyond what is literally inscribed on the page, basing its interpretive burden of proof on the life rather than the text" (20). See also Peck (20–22).

9   Bal extends Genette's observations, arguing that "description is at the core of the novelistic genre" (571) by invariably moving us into a temporal realm in which some things take precedence over others, thus producing meaning. According to her, Proust preeminently "shipwrecks" any real distinction between narrative and description, since the latter is always pointing toward the former: "descriptions of the main characters—or rather, the difficulties of describing them—are the 'essence' of" *La Recherche* (Bal 585).

10 In 1911, the abstract expressionist Wassily Kandinsky, who painted *The Blue Rider* (1903), formulated ideas about color symbolism, and the "inner resonance" by which color touches the soul of the viewer. He claimed in particular that "Depth is found in blue, first in its physical movements (1) of retreat from the spectator, (2) of turning in upon its own centre. It affects us likewise mentally in any geometrical form. The deeper its tone, the more intense and characteristic the effect. We feel a call to the infinite, a desire for purity and transcendence. *Blue is the typical heavenly color*; the ultimate feeling it creates is one of rest." (58). In 1924, as part of the Bauhaus group, he was one of "Die Blaue Vier" (Blue Four) who lectured and exhibited in the USA.

11 Michael Leddy has commented on striking imagistic parallels, while Anne Moseley provides a useful assessment of the novel's structural tensions that in some ways anticipates my analysis.

12 See Hermione Lee (242, 255–56) and Demaree Peck (189–217).

13 Thomas Strychacz (56) and Marilee Lindemann (104) indict Tom Outland for allegedly treating the archaeological sight as his own. Yet my claim is the contrary, that Tom's anger at Roddy results from his recognition that no one *does* possess the artifacts.

14 Hermione Lee anticipates aspects of this discussion, but her chapter on the novel (significantly entitled "Taking Possession") argues that Tom's paring down of speech is a "paradoxical disclaimer" (253).

Chapter 2

OSCILLATION IN *LOLITA* (1955)

Thus it appeared, I say, but was not. It was my antagonist—it was
Wilson, who then stood before me in the agonies of his dissolution.
His mask and cloak lay, where he had thrown them, upon the floor.
Not a thread in all his raiment—not a line in all the marked and
singular lineaments of his face which was not, even in the most
absolute identity, *mine own*!

—Edgar Allen Poe, "William Wilson" (130)

Quite an unwholesome book.

—Adolf Eichmann, commenting on Lolita to his jailer while
awaiting trial for crimes against humanity in Jerusalem,
Hannah Arendt (49)[1]

At this superhigh level of art, literature is of course not concerned
with pitying the underdog or cursing the upperdog. It appeals to
that secret depth of the human soul where the shadows of other
worlds pass like the shadows of nameless and soundless ships.

—Nabokov, Nikolai Gogol (149)

Cather's visionary efforts that exhilarate characters and readers alike
becomes for Nabokov at once more one-sided (favoring the reader
alone) and far less ethereal. Still, the fact that two such different
authors, invested in such disparate narrative projects, should share so
closely the narrative ambition of readerly transformation is itself
cause for surprise. Cather remarkably anticipates Nabokov's claim
that *Lolita* "affords me what I shall call aesthetic bliss, that is a sense of
being somehow, somewhere, connected with other states of being"
(314), in her own tacit aims for *The Professor's House*. And while his
"bliss" may differ from her "epiphany," it does so through the reader's
more unsettling engagement with words revealed as autonomous
linguistic structures that do not invariably align with the phenomenal

worlds they silently represent. In this, Nabokov advances Cather's agenda from an experience narrated by characters, then replicated for readers, to one now exclusive to readers alone, in the galvanizing lexical disjunctions that both submerge us *in* a novel and simultaneously make us aware *of* a novel being read. The seductiveness of Cather's lyric descriptions that immerse us in moments of awe becomes no less seductive in Nabokov's stylistic flamboyance, though he persists in drawing the reader's attention to his stylistic legerdemain, as if perversely withholding the possibility of a suspension of disbelief. Unselfconscious immersion in narrative, even Cather's narrativizing reduced to sheer description, no longer seems enough for Nabokov, who thinks of readerly transformation as a process of disorientation. It is as if *Lolita* represented the perfect example of Roland Barthes's "text of bliss," which singularly "brings to a crisis [the reader's] relation with language."[2]

That crisis can of course emerge from many forms of literature, as Barthes acknowledged, but Nabokov's novel marks a notably deliberate assault on expectations in its startling disruption of the conventional status of language itself. For in alternating between words that map a realm imagined as potentially real, and words that register nothing more than their own self-contained linguistic play, *Lolita* would seem to waver between the modernism of Cather, Faulkner, and Hemingway on the one hand and what would become the postmodernism of Thomas Pynchon, Donald Barthelme, William Gaddis and William Gass, Don DeLillo and Kathy Acker on the other.[3] Nabokov delineates that seesawing effect, as many have observed, in the intersection between full-fledged characters and sound effects, between supposedly virtual figures and mere rhetorical figures of speech. John Ray, Jr., Ph.D. offers an opening assessment that speaks to the former possibility, in touting the novel as a lesson that encourages "the task of bringing up a better generation in a safer world" (*Lolita* 6). Protesting this, the "Afterword" (ostensibly in Nabokov's own voice) argues that "*Lolita* has no moral in tow. For me a work of fiction exists only insofar as it affords me what I shall bluntly call aesthetic bliss, that is a sense of being somehow, somewhere, connected with other states of being where art (curiosity, tenderness, kindness, ecstasy) is the norm" (314–15). Presciently, these two bookended declarations anticipate nearly all subsequent interpretations, even as they would become caricatures in their unyielding resolve of broader critical positions.[4]

Taking a larger view, we find that *Lolita* might be said to expose what all novels do (if rarely so theatrically): offering an account of characters engaged in morally consequential behavior through a style so consummate as to divert attention to something other than the sheer account itself. Nabokov simply exaggerates that "diversion" unconscionably, in the absolute divorce between aesthetic pleasure and considerations that arise in an imagined narrative realm, as if flouting not only immediate ethical reassurance but Keats's larger conclusion that "Beauty is truth, truth beauty." Indeed, Nabokov's choice of the most scabrous of scenarios seems deliberately intended to inflame the issue, even as it reveals that issue (however toned-down) as lying at the heart of all literary texts. For while not apparent at first, *Lolita* raises the vexed question of how language in general is meant to work, whether as mere neutral reflector of autonomous reality or as artistically shaping and virtually constituting what it represents (autonomous itself). These alternatives have long fueled a classic philosophical debate, though it comes as little surprise that Nabokov simply cut the Gordian knot, dismissing doubts with customary aplomb by denying that phenomena could ever be perceived without betraying a perspective:

> The trouble is that bare facts do not exist in a state of nature, for they are never really quite bare: the white trace of a wrist watch, a curled piece of sticking plaster on a bruised heel, these cannot be discarded by the most ardent nudist . . . I doubt whether you can even give your telephone number without giving something of yourself.
>
> *Gogol* 119

And for that reason, the truth of another's life remains inaccessible, "because thought cannot help distorting whatever it tries to encompass" (Cited by Alexandrov 34).[5]

Lolita is perfectly attuned to the stakes involved in this clear-cut distinction—of accurately representing phenomena independent of one's blinkered point of view versus automatically projecting assumptions one fails to realize are assumptions at all. After all, that is Humbert Humbert's central ploy, detailing a set of alleged historical facts whose status as history he regularly undermines through the inscribed, wrought, *written* status of his narrative. The reader, buffeted back and forth between seemingly exclusive modes of reading, is swayed into fleeting sympathy with characters *in* the text even as the novel exposes character itself as mere lexical prestidigitation, a scintillating performance of verbal smoke and mirrors. Yet if this oscillating strategy suggests that ethical considerations can flower only in the absence of aesthetic enjoyment, we also become magically mindful of their mutual involvement, as if each existed only in the presence of the other, with the stripped-down style of historical verisimilitude more fully apparent by contrast with the defiantly flamboyant, self-consuming style of harmless aesthetic play. The sharp contrast between these discursive modes establishes how each can be separately read, and in turn *Lolita* reveals in bold strokes the way other novels work, if more surreptitiously.

Few readers, however, appreciate how fully its oscillating textual rhythms accentuate its ethical claims, or how much Humbert's sometimes passionate, sometimes aggrieved, sometimes wistful verbal choices constitute the very subject they represent, and in so doing unsettle any stable understanding, any settled response of either aesthetic bliss or ethical outrage.[6] "My characters are galley slaves" (*SO* 95), Nabokov once rebuffed an interviewer, and in the duplicitous pun between ship's chattel and lead type he trenchantly illustrates the alternation his novel sets in motion between people and words, modernism and postmodernism, ethics and sheer bliss. While this shape-shifting mode has admittedly drawn considerable critical attention, rarely has it been claimed to constitute the basis of our "mere reading" of the novel. In the following, I argue that *Lolita* requires an oscillating perspective, never allowing the reader to settle into either unearned sympathy or sheer verbal delight, keeping ever before us the tantalizing impossibility of joining two antithetical modes together.

I. Style and Desire

Turn first to the ostensible plot of the novel, since readers *do* ineluctably project a life into a name, imagined characters into events, and since Humbert does so often implore belief in his account. Even before he begins, his editor John Ray, Jr. offers to reveal the "destinies of the 'real' people beyond the 'true' story" (*L* 4), a hoary ploy meant to dissolve the verbal texture of the narrative that ensues, persuading us of some flesh-and-blood reality independent of words. Teasingly, we are informed that "Mrs. 'Richard F. Schiller' died in childbed, giving birth to a stillborn girl, on Christmas Day 1952, in Gray Star, a settlement in the remotest Northwest" (4)—this, hundreds of pages before we learn she is the novel's eponymous figure—as if to establish an unframed, unstoried dimension beyond narrative, where historical documentation can challenge Humbert's construction for the reader careful enough to remember the facts. Humbert himself invokes history as confirmation of his account, offering a chronicle that roots the whole in a quotidian world. "The reader may check the weather data in the Ramsdale *Journal* for 1947" (40), he assures the dubious, in a Stendhalian gesture that echoes John Ray Jr.'s exhortation: should Humbert's crime seem merely fictional, look at "the daily papers for September–October 1952" (4). Contributing to this effect is a wealth of references to popular culture, from western motels and hit tunes to fast food and teen magazines, all of which lend an air of history to the narrative even as they undermine themselves, including Humbert's masking of people's names in mock simulation of crime journalism, to protect the innocent. Actual figures seem to loom behind their fictional pseudonyms, even as pseudonyms are meant to evoke a tinge of character itself. As the double-monikered Humbert Humbert admits, he even toyed with other fake names for himself, "but for some reason I think my choice expresses the nastiness best" (308).[7] Likewise, Humbert's description of the letter Lo finally sends, pleading for help, jumbles together actual dates and fictionalized places to reinforce his account's authenticity: "The letter was dated September 18, 1952 (this was September 22), and the address she gave was 'General Delivery, Coalmont' (not 'Va.,' not 'Pa,' not 'Tenn.'—and not Coalmont, anyway—I have camouflaged everything, my love)" (267). The very invocation of so many other "Coalmonts" (which turns out not to be the name anyway) establishes the map of a national landscape (with an actual Coalmont in every state Humbert mentions as well as in Indiana and Colorado) at the same time that it makes Humbert's narrative seem plainly invented. Whenever we sense the novel is becoming momentarily realistic, with characters taking on flesh and blood, we're reminded of the elaborate machinery producing that effect, eroding our projected belief, stripping them back to verbal skeletons.

In his Afterword, Nabokov called "the task of inventing America" essential to the novel, but only by "the obtaining of such local ingredients as would allow me to inject a modicum of average 'reality' (one of the few words which mean nothing without quotes) into the brew of individual fancy" (312). That air of "reality" was the result of his extensive experience in America, teaching in New England, butterfly collecting in Colorado, staying at assorted motels, even doing "field research" on bus rides with school girls to learn how they behaved.[8] Nabokov's eye for the telling detail, exact in its placement, is nonetheless at the service of a fanciful imagination, and the panorama that Humbert paints of American landscape regularly alternates between lyric evocation, mordant wit, and realist deflation:

And as we pushed westward, patches of what the garage-man called 'sage brush' appeared, and then the mysterious outlines of table-like hills, and then red bluffs ink-blotted with junipers, and then a mountain range, dun grading into blue, and blue into dream, and the desert would meet us with a steady gale, dust, gray thorn bushes, and hideous bits of tissue paper mimicking pale flowers among the prickles of wind-tortured withered stalks all along the highway; in the middle of which there sometimes stood simple cows, immobilized in a position (tail left, white eyelashes right) cutting across all human rules of traffic.

153

Even here, in the surfeit of mid-American landscape details, a splashy style trumps realism in the curious intrusion of "mysterious outlines" and "ink-blotted with junipers," anticipating Humbert's painterly eye that traces shades from "blue into dream." The alliteration of "wind-tortured withered stalks" is as mannered as the mordant observation of cows "cutting across all human rules of traffic." And this is only one of many passages offered up as descriptively impressionist *tours de force*, linking the landscape with Humbert's dreamlike impressions, drawing our eye persistently back from hard fact to feverish sensibility.

Yet this descriptive zeal also serves as foil to less fervid occasions when something besides style is apparent, hinting at an actual situation lurking just beneath the lapidary prose. This register occurs most obviously at more temperate emotional moments for Humbert, especially when Lolita is not an object of yearning for him and he feels compelled to acknowledge his effect on her. On these occasions, an ethical strain ineluctably emerges in the admission of pain that itself becomes the currency of realism in their relationship, defining what is actually exchanged between them: "For a second I held her. She freed herself from the shadow of my embrace—doing this not consciously, not violently, not with any personal distaste, but with the neutral plaintive murmur of a child demanding its natural rest. And again the situation remained the same" (*L* 130). The understated quality of this description—in poetic rhythms that patiently reiterate Lo's own resistance (the repeated "not ... not ... not ... ") and that for once recognize her poignantly as "a child demanding its natural rest"—seems less fictional than other moments described by Humbert, precisely because the passage is stylistically muted. As well, the scene corresponds to more conventional prose norms, in contrast to Humbert's otherwise inflated lyrical invocations. Though just as calculatedly crafted, the passage encourages us to respond as if it were less invented. And it is the novel's magical oscillation between registers that contributes to this artistic deception, lending a sense of authenticity to the scene in the very contrast with Humbert's more flamboyant effusions.

Shortly thereafter, Humbert acknowledges "something torn" inside Lolita that has brought tears to her eyes: "This was an orphan. This was a lone child, an absolute waif, with whom a heavy-limbed, foul-smelling adult had had strenuous intercourse three times that very morning. . . . I had been careless, stupid, and ignoble. And let me be quite frank . . ." (*L* 140). Again, the pathos of Lo's circumstances speaks as directly to the reader as it does to Humbert, diverting attention from the wooden clichés, the cartoon-like representations that he invokes to describe their situation—or rather, once again lending authenticity to seemingly actual events because *of* those clichés. And that, of course, is also part of Humbert's aesthetic contrivance. When he then poignantly admits her isolation—"You see, she had absolutely nowhere else to go" (*L* 142)—the spare understatement of Lolita's plight all but calls for an ethical response. The aesthetic may seem to dissolve in the direct claim for a girl's consternation, in her projected helplessness facing a world gone horribly awry, but even here Humbert does not quite capitulate to sentiment. We may momentarily assume her pain put paid to any aesthetic enjoyment she might arouse, but we are never bereft of style, never simply left alone with another consciousness, however tormented.

Analogously, the sheer vulgarity of Humbert's desire defies lyrical transformation (if not aesthetic rendition), further enforcing an otherwise suspended sense of phenomenal reality. Consider one of those moments when he gains Lolita's compliance, bribing her for sexual favors: "I . . . unbuttoned my overcoat and for sixty-five cents plus the permission to participate in the school play, had Dolly put her inky, chalky, red-knuckled hand under the desk" (*L* 198). Any possibility of lyrical *frisson* is coldly excluded in the stark depiction of Humbert's need, though the careful adjectives describing her hand ("inky, chalky, red-knuckled") evidence an ever-present verbal craftsman. More generally, encounters whose sordidness is described so abruptly tend to inflame our moral sympathies to the exclusion of any other response. And the recurrence of these encounters—or more particularly, of depictions at once condensed, understated, and raw—reinforces solicitude and precludes aesthetic delight. Regularly, Humbert's sadism ("How sweet it was to bring that coffee to her, and then deny it until she had done her morning duty" (*L* 164)) vies with his appallingly mild chagrin (when "the operation was over, all over, and she was weeping in my arms;—a salutary storm of sobs after one of the fits of moodiness that had become so frequent with her in the course of that otherwise admirable year!" (*L* 169)). In either instance, either sadism or chagrin, any inclination to see this as merely a play of verbal possibilities has been disrupted. Granted the fictionality of Humbert's world, what has also been disrupted is an acceptance of even imagined behavior so otherwise immoral in everyday life.

In short, inducing ethical consciousness is part of the novel's oscillating strategy, as if the usual response to *Lolita* as verbal bonbon were misdirected, or at least only partially true. This realization begins with the moderately obtuse fictional editor, John Ray, Jr., describing his decision to keep some "'aphrodisiac'" scenes in the final version, "since those very scenes that one might ineptly accuse of a sensuous existence of their own, are the most strictly functional ones in the development of a tragic tale tending unswervingly to nothing less than a moral apotheosis" (*L* 4–5). Ray's tone-deaf sensibility coincides with a puerile conception of literature that makes him a figure easy to dismiss. Still, his trust in our "compassion for Lolita" (*L* 5) hardly lacks merit, being borne out by decades of interpretation (including Nabokov's own) that cringe at a childhood so foreshortened by Humbert's desires. And the projection of an actual fate onto the conjured figure of Lolita is so irrepressible that the question of ethics can never be simply dismissed, as many have observed, if only because we hear it given voice in the shift to an apparently unselfconscious register, in tones direct and discursively flat (a register every bit as constructed as any other). A world, it would seem, swims into view beyond the words that invoke it.

Humbert himself flamboyantly invokes just such moral considerations, repeatedly addressing the question of how people ought to behave. He admits, following Charlotte's death, to being "obsessed by all sorts of purely ethical doubts and fears" (*L* 105), though those fears turn out (in a parody of striving parents' aspirations everywhere) to be about Lo's new social coups. Later, the measure of his ethical vacancy emerges in the exaggerated split between his benign self-characterization and the malignant examples invoked to support it: "I itemize these sunny nothings mainly to prove to my judges that I did everything in my power to give my Lolita a really good time" (*L* 163). "Good time" indeed, or as he admits on the very next page, "I would lead my reluctant pet to our small home for a quick connection before dinner" (*L* 164). Humbert's tone, so often hard to pin down, wavers between the deliberately mindful (admitting he wants to minimize criminal conduct) and the blithely unintentional (blind and deaf to what he is doing). At other times, he takes delight in behavior that has just elicited remorse, rendering the remorse either simply evanescent or invoked after the fact merely to win readerly sympathy. A similar turn occurs in Humbert's recollection of masturbating against Lolita on the davenport, when he admits to first distress, then relief that "I had stolen the honey of a spasm without impairing the morals of a minor" (*L* 62). Again, the confession is aestheticized by its carefully balanced locutions, which detract from the ethically serious mood he purportedly hopes to create. It is as if Humbert, despite his callous lust, verged on the edge of moral sympathy but is diverted (and thus diverts us) from any more complete identification with his victim by stylistic aplomb.

The davenport scene raises a further issue, however, as Humbert wonders whether the flesh-and-blood creature he has secretly abused is no more than a fitful projection of his own desires. The link between elaborate fantasy and the ostensible Lolita who sits on his lap, between an overactive imagination and the vibrant girl alive in the novel, is one he conveniently elides, claiming that "What I had madly possessed was not she, but my own creation, another fanciful Lolita—perhaps, more real than Lolita; overlapping, encasing her; floating between me and her, and having no will, no consciousness—indeed, no life of her own" (*L* 62). Yet in a novel where he himself exists as Nabokov's artfully invented construction, such metaphysical sophistry hardly undermines the ethical dilemma. He may persist in claiming, "The child knew nothing. I had done nothing to her. And nothing prevented me from repeating a performance that affected her as little as if she were a photographic image rippling upon a screen and I a humble hunchback abusing myself in the dark."[9] His perverse analogy here only complicates, not excuses, their imagined relations, and even his assorted excuses—including the revelation (true? false?) that she was not a virgin, indeed that she had first seduced him—later collide with her plaintive statement that "you raped me" (*L* 202). In short, the question of whose account to credit seems beside the point, since Humbert as guardian is culpable ethically in either case, true *or* false. Yet the persistence with which that understanding recedes before us owes to the power of Humbert's stylistic legerdemain, which persistently relaxes the purchase of any ethical hold.

Perhaps to reinforce that effect, Humbert keeps ironically reintroducing ethical considerations, occasionally in situations that seem less than immediately relevant. Speaking of Charlotte's clichéd romantic accounts, he announces: "The sincerity and artlessness with which she discussed what she called her "love-life," from first necking to connubial catch-as-catch-can, were, ethically, in striking contrast with my glib compositions, but technically the two sets were congeneric since both were affected by the same stuff (soap operas, psychoanalysis and cheap novelettes) upon which I drew for my characters and she for her mode of expression" (*L* 80). What does "ethically" mean here—that she is telling the truth and he is making things up? That she is talking about her marriage and he about his affairs? Or that she is artless and he is glib? This, the first of three invocations of the word by Humbert, seems curiously misdirected, in representing "ethics" as an aspect of writing-as-action (characterizing the ends to which a verbal account is put) or even writing *per se* (artless vs. glib), and not physical action itself or the situation that writing represents. Instead of accounting for peoples' behavior, ethics here refers to the accounts *of* that behavior and how they are to be used. Charlotte's impassioned investment in a derivative, sentimental history offers (so Humbert seems to say) a certain *ethical* distinction from his own invented account. This applies only because of the "glib" nature of its construction, as if her very indifference to ideological premises was itself an ethical flaw. Whether that actually renders her account ethically better or worse is never clear—whether belief in a clichéd, tired version of events is a sign of ethical vitality, somehow making the ethical come alive, or whether instead Humbert's sophisticated contempt for the sentimental conceits he indulges serves as sign of ethical consciousness. The only certainty here is that the ethical and the writerly are linked.

This vision of ethics will develop over the course of the novel into a more familiar concern with actual events rather than curious accounts of them. And it coincides with Humbert's adoption of this conventional understanding, in recognizing Lolita as a person, not simply a figment of imagined desires. A plaintive strain emerges near the conclusion in his rueful recollection of hearing "the melody of children at play," when he realizes "that the hopelessly poignant thing was not Lolita's absence from my side, but the absence of her voice from that concord" (*L* 307–8). Ostensibly, Humbert has made a transition from selfish perversion to compassionate regret, from narcissistic obsession to a sense of parental responsibility. But even that transition is less than clear, in part because his stylistic *tours de force* have made us wary of his claims, especially those that seem to speak from the heart.[10] There is something suspicious in a narrator who, having opened with pathological lyricism meant to help explain his monstrous excess ("Lo-lee-ta"), presents himself as transformed in the course of his narrative into a person like us, capable of remorse. We are left undecided between accepting his confessional tone and rejecting it as part of an overall strategy meant to reduce his criminal sentence (for the murder of Quilty? for the abuse of Lolita?). After all, we never know his motives for making an account in the first place. And only once does he acknowledge writing that account retrospectively, undermining the status of his alleged transformation in the exuberant delight with which he now (supposedly after his expressed remorse) revels in Lolita's nymphet status. We are caught in a verbal hall of mirrors that reminds us of Humbert's earlier self-depiction as he watches Charlotte swimming, imagining her murder "with the stark lucidity of a future recollection (you know—trying to see things as you will remember having seen them)" (*L* 86). In short, determining whether Humbert is converted or unredeemed, sincere or simply manipulative, can never be adequately answered. Even his promising depiction of metamorphosing into a compassionate paternal figure conforms rather obviously to a contrition-and-conversion narrative, the kind of canned testimonial concocted to win a parole board's sympathy.

In contrast to that shaping of louche events into probable narratives, which incites our dubiety in being so apparently calculated, Humbert more often diverges from predictable narrative patterns as a means of establishing a seemingly non-fictive identity, sometimes by forgoing explanatory connectives, at others by offering unaccommodated nouns or adjectives, often parenthetically. The most striking instance occurs early on—"My very photogenic mother died in a freak accident (picnic, lightning) when I was three" (*L* 10)—as if to confirm through two words the most condensed of narratives, left undetailed for the reader to parse out. The effect of these occasions is once again to draw attention from proffered words to events that lie supposedly behind them. First laying eyes on Lolita, for instance, he's reminded of his long-lost Annabel, "as if I were the fairy-tale nurse of some little princess (lost, kidnapped, discovered in gypsy rags through which her nakedness smiled at the king and his hounds), I recognized the tiny dark-brown mole on her side. With awe and delight (the king crying for joy, the trumpets blaring, the nurse drunk) I saw again her lovely indrawn abdomen where my southbound mouth had briefly paused" (*L* 39). The fairy tale invoked elliptically begins by evincing Humbert's flamboyant delight, offering the reader a familiar genre in which to map his memory of Annabel. But suddenly the genre shifts, with a drunken nurse Humbert salivating over his lover's body, as we try to break through the figurative language to comprehend the separate bodies of Lolita, Annabel, the fairy tale princess. For even while attempting to press the scene into a predictable plot—which locks Lolita prospectively into a prescribed role—we find ourselves, through narrative gaps and disjunctions, granting her a seemingly autonomous stature outside a completed narrative, in the fissures of figuration itself.

The same is true of Charlotte's fatal accident, as Humbert in shocked delight reconstructs it imaginatively: "Within the intricacies of the pattern (hurrying housewife, slippery pavement, a pest of a dog, steep grade, big car, baboon at its wheel), I could dimly distinguish my own vile contribution" (*L* 103). The very sequence of parenthetical predicates—not quite incoherent yet not structured as plot—registers a certain non-narrative reality, as Humbert constructs an explanation for his happy change of marital fortune. In the end, of course (as almost everywhere else in the novel), it is unclear whether these instances confirm an autonomous reality (since *not* plotted, but left in a weak paratactic arrangement), or instead point to the account's utter verbal inventiveness.[11] Humbert himself teeters once again between the two, though the latter exerts a greater hold on his imagination as he gives reign to erotic fantasies, acknowledging the confectionary quality of his narrative: "A shipwreck. An atoll. Alone with a drowned passenger's shivering child. Darling, this is only a game! How marvelous were my fancied adventures" (*L* 20). The responsive reader wavers back and forth, see-sawing between mutually exclusive prospects, caught unable to settle into an acceptable readerly role.

II. Evasions and Oscillations

If such scenes are hardly Humbert's dominant stylistic mode, they nonetheless suggest one of the novel's central motifs: that amid the absent connectives, missed transitions, and suppressed explanatory clauses, we are left in doubt of the extent to which authors are ethically liable for the acts they perform on their characters. What are the ethics, then, not of actually treating others in such and such a fashion, but of writing them into imagined plots that end with their equally imagined demise? True, moral philosophy is full of examples weighted in ethical ways, but only because principles need be tested in imagined worlds before being applied in the here and now. Yet if no one is hurt by imagined behavior, what ethical discriminations apply? And the question is compounded by Humbert's inordinate style, so far in excess of a conceivable reality that only John Ray's tone-deaf colleagues persist in invoking moral considerations. From the outset, Humbert's flamboyant indulgences fix our eye on the textual surface, refusing to draw it through to some space beyond: "Lolita, light of my life, fire of my loins" (*L* 9). Here, in contrast to the less gaudy moments cited above, is a narrator in love with words at least as much as with nymphets, constructing a figure from language, concerned less with confirming an independent reality than evoking a figment of possibilities—indeed, with drawing a reader's attention to the figures we use to create figments. Even simply driving with Lolita in the "hot car . . . her mouth working violently on a piece of chewing gum," Humbert cannot resist recalling how "we sped through the striped and speckled forest" (*L* 111), transforming the nominal scene through diction and alliteration into a strangely poeticized moment. More vulgarly, he earlier admits, "I gave her to hold in her awkward fist the scepter of my passion" (*L* 15), undermining through the locution's absurd blend of archaism and euphemism the very spectacle it is meant to represent. When first considering a move to Ramsdale, having accepted the offer of a room in a house where a twelve-year-old girl lives, Humbert imagines "in all possible detail the enigmatic nymphet I would coach in French and fondle in Humbertish"—only to have the house burn down on his arrival, "possibly, owing to the synchronous conflagration that had been raging all night in my veins" (*L* 35). Even when Humbert seems intent on a realistic account, his descriptions regularly delight in their own construction.

This spinning out of scenes whose very renditions subvert their imagined reality is compounded by Humbert's treatment of characters as themselves self-divided. As he announces when he learns of his wife Valeria's revelation of adultery, "Humbert the Terrible deliberated with Humbert the Small whether Humbert Humbert should kill her or her lover, or both, or neither" (*L* 29–30). Characters are regularly fissured, broken apart, exposed as verbal artifacts, much like Duchamp's cubist demolition of his descending nude into constituent forms. Charlotte's entry offers an exemplary instance: "presently, the lady herself—sandals, maroon slacks, yellow silk blouse, squarish face, in that order—came down the steps" (*L* 37). But other iconic figures—like the Shirley Holmes who runs Camp Q (making only a fleeting appearance), or Miss Opposite, Humbert's prying Ramsdale neighbor, who has one feeble hand-waving scene—confirm how fully character in this novel can seem simply a function of verbal legerdemain. As Nabokov himself remarked of *Dead Souls*, "the peripheral characters of [Gogol's] novel are engendered by the subordinate clauses of its various metaphors, comparisons and lyrical outbursts. We are faced by the remarkable phenomenon of mere forms of speech directly giving rise to live creatures" (*Gogol* 78). Or conversely, of creatures who everywhere turn into forms of speech, then back into characters again.

More generally, Humbert repeatedly draws attention to words *as* concocted for the occasion, self-confirming and non-referential, all but written as we read. Even common figures of speech are pointedly parsed ("This, to use an American term, in which discovery, retribution, torture, death, eternity appear in the shape of a singularly repulsive nutshell, was *it*" (*L* 235)). Or Humbert parenthetically denies what he at the same time asserts as true: "She and the dog saw me off. I was surprised (this is a rhetorical figure, I was not) that the sight of the old car in which she had ridden as a child and a nymphet, left her so very indifferent" (*L* 280). Or, he toys with the purported capacity of words to represent events *in extremis*, as when Charlie Holmes has just been killed: "I said didn't she think '*vient de*,' with the infinitive, expressed recent events so much more neatly than the English 'just,' with the past?" (*L* 290). The strange self-congratulation expressed in these various verbal gymnastics offers simply another aspect by which Humbert detaches the reader from a projected belief in character. On other occasions, statements resonate more at a secondary than a primary level, as in his late demand to Lolita "to leave your incidental Dick, and this awful hole, and come to live with me" (*L* 278). The salaciousness here is the opposite of pornographic, since the words function as impoverished puns, invoking referents effaced as they appear, drawing attention again away from an imagined scene to a verbal scrim—functioning much as they do in Humbert's first masturbatory scene, when "I crushed out against her left buttock the last throb of the longest ecstasy man or monster had ever known" (*L* 61). Hyperbole so adorns the scene that it sinks from serious consideration as an event involving actual people into a play of verbal artifacts. Perhaps the novel's most stylistically varied sequence, bankrupting conventional considerations, is Humbert's purported recollection of his lost pocket diary for June 1947, the month he first met Lolita and moved into Charlotte's house. The chapter's staccato rhythms, unanswered queries, and irrelevant observations, its tireless bricolage of sociological observation, French phrases, class lists, and lyric brio, suggests an eclectic diary format (as well as a madman's psychosis). All the while the reader struggles to stitch together a narrative commensurate with the experience represented, even as that purported experience is passionately overwritten.

Not only do weirdly improbable moments proliferate but wildly far-fetched renditions of otherwise hackneyed moments as well—"*Woof*, commented the dog perfunctorily" (*L* 269). At other times, banal contexts are transformed not through inventive verbal renditions but as an allegorical sign itself, with the physical become a semiotic system. When Humbert first views Charlotte's rooms, he peers into the common bathroom, "with limp wet things overhanging the dubious tub (the question mark of a hair inside)" (*L* 38)—thus intimating not only the questionable nature of this rental for a fastidious foreigner but also (even before Lolita appears) her own questionable presence. That conjunction of tangible and symbolic exemplifies a novel where both are the same, if not always so obviously. Later, Humbert registers a similar consciousness just as he is about to seduce Lolita in The Enchanted Hunters Inn, observing that "her lightly veiled body and bare limbs formed a Z" (*L* 128)—as if the inert child embodied, in her recumbent state itself, the conventional comic book representation for sleep as ballooned Z's.

Compounding Humbert's defiance of probable cause and realist expectation is his repeated exposure of his own authorial fabrication, revealing how fully actual events are in fact embroidered: "I want my learned readers to participate in the scene I am about to replay. I want them to examine its every detail and see for themselves how careful, how chaste, the whole wine-sweet event is if viewed with . . . 'impartial sympathy.' So let us get started" (*L* 57). Instead once again of pulling us through the narrative surface, making it disappear, he flaunts it openly: "As greater authors than I have put it: 'Let readers imagine' etc. On second thought, I may as well give those imaginations a kick in the pants" (*L* 65). Later, he coyly anticipates his own plot: "A few words more about Mrs. Humbert while the going is good (a bad accident is to happen quite soon)" (*L* 79). When Charlotte on the next page insists Humbert confide a chronicle of his past affairs, his narrative embraces clichés that puncture the very account they authenticate: "So I presented my women, and had them smile and sway—the languorous blond, the fiery brunette, the sensual copperhead—as if on parade in a bordello" (*L* 80). Only dim-witted Charlotte might credit these flitting figures as actual women. Yet belief hardly matters in a narrative where words disrupt belief to whimsically lead a life of their own. Occasionally, that disruption occurs gratuitously in terms of easy puns, as in "'Lo!' cried Haze . . . 'And behold', said Lo (not for the first time)" (*L* 50–51). Indeed, Humbert is amused enough to repeat the pun himself—"and, lo (she was not interested but the reader may be)" (*L* 210); or, "I looked up from the letter and was about to=MThere was no Lo to behold" (223). Yet his beloved nymphet's name is hardly the only sound arousing such playfulness, and familiar figures of speech come in for their share of defamiliarizing: "'Let me follow a train of thought.' I thought. More than a minute passed. 'All right. Come on.' 'Was I on that train?' 'You certainly were'" (*L* 85). Characters themselves are reduced to aspects of their names, as when Humbert ruefully observes that "to think that between a Hamburger and a Humburger, she would—invariably, with icy precision—plump for the former" (*L* 166). Or, in a more celebratory mood, he exults in Lolita's class list: "A poem, a poem, forsooth! So strange and sweet was it to discover this 'Haze, Dolores' (she!) in its special bower of names, with its bodyguard of roses—a fairy princess between her two maids of honor" (*L* 52). And the reader must revert to the list to realize the pun.

Humbert simply cannot curb his obsessive graphorrhea, ready at a moment's notice to shift attention from his subject to the verbal arsenal invoked to describe it. His neighbor occasionally "barbered some late garden blooms or watered his car, or, at a later date, defrosted his driveway (I don't mind if these verbs are all wrong)" (*L* 179). Later, Humbert takes a walk among "a conspiracy of poplars ... I loafed and leafed, as it were, through one long block" (*L* 224)—with an alliterative linking of verbs so dissimilar that we shift from referent to sonic signifier in a mental transition that pointedly defies the walk he purportedly takes. Still later, driving from Wace, Colorado, he "turned into the shadow of a picnic ground where the morning had dumped its litter of light on an empty table" (*L* 227). Sometimes, he simply indulges in nonsensical, half-remembered phrases: "O my Carmen, my little Carmen, something, something, those something nights, and the stars, and the cars, and the bars, and the barmen" (*L* 61). More generally, he delights in the multifarious contingencies evoked by language as sonority, as if it were a game based entirely on unexpected phonic links. At its simplest, this involves the invention of portmanteau words— "They were going to India for their honeymonsoon" (*L* 266)—or weird neologisms: "how eventually I might blackmail—no, that is too strong a word—mauvemail big Haze" (71). The sign of Humbert's success is that the reader delights as well in this verbal prodding and probing, in turning our mental gaze to the figurative hardware that serves as a supposedly simple tool, revealing its complexity by tustling it into newly revelatory insights.

Far from hiding his creative efforts, Humbert regularly parades them before the reader: "I have to put the impact of an instantaneous vision into a sequence of words; their physical accumulation in the page impairs the actual flash, the sharp unity of impression: Rug-heap, car, old man-doll, Miss O.'s nurse running with a rustle, a half-empty tumbler in her hand" (*L* 97). Once again, the priority of an extra-verbal world is drawn into question by the narrative pyrotechnics that give us merely the illusion of that world. And Humbert's confession to narrative tics bolsters his status as the shape-shifting writer: "every once in a while I have to remind the reader of my appearance much as a professional novelist, who has given a character of his some mannerism or a dog, has to go on producing that dog or that mannerism every time the character crops up in the course of the book. There may be more to it in the present case" (*L* 104). Exhausting every means possible, Humbert repeats the tic—the reminder that he is creating a narrative, writing after the fact, closeted in a prison cell, and even when he attempts to dramatize the fact of *not* writing, *not* sitting in a cell, he cannot help but ironically confirm his fictional status. Late in the novel, hurrying through Ramsdale, he shuttles unstably between the two realms, admitting: "I had been keeping Clare Quilty's face masked in my dark dungeon, where he was waiting for me to come with barber and priest … I have no time right now to discuss the mnemonics of physiognomization—I am on my way to his uncle and walking fast—but let me jot down this: I had preserved in the alcohol of a clouded memory the toad of a face" (*L* 290). Humbert the maker evokes himself as creating intelligence whenever the opportunity arises, even walking to the dentist, though later recalled by prison-bound Humbert transforming that earlier experience into verbal conceits.

At this point, it is worth recalling that the novel's lyricism is part of a celebrated literary tradition in which a flesh-and-blood beloved becomes merely the occasion for poetic praise. Lolita follows in a long line of such romanticized figures, as Humbert himself observes in invoking Petrarch, Dante, and Shakespeare. Yet carrying this tradition to an extreme and disrupting his basic premise, he intimates throughout that Lolita is created *by* him, through his written-out adulation, nothing more than the effect of his pen. As he invokes her, "the eternal Lolita as reflected in my blood" (*L* 65), we wonder at detail so precise as to overwhelm the possibility of an actual adolescent girl: "the little bone twitching at the side of her dust-powdered ankle … The glistening tracery of down on her forearm" (41). Paeans to Lolita's beauty punctuate the narrative, of course, though it reaches its most rhapsodic pitch at the Colorado resort where she plays tennis, "with her apricot-colored limbs, in her sub-teen tennis togs. Winged gentlemen! No hereafter is acceptable if it does not produce her as she was then" (*L* 230). Humbert's obsession here acquires a life all its own, measured in the extremes to which he imagines her physically, indeed claims to see what might only actually be imagined—detail so fine as either to be beyond a viewer's normal ken or (even less realistically) to be imagined only internally, anatomically. As Humbert confesses, in a description whose lyrical charm is exceeded only by its perverse perspective, "My only grudge against nature was that I could not turn my Lolita inside out and apply voracious lips to her young matrix, her unknown heart, her nacreous liver, the sea-grapes of her lungs, her comely twin kidneys" (164–65). Earlier, after she has eaten a candy bar, he even imagines her alimentary canal: "Lo, whose lovely prismatic entrails had already digested the sweetmeat . . ." (*L* 116). And he takes that same inner view of himself, strangely linking him with Lolita in some thoroughly imagined, internal space. "I put a gentle hand to my chest as I surveyed the situation," he says when first apprised of Quilty's effect on Lolita; "The turquoise blue swimming pool some distance behind the lawn was no longer behind that lawn, but within my thorax, and my organs swam in it like excrements in the blue sea water in Nice" (237). Moments later, he magically vomits up that undigested vision, "a torrent of browns and greens that I had never remembered eating" (238). Colors and shapes seem to have become little more than verbal mouthfuls, motifs regurgitated mentally, part of the half-configured materials of thoroughly imagined scenes that are returned to us undigested—as if in a strange analogy to the process by which the novel itself refuses to cohere.

The intimation that Humbert's experience of Lolita is more imagined than real—the triumph of aesthetic obsession rather than the trace of an actual crime—emerges in the most intensely lyrical evocation, the mural he exultantly imagines painting of her in The Enchanted Hunters hotel. Not Lolita herself but the joy she elicits is expressed through a scene equal parts kitsch, pornography, and adulation, all couched in the past perfect conditional to stress the scene's hypothetical, counterfactual state:

There would have been a lake. There would have been an arbor in flame-flower. There would have been nature studies—a tiger pursuing a bird of paradise, a choking snake sheathing whole the flayed trunk of a shoat. There would have been a sultan, his face expressing great agony (belied, as it were, by his molding caress), helping a callypygean slave child to climb a column of onyx. There would have been those luminous globules of gonadal glow that travel up the opalescent sides of juke boxes. There would have been all kinds of camp activities on the part of the intermediate group, Canoeing, Coranting, Combing Curls in the lakeside sun. There would have been . . .

L 134

The passage might be said to form a neat synechdoche of the novel, representing in miniature Humbert's heated aestheticizing of every aspect of his nymphet-loving experience.[12] The riotous contagion of images creates a surreal vision, half-exotic, half-banal, that defies attempts to visualize the whole even as it vaunts Humbert's sexualized desires. The sultan's "caress," the slave ascending "a column of onyx," the "globules of gonadal glow," the "choking snake sheathing whole the flayed trunk of a shoat": all evoke the sensual liaison Humbert imagines with Lolita (even if these images are linked to activities so flatly conventional that Humbert plucks them from his well-studied volume C of the *Girls' Encyclopedia*). Unabated urgency emerges from the passage's repeated anaphora ("There would have been . . . There would have been . . ."), an urgency only momentarily tempered by the alliteration of those benignly domestic encyclopedic references. More generally, the passage in nearly all its details—from tigers to birds of paradise, from callypygean slaves to the encyclopedia Cs—attests to a profound literary intelligence in which words contribute less to narrative sequence than to a florid series of images meant to draw attention to their creator's stylistic verve (and imaginative desire).

In contrast to this intensely lyric celebration, consider the moment when Humbert finally catches up with a pregnant Mrs. Richard F. Schiller:

> Here she was with her ruined looks and her adult, rope-veined narrow hands and her goose-flesh white arms, and her shallow ears, and her unkempt armpits, there she was (my Lolita!), hopelessly worn at seventeen . . . and I looked and looked at her, and knew as clearly as I know I am to die, that I loved her more than anything I had ever seen or imagined on earth, or hoped for anywhere else. She was only the faint violet whiff and dead leaf echo of the nymphet I had rolled myself upon with such cries in the past; an echo on the brink of a russet ravine . . .
>
> *L* 277

Beginning in a distinctly anti-lyric mode, Humbert describes straightforwardly the haggard body of his beloved, and yet the very intensity of his gaze ("I looked and looked at her") revives not only his passion but the lyric itself as a mode of celebration and commemoration ("the faint violet whiff and dead leaf echo"). As clear as anywhere in the novel, Humbert projects his affection and obsessions *on* the body before him, with the paradoxical effect that Lolita's reality is attested precisely by the absence of nymphethood. That category, delineated earlier so carefully, can only be attributed imaginatively, via his own agency, in contrast to qualities intrinsic *to* her. Lolita herself is (always was) merely an occasion for obsession, and the disparity between the lyric and realistic modes suggests an actual realm beyond Humbert's creation even as it confirms the aesthetic pleasure *of* that creation. Unsurprisingly, he states it best: "the very attraction immaturity has for me lies not so much in the limpidity of pure young forbidden fairy child beauty as in the security of a situation where infinite perfections fill the gap between the little given and the great promised—the great rosegray never-to-be-had" (*L* 264). That perfectly pitched balance can never sustain itself, however, as Humbert realizes: "and Eve would revert to a rib, and there would be nothing in the window but an obese partly clad man reading the paper." Humbert realizes how much of his past is filled with moments when "the promise of reality" could only be "simulated seductively."

The questionable status of that simulation lies at the heart of Humbert's larger ethical standing, in a novel whose evocations dip with quicksilver dispatch from idealized (purely textual) "nymphet" to realistic (recognizably uncouth) pre-teen. As Humbert admits: "What drives me insane is the twofold nature of this nymphet—of every nymphet, perhaps; this mixture in my Lolita of tender dreamy childishness and a kind of eerie vulgarity" (*L* 44). And that view becomes contiguous with the reader's own unstable experience, in his contrast between "the eternal Lolita as reflected in my blood" and another creature, strident, sticky, crass, burdened with "vulgar vocabulary—'revolting,' 'super,' 'luscious,' 'goon,' 'drip'—*that* Lolita, *my* Lolita" (65). In this oscillation between rapture and revulsion, Humbert alternately sings her praises poetically and dismisses her rudely as "a most exasperating brat, ... a disgustingly conventional little girl" (*L* 148). Where lyric praise invariably calls attention to its own artful forms, this more straightforward irritation with Lolita registers in curt tones and minimal imagery a figure as independent of his will as of his prose. And the triumph of the novel is to make us falter between these distinct imagined realms, one of which implicitly defies an ethical response (since we rarely consider moral discriminations among verb tenses, rhetorical figures, and ornate imagery), while the other implicitly demands it (since accounts of those we take as even imaginatively real elicit from us principled considerations).

Keep in mind that Humbert waxes poetic about Lolita not just when inflamed with sexual desire but at other moments as well, lending to even her most unerotic gestures a saving grace. The most lyrical of such invocations occurs as he watches her play tennis: "The exquisite clarity of all her movements had its auditory counterpart in the pure ringing sound of her every stroke. The ball when it entered her aura of control became somehow whiter, its resilience somehow richer, and the instrument of precision she used upon it seemed inordinately prehensile and deliberate at the moment of clinging contact" (*L* 231).[13] Here, something like a magical metamorphosis occurs, wrenching what we presume to be reported experience into another realm. Beginning with Lolita's own apparent transformation of "make-believe" into "the very geometry of basic reality," the process continues in Humbert's conversion of a game into something aesthetically rich and erotically tinged (in the "somehow whiter" ball in "clinging contact" with her racket). Humbert continues for pages in rapt celebration of Lolita's prowess—the "vital web of balance between toed foot, pristine armpit, burnished arm and far back-flung racket"—that finally allows him to rest "within the innocence of her style, of her soul, of her essential grace" (*L* 233). And what is most striking in this apotheosis is our focus on Humbert's grace in describing Lolita, effectively masking her as other than a constellation of breathtaking attributes. The scene embodies the novel's larger alternation between narrative transparency (a girl playing tennis) and its lyrical opacity (a deification of arabesques and stylish riffs), sustaining an oscillating rhythm between everyday reality and flights of fancy, ethics and excess.

The very premise of the novel enhances this oscillation, displacing the plot as a series of events recalled, with Humbert rarely reporting directly and otherwise compelled to re-imagine everything that has occurred long in the past. This premise raises an insoluble question about the status of all sorts of imaginings and their connection with actual experience, since fantasy remains unfettered and private imaginings are only policed by one's superego. On the one hand, of course, Nabokov's novel is clearly fictional, and he regularly took offense at readers who presumed anything about his own life from their reading. On the other hand, within the fiction *of* the novel, Humbert presents his account at times as legal brief ("Frigid gentlewomen of the jury!" [*L* 132]), at others as psychoanalytic confession ("I am so oppressed, doctor" [15]), in both of which private imaginings have a public role, impinging on history, dictated by shared experience, introducing a condition of accountability. And not only do we hesitate between these realms, but even they are separately rendered unstable. Humbert, for instance, reminds the reader he is creating a narrative, writing it "in the opaque air of this tombal jail" (*L* 109), left alone with only his imagination (the sole documentary exception being a transcribed page from a prison library book (31–32)). Yet he also claims to rely on a memory of actual past events, and *that* premise—of writing a true memoir or "confession"—immediately invokes ethical considerations appropriate to that genre, even if within a fictional realm.

The problem lies in our customary impulse to separate different registers even as the novel collapses them. Humbert may after all admit "I have only words to play with!" (*L* 32), but he nonetheless regularly strives to identify exact dates, to represent allegedly real people faithfully, to recall conversations exactly as they occurred: "That must have been around August 15, 1947. Don't think I can go on. Heart, head—everything" (109). Further confounding the fictional frame is Humbert's pocket diary, the purported basis of the novel, which he admits was "destroyed five years ago and what we examine now (by courtesy of a photographic memory) is but its brief materialization" recopied out in his microscopic hand (*L* 41). The contention for documentary evidence is invoked only to be subverted, just as claims for actual persons projected into the past are made to be denied. The very duplication of written evidence seems, once again, simultaneously to enforce and undermine belief in an original text, and even more, the prior textualized event. Compounding this instability in our reading is the uncertainty of the novel's informing premise, that Humbert is blessed with a "photographic memory" (*L* 214). Yet he also admits the contrary (helping explain why he keeps a diary): "Being a murderer with a sensational but incomplete and unorthodox memory, I cannot tell you, ladies and gentlemen, the exact day when I first knew with utter certainty that the red convertible was following us" (*L* 217). And those criss-cross admissions recur throughout, as when certain occasions are not "sharply engraved on my mind" (*L* 242), or he simply admits that "I notice I have somehow mixed up two events" (*L* 263). Humbert invents, adds, and alters according to whim, casting his assertions of accuracy in doubt. John Farlow's offer to fetch Lolita is slyly amended: "'why don't I drive there right now, and you may sleep with Jean'—(he did not really add that but Jean supported his offer so passionately that it might be implied)" (*L* 100). What are we to make of a narrator who so readily shades the truth? Earlier, Humbert edits Charlotte's love letter to him:

"What I present here is what I remember of the letter, and what I remember of the letter I remember verbatim (including that awful French). It was at least twice longer" (*L* 68). Compounding this confession of faulty memory, he then admits that, verbatim assurances aside, there is "a chance that 'the vortex of the toilet' (where the letter did go) is my own matter-of-fact contribution" (*L* 69). And what of other such contributions? When Humbert finally pleads with Lolita to "'come to live with me, and die with me, and everything with me' (words to that effect)" (*L* 278)—the breach between historical record and imagined scene is all but complete.

Collapsing that division are frequent eruptions of the present into the past, as if the novel's preoccupation with entangled opposites (aesthetic and ethical) extended to temporal dislocations as well. This happens in Humbert's appeals to the reader but is also registered in other ways, as when he imagines murdering Charlotte swimming in Hourglass Lake: "as I watched, with the stark lucidity of a future recollection (you know—trying to see things as you will remember having seen them)" (*L* 86). It is as if Humbert were evoking the topsy-turvy, dream-like nature of *Lolita*—and this strange conflation of memory with future event is compounded by being recalled in his cell, as he narrates retrospectively a vividly anticipatory moment. Later, he will plead with us to believe in "destiny in the making" (*L* 210), as if his narrative elisions and conflations were meant to enforce a belief that all had been fated. Whether or not the future is as fixed as the past (as he seems to claim), ostensible events are represented in a form that draws attention to their crafted quality, as if out of time. This confusing yet exhilarating mixture keeps reflecting back on itself, with Clare Quilty's play, *The Enchanted Hunters*, itself seeming to incorporate the self-created, self-revealing principle of the novel: "a seventh Hunter (in a *green* cap, the fool) was a Young Poet, and he insisted, much to Diana's annoyance, that she and the entertainment provided (dancing nymphs, and elves, and monsters) were his, the Poet's, invention" (*L* 201). Humbert is suitably caustic about the play's otherwise conventional plot, although Diana's concluding kiss of the poet is meant to deny his presumptive claim, enforcing "the play's profound message, namely, that mirage and reality merge in love" (*L* 201). The promise of such a merging might as readily be thought of as the "message" of Humbert's narrative, though it remains only a promise. And in that constantly deferred fusion of aesthetically rich "mirage" and painfully fraught "reality," the novel achieves its sustaining tension.

III. Dualities, Indeterminacy, Literature

Lolita's unending oscillation means we never rest easy, neither settling for characters quite like ourselves nor taking them as mere flickering shapes on a page. Those many readers who therefore resolve on either an exclusively ethical or an aesthetic response seem driven more by private predilections than by the novel's shifting rhythm.[14] After all, the very trajectory of the novel in the twentieth century has been from the ostensible formal transparency of realism, to modernism's experimentations with form, to postmodernism's claims for nothing knowable beyond form, to late modernist efforts to rejoin earlier prospects. And that trajectory has traced our shifting relation to those we are asked to imagine, altering ethical considerations in novels that ever depict events akin to those we encounter in everyday life.[15] Of course, part of what it means to be considered "literature" rather than simple report involves words and narratives not self-evidently what they seem, introducing an unending engagement with slippery categories, forcing us to oscillate back and forth between crafted surface and the resonances lying beneath. We alternate between standing in- and outside the frame of novels, shifting back and forth as they enforce yet undercut their figures, both literal and rhetorical. Or perhaps it is more accurate to say that we alternate *within* the frame, which demonstrates the magic (and the genuine paradox) of literature more generally, compelling us through aesthetic legerdemain to do the impossible, inhabiting different cognitive realms, suspending some as we draw on others.

This strange effect is apparent in Humbert's repeated (and increasingly panicked) beseechments to interlocutors (readers, jurors, psychoanalyst), which themselves oscillate, demanding we believe *in* him in prose that persistently undercuts the possibility: "do not skip these essential pages! Imagine me; I shall not exist if you do not imagine me; try to discern the doe in me, trembling in the forest of my own iniquity; let's even smile a little" (*L* 129). The figurative playfulness of this bizarre injunction exposes the fabricated condition of Humbert's persona, as if his importunity itself belied the contrived status of his position, introducing hysterical artfulness into the equation just when a calm sense of transparent reality is called for. This is, of course, the inauguration of a new self-consciousness about fabrication that identifies Nabokov's novel as a transition from modernism to postmodernism, where figures defy ethical treatment by their very two-dimensionality, the ironic perspective within which they are presented.

Nowhere is this clearer than in Humbert's alter-ego Quilty, whose name itself invokes a dual sense of realistically entrenched guilt as well as the surreally textured fabric in which such guilt is transmuted. And yet Nabokov never quite capitulates to suasions away from realistic representation, always keeping one foot in the world of our normal moral projections, in part simply by hinging Humbert's existence on the reader's need to believe in him, even if that need for belief already places that existence in jeopardy.[16] This weirdly unstable aspect of Humbert Humbert, as pseudonymous narrator drawing attention to his own creation, is akin to the outlined hand drawing itself into existence in an M. C. Escher engraving. And Nabokov himself was keenly aware of this paradoxical effect, revealed again in his admiring claim for a character in Gogol: "not quite knowing whether he is in the middle of the street or in the middle of the sentence, these details gradually dissolve the clerk Akaky Akakyevich so that towards the end of the story his ghost seems to be the most tangible, the most real part of his being" (*Gogol* 146). The description could not better characterize Humbert Humbert himself.

Yet an even more compelling claim for indeterminacy in our reading of *Lolita* emerges from the novel's subject, which is so excessive as to defy all predictive rules. Humbert expresses this boundlessness on (at least, allegedly) hearing Lolita's initial proposal of sex with him: "gradually the odd sense of living in a brand new, mad new dream world, where everything was permissible, came over me as I realized what she was suggesting" (*L* 133). Here, the wondrousness of what might seem simply perverse is unsurpassable, and in the surprise of Lolita's forwardness we are made (at least, momentarily) to feel that conventional rules no longer apply. It is as if the supposed "dream" of pedophilia was, in Humbert's view, equivalent to that of novel writing itself, in the transcendence of narrow ethical imperatives and the concession to full imaginative play. His very reticence about the crude activities that then ensue—that might be predictably, all too conventionally depicted—confirms his decision to remain in an unfettered imaginative realm. A reader's counter desire for transgression depicted, with ethical strains more neatly defined, is met by Humbert's coyly anticipatory demurrer: "But really these are irrelevant matters; I am not concerned with so-called 'sex' at all. . . . A greater endeavor lures me on: to fix once for all the perilous magic of nymphets" (*L* 134). The magic is perilous precisely because it verges so closely on the perverse as well as the unexpressed.

Nabokov deliberately conceives the most extreme version of the "literary," encouraging readers into moral considerations that seem at last irrelevant, if only because the murderous Humbert is no more than the effect of his "fancy prose style," alternating between a self-indulgent verbal excess and a professed effort at realistic transparency that seems equally constructed. Slyly cognizant of the way we process fictional accounts, he projects emotional and ethical judgments onto the page much as we do in everyday life, filling out details, inferring causes and connections, presuming a larger pattern that involves conventional moral and aesthetic ideals. Yet Nabokov the author perpetually turns the tables, never quite allowing us to conceive of Lolita, Humbert, Quilty, or anyone else as actual or even wholly fictional characters (a quality that has regularly defeated efforts to turn the novel into a successful film). Whatever outrage we feel at Humbert's victimization of Lolita is deflected by the delight the novel takes in its own extravagant wordplay, its mix of literary allusion and lyrical depiction, of parody and puzzling cross reference. Like *Alice in Wonderland*, the novel creates a realm in which letters (e.g., Q) and numbers (e.g., 342) enjoy the same full (or, if you want, impoverished) "reality" that characters do, reappearing with coincidental regularity, helping to shape the plot.[17] Gruesome events become mordant occasions for humor we would never otherwise countenance—as when Humbert thinks back on his "best moments" with Lo, when they "played a childish game of cards, or went shopping, or silently stared, with other motorists and their children, at some smashed, blood-bespattered car with a young woman's shoe in the ditch (Lo, as we drove on: 'That was the exact type of moccasin I was trying to describe to that jerk in the store')" (*L* 174). Here, as sardonically as anywhere in the novel, two registers deftly defy one another.

Lolita is at its most ambitious in exploring the status of literature itself, arousing ethical considerations about the most profoundly transgressive of human activities—considerations it blithely fails to resolve but never quite ignores. Yet the fact that we *do* bring to *Lolita* a well-worn array of moral baggage does prove any reading of Humbert Humbert an unsettling one. After all, we live not simply in the details, in the brilliant passages of excoriating prose, but as well in the connections those details make with larger ideals of how we want to live. That does not mean we agree with John Ray, Jr. Ph.D., who brings a solidly obtuse "moral in tow" to his reading of the novel. But we realize how irrepressible the impulse is when even those most opposed to an ethical reading end up dragging ethics in via another route. Recall that Nabokov, that notorious aestheticist, described "aesthetic bliss" as the "sense of being somehow, somewhere, connected with other states of being where art (curiosity, tenderness, kindness, ecstasy) is the norm." That sequence of four descriptive nouns entered parenthetically ("curiosity, tenderness, kindness, ecstasy") offers a curious re-introduction of the ethical back into the novel, and in so doing establishes the terms by which a reading of Humbert should be pursued. After all, kindness, curiosity and tenderness are the very virtues he lacks in his narcissistic subjugation of Lolita—a subjugation we eerily reinforce in our own delight at his dazzling verbal skill.[18] But as well, consider how the first three nouns (all ethical) require prepositions, involving others—curiosity *about*, tenderness *towards*, kindness *for*—while ecstasy is something that can be achieved alone, requiring neither preposition nor an ethical component. All literature taxes us in this vexingly paradoxical fashion by transforming human experience into something as interesting for its verbal representations as for its represented experience, as interesting for its aesthetic as for its ethical qualities. Sensitivity to the one may help sensitize us to the other, but no more certainly than any of countless other activities. Part of the problem is simply that far less clarity exists about ethical than aesthetic issues, if only because the ethical more often becomes a translation out of the text into another form, a supposedly untextualized form, where values are not seen to clash and where a *summum bonum* is presumed to exist.

What invariably raises moral questions is the realm of actual lived events, a realm one distinct remove from where Humbert persistently places himself. Yet, if distinct, that remove is still not far away, defined by a very fine line, as Nabokov himself observed in a predictably playful verbal formulation: "the difference between the comic side of things, and their cosmic side, depends upon one sibilant" (*Gogol* 142). The aesthetic and the ethical, in short, define themselves against one another, linked in such a way that never allows us to rest assured in either inconsequential formal delight or pat moral maxims. Perhaps the best explanation is, once again, Nabokov's own as he tries to calibrate the effect of Gogol's peculiar literary vision: "There can be no moral lesson in such a world because there are no pupils and no teachers: this world *is* and it excludes everything that might destroy it, so that any improvement, any struggle, any moral purpose or endeavor, are as utterly impossible as changing the course of a star. It is Gogol's world and as such wholly different from Tolstoy's world, or Pushkin's, or Chekhov's or my own. But after reading Gogol one's eyes may become gogolized and one is apt to see bits of his world in the most unexpected places." (*Gogol* 144). Here, style defiantly trumps ethics in the sure strokes of Nabokov's mandarin tones. Yet if the exclusion of any "moral lesson" results from the fixed narrative pattern of Gogol's world—as fixed as Tolstoy's, Pushkin's, Chekhov's, Nabokov's and every other artist's—the possibility of reintroducing ethics back into such worlds occurs because (as Nabokov ends by acknowledging) those worlds become part of our own, transforming the way we see, altering not merely our aesthetic assumptions but our moral ones as well. That is not a "lesson" we can extract from the oscillations of literature, but it *is* a reminder that the most accomplished novels never fail to embrace our world as fully as they rebuff it.

Notes

1 See Frederick Whiting, 833.
2 The full quotation is: "Text of pleasure: the text that contents, fills, grants euphoria; the text that comes from culture and does not break with it, is linked to a *comfortable* practice of reading. Text of bliss: the text that imposes a state of loss, the text that discomforts (perhaps to the point of a certain boredom), unsettles the reader's historical, cultural, psychological assumptions, the consistency of his tastes, values, memories, brings to a crisis his relation with language" (*Pleasure* 14).
3 Trilling concludes his perceptive review with an observation that anticipates the directions of this chapter: "Indeed, for me one of the attractions of *Lolita* is its ambiguity of tone . . . and its ambiguity of intention, its ability to arouse uneasiness, to throw the reader off balance, to require him to change his stance and shift his position and move on. *Lolita* gives us no chance to settle and sink roots" ("Last Lover" 102).
4 From its first appearance, readers have viewed it as monstrous yet comically brilliant, pornographic yet poetic, deeply offensive yet endearing—a mixed reception that remains unchanged even as critical judgments have grown more refined. Those troubled by its ostensible subject matter were reassured by John Hollander as early as 1956 that "*Lolita*, if it is anything 'really,' is the record of Mr. Nabokov's love affair with the romantic novel" (Page 91). Howard Nemerov went further, arguing that "Nabokov's own artistic concern, here as elsewhere . . . has no more to do with morality than with sex" (Page 91). Those judgments resonate through countless critiques of the novel over half a century, championed most vigorously by Nabokov's former student and indefatigable editor of *The Annotated "Lolita"*, Alfred Appel, Jr. On the other side are readers like Lionel Trilling, who considered the novel a "love story" but admitted, "less and less, indeed, do we see a *situation*; what we become aware of is people" (Page 94). And it is those "people" who focus Richard Rorty's earnest reading of the novel, in his claim that "literary interest will always be

parasitic on moral interest. In particular, you cannot create a memorable character without thereby making a suggestion about how your reader should act" (Rorty 167). Extending this observation to the subject of child abuse itself, Linda Kauffman indicts Nabokov for celebrating incest, claiming "the incestuous father's tyranny is clinically verifiable in this novel" (166).

Even Nabokov chimed in, insisting to Edmund Wilson that his novel was in fact "a highly moral affair" (Karlinsky 298). Reinforcing this point (and in the process confounding those who assume his true voice can be found in the Afterword), he elaborated in an interview: "I don't think *Lolita* is a religious book, but I do think it is a moral one. And I do think that Humbert Humbert in his last stage is a moral man because he realizes that he loves *Lolita* [sic] like any woman should be loved. But it is too late, he has destroyed her childhood. There is certainly this kind of morality in it" (Alexandrov 160–61). The surprising sentimentality here aside, it's hard to know what *other* "kind of morality" Nabokov valued in the novel, since this kind is so patently what most readers acknowledge as central to their reading.

5   Seven years earlier, prompted by Pushkin, he had addressed the issue more narrowly: "Is it possible to imagine the full reality of another's life, to relive it in one's mind and set it down intact on paper?" The answer was clear: "I doubt it: one even finds oneself seduced by the idea that thought itself, as it shines its beam on the story of a man's life, cannot avoid deforming it. Thus, what our mind perceives turns out to be plausible, but not true" (Alexandrov 137). Plausibility, a narrative function, may satisfy conventional expectations, but truth to the facts rarely offers neat edges and predictable norms.

6   Early on, Michael Bell acutely observed: "The book itself works to supplant the absolutist terminology in which it is often discussed" (171). And he anticipates my reading with his conclusion: "*Lolita* creates a final state of mind that resists either a purely 'aesthetic' formulation or moralistic reduction" (184). More recently, Eric Naiman offers a salutary reading of critics who are caught between these two prospects. Michael Wood nicely observes of Nabokov: "doubt is what we find lurking in his apparent assurance, like death in Arcady" (*Magician's* 8). And his chapter on *Lolita* slips back and forth between the modes of ethics and aesthetics, without ever quite claiming that they rely on each other.

7   As if to compound the confusion between actual and fictional, Nabokov independently admitted of the name: "The double rumble is, I think, very nasty, very suggestive. It is a hateful name for a hateful person." (*Strong Opinions* 26)

8   Alfred Appel, Jr. briefly describes these efforts (xl).

9   Gladys M. Clifton claims: "It is fitting and funny that Humbert's one flight into erotic writing is couched mainly in a beautiful parody of the florid prose style of Victorian pornographers. Humbert acknowledges that he has

possessed not Lolita herself, 'but my own creation ...' Humbert's error in
attempting to live his fantasies is finally understood even by him. The
barrier between fantasy and reality cannot be crossed, as he acknowledges
in one of his more sober passages of self-analysis" (68).

10 As Alfred Appel, Jr. observes: "The reader sees Humbert move beyond his
obsessional passion to a not altogether straightforward declaration of
genuine love (pp. 277–78) and, finally, to a realization of the loss suffered
not by him but by Lolita (pp. 307–08). It is expressed on the next to the last
page in a long and eloquent passage that, for the first time in the novel, is in
no way undercut by parody or qualified by irony" (lxiv). Earlier, F. W.
Dupee had stated: "Humbert's remorse is more effective for not clothing
itself in abstractly moral terms. He feels, not that he has betrayed a 'trust' of
the kind that traditionally inheres in parenthood, but that he has horribly
let Lolita down as lover, friend, and fellow human being, as well as in his
capacity as father" (*Nabokov: CH* 89).

By contrast, Michael Wood believes Humbert is "protesting too much
... [T]he claim seems mawkish and self-regarding, altogether too good to
be true, 'dictated by some principle of compensation,' as Dupee says.
Humbert's fussy prose, elsewhere so resourceful and acrobatic, here
manages to seem both artful and hackneyed." In a more precise analysis,
Wood states: "the soft-spoken, Edwardian diction of the passage (melody,
vapour, limpid air, magically, divinely, demure, murmur, and the sickly
concord) suggests two minds, Humbert's and Nabokov's, trying hard for a
tone to which they are not accustomed: Humbert because he is seeking,
sincerely or not, to sound contrite, Nabokov because he is allowing the
moralist in himself to have one of his rare canters in the open. This elegant,
slightly over-beautified language is Nabokov's signature when he takes a
break from irony; as if in compensation, sardonic control gives way to a
maudlin recommendation" (*Magician's* 139–40, 25).

Brian Boyd most clearly condemns Humbert in this passage, based on
its timing alone (253–54).

11 Another instance occurs on arriving at camp: "Let me retain for a moment
that scene in all its trivial and fateful detail: hag Holmes writing out a
receipt ... photographs of girl-children; some gaudy moth or butterfly, still
alive, safely pinned to the wall ... the sound of trees and birds, and my
pounding heart" (*L* 110).

12 James Phelan reads (part of) this passage as "utterly reliable" (180), as
"metaphors of Humbert's predatory behavior toward Dolores that suggest
something of the 'animality' of that behavior," in focusing "on his own
desire even as its mini-allegory" (181–82). By contrast, Eric Naiman reads
the passage as "predicated on a rereader's fondling of details, including
sexually charged lexical elements ... if the reader is going to reject the
pleasure offered by this passage, he must also reject the pleasures and
methods that make *Lolita* worth reading" (159).

13 For an incisive reading of this passage, see Rampton (116–17).

14 Even Michael Wood, in an otherwise sensitive reading, asks: "But can we
   sensibly speak, as I just have, of a substantial American child? Aren't all the
   characters made of words, here as everywhere else in literature?" Wood goes
   on to suggest, in a reading that offers a person behind or beyond words, that
   "The 'actual' Lolita is the person we see Humbert can't see . . . In this sense she
   is a product of reading." Wood, in short, is attempting to still the oscillation by
   merging two mutually exclusive positions, acknowledging partially true
   (fictional) facts: "we can't question Humbert's interpretations . . . if we don't
   grant some sort of stability to the material he is interpreting" (*Magician's* 117).
15 Nabokov himself was not immune to conventional (even banal) ethical
   thinking, as Ellen Pifer notes in quoting him: "'I have reached the original
   conclusion that if one performs at least one good act per day (even if it is
   nothing more than giving one's place to an elderly person on the tram) life
   becomes exceedingly more pleasant. In the final analysis everything in the
   world is very simple and founded upon two or three not very complicated
   truths.' Thus the young Vladimir Nabokov wrote to his mother in
   September 1924, at the age of twenty-five. Have we caught the young dandy
   napping . . .?" (1). As David Rampton also observes, "*Lolita* . . . offers a less
   doctrinaire and more complex view of the subject than Nabokov's own
   comments generally do" (116). In 1965, Nabokov himself responded to an
   interviewer's question in a highly moral vein: "'*Which is the worst thing men
   do?*' 'To stink, to cheat, to torture.' '*Which is the best?*' 'To be kind, to be
   proud, to be fearless'" (*Strong Opinions* 152).
16 Or as Michael Bell states, "he meets the emotional crisis within the story by
   placing himself half outside the narrative frame—the writing of the story
   placing him within a frame and the treatment of Quilty helping to move
   him out of it" (178).
17 This is one among many aspects of the novel's dip into a postmodern realm
   in which authenticity is dropped along with subjectivity, while
   characterization becomes simply a matter of naming, of textual cross-
   referencing.
18 "The Russian text translates exactly those four words in parentheses, but
   adds, between kindness and ecstasy, 'harmony' ['*stroynost*'], apparently
   another essential element of art that occurred to Nabokov after the original
   publication of the essay. It is interesting, in light of the accusation often
   leveled at Nabokov of being a 'formalist,' ostensibly unconcerned with the
   moral content of his fiction, that he at first defined art exclusively in terms
   of moral categories and only added a formal category as an afterthought"
   (Clifton 189).
       Frederick Whiting offers another perspective: "The first three terms that
   Nabokov places in parenthetical apposition to aesthetic bliss—curiosity,
   kindness, and tenderness—import into his purely aesthetic model the very
   moral register he seems bent on avoiding. . . . Their publicness stands in
   marked contrast to the connotations of privacy that surround the last term
   in the series, ecstasy" (854–55).

Chapter 3

HOSPITALITY IN *HOUSEKEEPING* (1980)

We dress our garden, eat our dinners, discuss the household with
our wives, and these things make no impression, are forgotten next
week; but in the solitude to which every man is always returning, he
has a sanity and revelations, which in his passage into new worlds
he will carry with him.

—Ralph Waldo Emerson, "Experience" (*F&S* 262)

Because no man can ever feel his own identity aright except his eyes
be closed; as if darkness were indeed the proper element of our
essences.

—Herman Melville, *Moby-Dick* (60)

The monosyllabic opening of Marilynne Robinson's *Housekeeping*, "My
name is Ruth" (25), immediately conjures up Melville's brash invitation,
"Call me Ishmael!" (3). Yet her own haunting spondaic rhythm serves as
a quiet drum roll for the funereal list of family members that follows,
until the style metamorphoses within a page, in Ruth Stone's account of
her grandfather's westering to a land of "uncountable mountains" (4).
Abruptly, time and space pull asunder as Fingerbone Lake floods the
family home, with Ruth scrambling descriptive tenses, gently echoing
herself, swelling lyrical in a recollection of then and now, there and here:

It seems there was a time when the dimensions of things modified
themselves, leaving a number of puzzling margins, as between the
mountains as they must have been and the mountains as they are
now, or between the lake as it once was and the lake as it is now.
Sometimes in the spring the old lake will return. One will open a
cellar door to wading boots floating tallowy soles up and planks and
buckets bumping at the threshold, the stairway gone from sight after
the second step.

H 4–5

The "puzzling margins" of things are puzzling first at temporal limits, as past and present collide (former mountains, older lake), before she veers into a future tense ("One will open") that paradoxically strains temporal limits, anticipating the novel's "resurrection of the ordinary" (*H* 18). It is as if the flooded basement itself provoked the emergence of a lyrical voice ("wading boots floating tallowy soles up and planks and buckets bumping at the threshold"), with water, air, vegetation, basement, all commingling, outdoors and in, while the tableau slips and slides among descriptive registers.

This forms a baffling dislocation of setting as well as style before we realize how fully the novel celebrates things out of place, not merely in scenes that defy conventional household management but in a narrative voice loosely constrained by figurative forms of housekeeping. Robinson's title refers to more than just keeping house, then, becoming a trope for strategies of imposition and order as well as for gestures of restoration and accommodation. The very word "housekeeping" registers this ambivalence: "the maintenance of a household; the management of household affairs," but also "keeping of a good table—hospitality" (*Shorter OED*). In turn, "hospitality" is cited as "the reception and entertainment of guests or strangers with liberality and goodwill." The tension between these polarities (of maintaining order, yet accommodating different standards of order) structures Ruth's efforts to assuage her feelings of abandonment, imagining the lost voices of her grandfather, grandmother, mother and sister as she plucks from memory the shards of a past that might help shape a tolerable future. Yet she does so in a mixed mode, both stylistically and narratively, defined by the twin poles of housekeeping: she grants the guests of her fragmented life a hospitable hearing, even as she organizes her account to ensure a suitable structure. This ambivalence is evoked towards the end in a telling simile when Ruth concedes that "even things lost in a house abide, like forgotten sorrows and incipient dreams" (*H* 207), acknowledging the ineffectiveness of too one-sided housekeeping in the very breath that fosters its restorative psychological analogies. And her narrative style pays tribute to her grandmother's striving for domestic harmony and order, even as she models herself on her aunt Sylvie's eccentric discombobulations by shifting registers, entertaining anomalies, embracing paradox and contradiction.[1]

In fact, the novel bridges the very tensions of its title, cherishing the recuperative possibilities of both housekeeping *and* narrative as if conceived reciprocally—of housekeeping as a form of imaginative accommodation akin to narrative, restoring a tentative order that nonetheless keeps ambiguity alive, paradoxically defying closure yet knitting a fragile resolution together. As Robinson elsewhere reminds us, "at a certain level housekeeping is a regime of small kindnesses, which together, make the world salubrious, savory, and warm. I think of the acts of comfort offered and received within a household as precisely sacramental. It is the sad tendency of domesticity—as of piety—to contract, and of grace to decay into rigor, and peace into tedium" ("My Western Roots"). The novel finally rests on this contradictory insight, in its narrative of borders breached and repaired, its recovery of a past suasive yet speculative, its ranging among stylistic registers without sequestering one from another.

Yet if Robinson brilliantly transforms a stereotypically female activity by exploring its covert implications, she also undertakes an ambitious version of literary housekeeping, heralded in Ruth's opening self-introduction that recalls a novelistic forebear as significant as any of her own lost family.[2] For that recasting of Melville initiates a complex engagement with a largely male tradition of American literature, ordering and accommodating it in the process of gradually engaging its central insights, and doing so by recasting its characteristic syntactic rhythms. As Linda Hutcheon has argued for "postmodern parody," such texts reincorporate past representations ironically, at once defining our severance from the past and restoring "the context of past representations" (94). Such self-reflexive moments are, as she adds, a particularly effective means by which feminist artists can write themselves into as well as deconstruct the gendered terms of representation they have inherited (Hutcheon 102).[3] "Housekeeping" thus becomes a radical metaphor for ways in which a woman leaves a conventional female identity behind and becomes herself by writing, revising the canon by inserting herself distinctively within it. That process initially takes shape in Sylvie's commitment to transiency, which quietly traces a debt to America's peripatetic grand narratives, from *Moby-Dick* (1850) and Thoreau's *Walden* (1854) to Whitman's "Song of the Open Road" (1856) and Twain's *Adventures of Huckleberry Finn* (1885); from Hemingway's *In Our Time* (1925), to Nabokov's *Lolita* (1955/58) and Kerouac's *On the Road* (1957). All anticipate Robinson's paean to the journey as road to self-discovery, even if her narrative comes to seem more provisional and (because of housekeeping itself) paradoxical. Perhaps a more salient tradition coyly intimated by Robinson's title flows from Edgar Allen Poe's "The Fall of the House of Usher" (1839), to Nathanael Hawthorne's *The House of the Seven Gables* (1851), to Edith Wharton's

The House of Mirth (1905), to Willa Cather's *The Professor's House* (1925), to William Faulkner's *Light in August* (1932) and *Absalom, Absalom!* (1936), each written under the working title, *The Dark House.* That is, the ambition of *Housekeeping* is to respond to these and other literary "houses," recasting their transformative ways of thinking about words and narrative, all as a kind of ode to the house of American literature itself, haunted by the echoing presence of authors who once again loom as large as Ruth's family. In short, Ruth's adaptation of her aunt Sylvie's example is analogous to Robinson's appropriation of earlier American novelists: in both cases, examples are transmuted via the underlying ambivalence of "housekeeping," as at once an ordering and an accommodation.

Given all this, it should come as little surprise that Robinson's multiple border-crossings have prompted readings equally diverse: as empowering indictment of patriarchal notions of a "woman's place" (Champagne, Foster, Geyh, Kaivola, Meese, Smyth); as account of the debilitating effects of abandonment and psychological trauma (Caver, Hedrick, McDermott, Mattessich, Ravits); less theoretically, as embrace of transience itself (Burke, Galehouse). What fascinates me as much as the variety of these critical engagements is the novel's resistance to totalizing assessment at every level (reinforced by ambivalence in the very meanings of "housekeeping"), but especially at the level of style. As Kristin King observes, "This poetic and dreamlike novel crosses voices, expectations, and roles to suggest some as yet unrealized hybridization from old categories" (568). King's silent concession of indeterminacy (via "suggest" and "unrealized") offers a salutary caution: that any reading of *Housekeeping* must first confront the novel's voice, which defies strict categories and refuses "to contract" (as Robinson warns of domesticity). My lead thus follows those who have responded to the novel's rejection of a "logic of exclusion" (Foster 88–89), offering instead interpretations that celebrate its narrative tensions, its ineluctable blending of fact and fiction, outside and in.[4] For Robinson dramatizes "how compelling it can be," in Karen Kaivola's words, "to try to overrun boundaries between self and other, to merge, to be absorbed. At the same time, she shows how dangerous it is to allow one's boundaries to be overrun" (688). That comprehensive vision underlies Robinson's claim for a more expansive sense of housekeeping, less ossified and tedious. In short, what I argue is that the novel denies prescriptive responses to vocation, to trauma, even to psychology, instead offering a vision of housekeeping (as the word implies) that begins literally as physical accommodation in creating household order, and ends figuratively by revising and re-envisioning one's sensibility. What first appears a cluttered style (describing a species of failed housekeeping) emerges as a more comprehensive if also more flexible means for grasping one's past and one's self, even as a slippery past and self ever elude that grasp.

I. Keeping House, Amid Loss

Published in 1980, seventeen years after Betty Friedan's *Feminine Mystique*, Robinson draws on a stereotypically female task—housekeeping—only to turn it figuratively on its head. At first glance, her novel seems as unassuming in scope as her title, as if to defy Ishmael's decree that "To produce a mighty book, you must choose a mighty theme. No great and enduring volume can ever be written on the flea, though many there be who have tried it" (Melville 497). Yet if housekeeping hardly resembles whaling, the more one pauses over Melville's epic, the more its curious alternation of hospitality and transience emerges as an informing pattern, in Ishmael's various interjections for an "attainable felicity" (456) (many on behalf of Queequeg) that contrast with Ahab's single-minded quest. Thoreau's analogous escape from Cambridge propriety to the freedom of Walden Pond involves him nonetheless with problems of keeping his new house, in maintaining at once his revived spirit and its dusty domestic order. Huck Finn's escape from Aunt Sally's "sivilizing" lands him on a raft drifting south, in scenes of illuminating companionship with Jim that alternate with hazards of all sorts. In each of these canonical texts, moreover, domestic security is threatened by indomitable bodies of water (the sea, Walden Pond, the Mississippi), in scenes where nature is pitched against whatever self-nurturing possibilities avail. Fingerbone Lake might be thought of as the culminating setting of a long line of watery texts. In short, Robinson's novel does seize a central, even "a mighty theme," and in a remarkably ambitious effort rewrites a tradition of American literature. Yet as Linda Hutcheon reminds us, she does this in a complex parody of her predecessors, as a kind of housekeeping that involves efforts large and small, in addressing the multiple contingencies in her title that inform narrative possibilities as well.

What makes us initially miss the literary ambitions of Robinson's novel is that, far more self-consciously than her predecessors, she everywhere engages the literal problems of keeping house, of maintaining domestic order. This begins with the disastrous rains that flood the Stones' parlor after Sylvie arrives, prompting a waltz in boots while "glyphs of crimped and plaited light swung across the walls" (*H* 63). As if disarmed by the disarray, Ruth collapses time itself in her recollection: "I remember precisely at this minute," she notes, writing the words (in a break of the narrative frame reminiscent of both Melville and Nabokov). This temporal dislocation augments the skewing of the physical world, with water seeping everywhere it shouldn't, including on top of the ice-bound lake. Conversely, during a night Ruth and Lucille spend in the woods, the wild appears tamed in a vivid description of the lake's "sheltered water," as if it were "a place of distinctly domestic disorder, warm and still and replete" (*H* 113). And later still, consciousness becomes water in a remarkable shape-shifting scene, as Ruth contemplates its unstable, effervescent quality: "What is thought, after all, what is dreaming, but swim and flow, and the images they seem to animate?" (*H* 162).

Given the physical effects of water—flooding the house, ruining furniture, disrupting behavior and sensibility alike—it is hardly surprising that figurative implications of housekeeping should first be ignored in favor of more conventional efforts. Threatened spaces demand attention more immediately than psychologies tormented by unaccountable loss. That explains Ruth's focus on her grandmother, who models the novel's most literal form of housekeeping after her husband dies, as if her assiduous efforts (doing laundry, baking bread, arranging flowers, making beds) might shield her children from adversity, even contingency. Yet the repetitiveness of her labor becomes as alarming as it is reassuring, inducing a disquieting sense of unease. And once her daughters have left, she cares for her granddaughters just the same, though now in a troubled mix of patience and incomprehension, trepidation and loss:

> She whited shoes and braided hair and fried chicken and turned back bedclothes, and then suddenly feared and remembered that the children had somehow disappeared, every one. How had it happened? How might she have known? And she whited shoes and braided hair and turned back bedclothes as if re-enacting the commonplace would make it merely commonplace again, or as if she could find the chink, the flaw, in her serenely orderly and ordinary life, or discover at least some intimation that her three girls would disappear as absolutely as their father had done.
>
> *H* 24–25

The repetitions here ("She whited shoes ... And she whited shoes ... as if ... or as if ...") echo the repetitive, restorative quality of the work represented, as activities never done and completed but needing to be repeated daily, weekly, with each generation, as granddaughters replace the daughters she has inexplicably lost. Yet the questions interrupting those recurrent activities are harrowing ("How had it happened? How might she have known?"), as if to intimate that housekeeping has not done its restorative work on the grandmother, who "suddenly feared and remembered that the children had somehow disappeared, every one." Against that chilling realization, she returns to domestic rituals that become the outward expression of a faith in order wrestable from chaos. The very confusion of the passage, unable to sort itself out, speaks to the futility of any such literal domestic efforts at achieving understanding.

When Sylvie finally arrives, talking "a great deal about housekeeping" (85), it is only to accentuate a practice at odds with her mother's: turning lights out, dining in the dark, welcoming the outside in for its (in Thoreau's words) "tonic of wildness" (575). That transgressive mode is epitomized in Ruth's half-fishy analogy: "Sylvie in a house was more or less like a mermaid in a ship's cabin. She preferred it sunk in the very element it was meant to exclude. We had crickets in the pantry, squirrels in the eaves, sparrows in the attic. Lucille and I stepped through the door from sheer night to sheer night" (99). Conventional efforts at imposing order (dusting, sweeping, picking up, keeping nature at bay) are abandoned in favor of a less exclusionary practice, registered in Ruth's description of their transition as one now from sameness to sameness ("sheer night to sheer night") that becomes in turn an invitation to enter a more diverse imaginative realm. And the success of Ruth's mastery of that realm is measured by her evocation of her aunt Molly as a *"fisher of men,"* a description that evokes Molly's sister, Sylvie:

Even now I always imagine her leaning from the low side of some small boat, dropping her net through the spumy billows of the upper air. Her net would sweep the turning world unremarked as a wind in the grass, and when she began to pull it in, perhaps in a pell-mell ascension of formal gentlemen and thin pigs and old women and odd socks that would astonish this lower world, she would gather the net, so easily, until the very burden itself lay all in a heap just under the surface. One last pull of measureless power and ease would spill her catch into the boat, gasping and amazed, gleaming rainbows in the rarer light.

Such a net, such a harvesting, would put an end to all anomaly.

H 91

It is as if Ruth's newly heterogeneous sensibility were sparked by Sylvie's literal practice of housekeeping, allowing her to transgress categories, styles, schemes of all sorts.[5] Molly's net would re-collect everything that had ever been lost, discarded, removed, including all buttons burst and spectacles mislaid, all toys cast off and cars abandoned. Ruth's whimsical conception of Molly "dropping her net" seems indebted to Thoreau's musings on "the long lost bottom of Walden Pond" (549), a body of water so transparent that he can look down at night to see its shores "strewed with the wrecks of the forest" (462). As Thoreau adds, in a Transcendental precept conjoining nature and psychology, thus "the beholder measures the depth of his own nature" (471). Melville characteristically alters this precept in depicting the cabin-boy Pip's figurative descent, "carried down alive to wondrous depths, where strange shapes of the unwarped primal world glided to and fro before his passive eyes; and the miser-merman, Wisdom, revealed his hoarded heaps; and among the joyous, heartless, ever-juvenile eternities, Pip saw the multitudinous, God-omnipresent, coral insects, that out of the firmament of waters heaved the colossal orbs" (466).[6] Robinson is troping a tradition of such scenes in Molly's imagined net, as Ruth intuits her gesture of physical re-collection would anticipate a fuller mental recollection. Yet Robinson reveals the resemblance of such weirdly figurative scenes to conventional housekeeping itself, in the process of "sweep[ing] the turning world," even as she quietly invokes Thoreau and Melville in their separate scenes imagining a marvelous review of all the things in our past long-forgotten, sheltered in odd mental corners, now allowing us to delight in their variety as life's salvage. Instead of reinforcing anomaly by segregating difference, Molly's effort (and Sylvie's) becomes comprehensive and inclusive.

And with such comprehensiveness, the implications of housekeeping and water blur, in conjoining domestic and natural, offering a dream of things at once ordered and accepted yet somehow neither unduly disciplined nor unexpectedly diminished. Ruth seems to have this in mind the night she speaks of "sheltered water" as domesticated though disordered: "Set apart from the drifts and tides and lucifactions of the open water, the surface of the bay seemed almost viscous, membranous, and here things massed and accumulated, as they do in cobwebs or in the eaves and unswept corners of a house" (*H* 113). The "domestic disorder" of this scene is its most comforting feature, offering an encouraging wholeness as Ruth realizes the need for forms of housekeeping that resemble Robinson's "regime of small kindnesses." Those forms represent an understandable urge to stave off chaos, disease, and disorder, but not at the expense of the generative flux of nature, in all its dizzying disruptiveness. Reconceived this way, housekeeping emerges as a blend of accommodation and imposition, a process of creating tentative household order that corresponds to the flexible ordering of a sensibility, in an effort finally to understand one's relation to the past. Emerson celebrated this apparent contradiction as a process of compensation, creating order out of natural disorder: "For every grain of wit there is a grain of folly. For every thing you have missed, you have gained something else; and for every thing you gain, you lose something" (*F&S* 57). Or as he concluded, "Things refuse to be mismanaged long" (*F&S* 58). Robinson, on the contrary, reveals her skepticism about Emerson here, as well as Thoreau in his own calm complacency: "The universe constantly and obediently answers to our conceptions" (399). Ruth's very silence before anything so confidently asserted suggests her wise consideration yet caution about the intersections between wild nature and a human propensity for order.

Sylvie's advent in Ruth's life represents a new mode of housekeeping but registers even more a different relation to things themselves, to houses well-kept along with the belongings they hold. She reminds us of Thoreau's notorious claim about property: "It is best to avoid the beginnings of evil" (376). And her doubt about the value of permanence or stability—about titles to assets and authorizations, about inherited possessions and appropriate wardrobes—initiates in Ruth a novel way of thinking about not only the present but the past as well, of what's to be kept, what discarded, and how in the process we discover memories for experiences we may never have had. Sylvie's eager habits of vagrancy, traveling light--refusing to settle into predictable patterns, other than transiency itself—offers Ruth once more a figurative model, though now for ways to be not in space but in time. And here, she parts with Lucille, who hates "transience," indeed hates any "invidious change" (*H* 103), imaged variously in the watery, rippling flow of possibility ever-present in Fingerbone's weather.[7] At one point, Ruth alludes to her sister's struggle with temporality, unsettled by the future's sheer potential for difference from the present: "Time that had not come yet—an anomaly in itself—had the fiercest reality for her" (*H* 93). Change, transitions, ephemerality, uncertainty all unsettle Lucille, which helps explain her staunch certitude, her penchant for unambiguous clarity. Her very name tips us off to the constitutional unease she feels at Sylvie's darkened dinners: "She insisted on a light at suppertime" (*H* 102). Unlike Ruth, who expresses the desire to disappear, to become unrealized potential, Lucille needs affirmation as a vivid presence here and now, without the threat of transformation there and then. And her view of others is equally indubitable, illustrated in the firm conviction that Helen was just like herself: "Lucille's mother was orderly, vigorous, and sensible, a widow . . . who was killed in an accident" (*H* 109). By contrast, Ruth is less inflexible, more uncertain, equally confused by Helen's death but unwilling simply to discount the dispiriting evidence of suicide.[8] In short, Lucille needs stability and finds the best means of controlling untoward events not only in conventional housekeeping but in a resistance to transiency, both literal and figurative. By contrast, when Lucille finally departs, Ruth's characteristic response is charitable to a fault, even finding admirable Lucille's effort to author herself, to forge her own identity in the absence of mothering.

Despite love of her sister, Ruth learns from Sylvie a valuable lesson, that her aunt's role as "unredeemed transient" (*H* 177) registers precisely the narrative habits that will allow her to cope with Lucille's desertion, and even more to understand her mother's suicide, her grandfather's death. For *Housekeeping* centrally forms a meditation on the processes of abandonment and loss, and on the commensurate ability to discover one's own divided voice in the midst of what is left, as a means of repairing a past that is always evanescent, always transient, altered in the very memory that re-members parts for whole. To that end, the novel repeatedly takes as its subject "the dear ordinary" (*H* 15), announcing that "the very ordinariness of the things would recommend them" (73), and in Ruth's voice presses remembrance as "a resurrection of the ordinary" (18). Yet if memory has a life-giving capacity for "rituals of the ordinary" (*H* 16), it functions best (as Ruth learns from Sylvie) in a state of transiency, of peripatetic expectancy shorn of habit and certitude. After all, "There is so little to remember of anyone—an anecdote, a conversation at table. But every memory is turned over and over again, every word, however chance, written in the heart in the hope that memory will fulfill itself, and become flesh" (*H* 194–95). Here is the novel's informing premise, of a traumatized Ruth as figurative transient of her own past, looking for means of self-restoration, hoping to bring the dead alive. And Ruth discovers that even the dislocations of flawed memory can serve her, adequately if imperfectly, shaping a narrative whose nuances illuminate even if the whole fails to hold together. The effort at narrative hospitality to the past always stands at odds with coherence and structured order, though Ruth is too alert to both aspects of housekeeping to allow either one to edge out the other. Like Melville's Ishmael, she embraces a peripatetic mode, not only physically in accompanying her transient aunt but figuratively, in adopting varied narrative strategies, shifting registers in an effort to sort out a bewilderingly mixed experience.

Ruth's sensitivity to blurred boundaries and fitful possibilities helps explain the visionary aspects of her narrative, which contributes detail she could not have known about her grandfather or her mother. In this, she responds most directly to Cather's *Professor's House*, in St. Peter's reconstruction of Tom Outland's experience on the Blue Mesa. Like a tailor repairing fabric, inserting material to match what is absent, Ruth seamlessly invokes and invents to make her larger recollection more sensible and complete. Or, to borrow her image of the bedroom furniture ornamented by her grandfather—designs painted over but emerging nonetheless years later—it is as if barely discernable memories "floated . . . just beneath the surface" (*H* 90). Ruth wants to recover these images, to discern a design to that past, especially in circumstances where so much has been displaced and forgotten. In fact, at one point she speaks figuratively of her own renewed sense of deprivation, and yet even so of restoration—"it seemed that something I had lost might be found in Sylvie's house" (*H* 124). The very formulation, expressing hope couched in a provisional "seemed," acknowledges an inability to ground knowledge in fact, memory in actual lived experience. But that inability does not curb her effort, as she elaborates recuperative possibilities of memory stitched together into narrative as something first surmised from Sylvie's example:

> what perished need not also be lost. At Sylvie's house, my grandmother's house, so much of what I remembered I could hold in my hand—like a china cup, or a windfall apple, sour and cold from its affinity with deep earth, with only a trace of the perfume of its blossoming. Sylvie, I knew, felt the life of perished things.
>
> *H* 124

To feel "the life of perished things" requires something like Sylvie's mastery of transience, a valuing of impermanence and imaginative detachment but also of crossed borders and blurred boundaries.[9]

II. "If I Had Been There"

Ruth, we learn early on, is quiet and withdrawn, the pale attendant on her more vibrant younger sister. As Kristen King observes, "It is as if she disappears in order to tell her story" (565). Suffering from a sense of invisibility as someone who doesn't "know what I think" (*H* 105), she draws on negative capability to merge imaginatively with others, in the process fostering a narrative recovery. And "foster" here is suggestive, as a verb that not only matches her mother's maiden name (evoking the past she needs to recover) but also intimating the necessary impermanence of that imaginative merging. Curiously, this process reverses the procedure by which Ruth was created, as a figure Robinson brought to life only by dividing her psychologically from others: "In order to create that feeling of dimensionality, I simply split up one woman and made her into a group of women" (Osen). Ruth complements Lucille and Sylvie, then, though she is the one still trying to merge, to imagine in others what she cannot know first-hand. And at such moments, she often pauses deliberately, drawing attention to the process of narrative-making. In this, *Housekeeping* again bears witness to Cather's *Professor's House*, which offers a strong precursor in its own taut balance of lyric description and narrative sequence. Yet the connection between these novels lies deeper, in Godfrey St. Peter's memorializing of Tom Outland, the beloved student he imaginatively inhabits. For Robinson adopts and extends Cather's visionary mode, making us appreciate through Ruth's metaleptic style the way in which two conceptual worlds have been effectively bridged.[10]

Early on, for instance, Ruth imagines the aftermath of her grandfather's death, leading us to wonder how she can know so many adduced details, when all of a sudden she enters her grandmother's consciousness:

> One day my grandmother must have carried out a basket of sheets to hang in the spring sunlight, wearing her widow's black, performing the rituals of the ordinary as an act of faith. Say there were two or three inches of hard old snow on the ground, with earth here and there oozing through the broken places, and that there was warmth in the sunlight, when the wind did not blow it all away, and say she stooped breathlessly in her corset to lift up a sodden sheet by its hems, and say that when she had pinned three corners to the lines it began to billow and leap in her hands, to flutter and tremble, and to glare with the light, and that the throes of the thing were as gleeful and strong as if a spirit were dancing in its cerements. That wind! she would say, because it pushed the skirts of her coat against her legs and made strands of her hair fly.

H 16

The passage begins with a strange shift in verb forms, from an initial "must have" that suggests the moment is unverifiable to the repeated imperative "Say" that builds the scene in almost incantatory tones. And that transition contrasts with Ruth's habit of stitching actual moments together with speculative transitions, as if she were figuratively combining housekeeping with transiency, an ordering narrative impulse with hypothetical meanderings. Here an initial fantasy is granted a gradual reality, with Ruth gaining access to her grandmother's thoughts, then gradually, inconspicuously *becoming* her grandmother. As Brian Gingrich has observed of this passage:

> reading becomes saying, and saying becomes creating. The text becomes something like a spell that must be read out by the reader in order to be cast. As details upon details are added to the scene—the three corners of the sheet, the strands of the hair, the smells of the snow, the half-a-day's walk—the image becomes too uncannily precise not to be true.
>
> But "say" is also like the word "if": it posits a certain set of circumstances ("if x is true ...") and then it imagines the probable consequences. What is interesting about this passage, and so many other similar instances in Ruth's narrative, is that the probable consequences are stated as fact. The "if" of the "if ... then ..." statement dissolves away ... and the narrative slips off into some secondary fiction-treated-as-reality. After the phrase "she would say," Ruth begins to speak only in the simple past ("pushed ... made ... came down ... smelled ..."). It's as if she's entered the consciousness of the version of her grandmother whom she imagines in the fantasy and she's speaking to us from there.
>
> 12

This description perfectly captures the transient nature of Ruth's consciousness, as she roams visually, syntactically across the narrative borders that otherwise secure such flights of self-sustaining fantasy from full factual knowledge. Only imperceptibly, moreover, does the narrative return to the Ruth of authenticated observation from the Ruth making it up, thus diminishing any anxiety about boundaries between assumed reality and momentary fantasy. Yet just as such narrative questions subside, she pauses to reflect again, reminding the reader how powerful the urge to fantasize is, as reverie bleeds into recollection and becomes lost within the plot. Cather had anticipated this strategy with "Tom Outland's Story," the recollected journal that breaks so abruptly into St. Peter's frame narrative. But Robinson seems here to invoke an even more powerful narrative precursor, in Quentin Compson's reconstruction of harrowing events half-a-century before he was born, based simply on imaginative possibilities and a shrewd sense of psychology. As he admits, "If I had been there I could not have seen it this plain" (Faulkner, *Absalom* 238)—a realization that seems to shadow Ruth's own reconstructions of the past.

Sylvie's influence is everywhere evident in this merging of invention and truth, of contemplation and knowledge. Her domestic approach to order parallels Ruth's efforts at resurrection, both vying to restore "the life of perished things." And notably, Ruth achieves transfigurations in both her account and her style, coming in part to understand those she's lost by merging with them imaginatively. The long flight of fantasy about her grandmother, for instance, continues to spread temporally, moving back and forth through her marriage to Edmund to her devastation at his death, then back to his love of eggshells in a pattern that rises again to an incantatory pitch through a series of anaphoras ("Say that . . ." shifting to "In a month . . ." shifting to "He would . . ."). Summarily, "the wind that billowed her sheets announced to her the resurrection of the ordinary" (*H* 17–18), preparing Ruth's grandmother for the epiphany Ruth imagines her experiencing as she digs up potatoes: "What have I seen, what have I seen. The earth and the sky and the garden, not as they always are. And she saw her daughters' faces not as they always were" (*H* 19). The fragmented, invented reminiscences merge in a vision paradoxically (if emphatically) "not as they always were," as if to evoke an effulgent divination of others as they *might* have been.[11]

Ruth's nuanced understanding derives from this capacity for inhabiting others so as not simply to reduce them to external features or predictable roles. She merges emotionally with others, a lesson learned inadvertently from her transient aunt, which she realizes walking behind Sylvie "as if I were her shadow" (*H* 144), without will or direction of her own. "All at peace, and at ease," Ruth concludes: "We are the same. She could as well be my mother. I crouched and slept in her very shape like an unborn child" (*H* 145). As with other such passages, this scene of potential empowerment is not unambivalent, suggesting as it does that the sacrifice of psychological autonomy may be needed for Ruth to achieve fuller insight. And significantly, the surgical separation of character that Robinson performed at the novel's inception is here briefly reversed, as they reunite, restored momentarily to something like psychological symbiosis. Shortly thereafter, that coalescence reaches its most intense pitch in a moment of epiphany as they roast marshmallows, then walk to a favored place Sylvie has discovered. Ruth gazes on a sunlit scene, covered with frost that seems like salt, prompting her to wonder at the convergence of desire and the world:

> and where the world was salt there would be greater need of slaking. For need can blossom into all the compensations it requires. To crave and to have are as like as a thing and its shadow. For when does a berry break upon the tongue as sweetly as when one longs to taste it, and when is the taste refracted into so many hues and savors of ripeness and earth, and when do our senses know any thing so utterly as when we lack it? And here again is a foreshadowing—the world will be made whole. For to wish for a hand on one's hair is all but to feel it. So whatever we may lose, very craving gives it back to us again. Though we dream and hardly know it, longing, like an angel, fosters us, smooths our hair, and brings us wild strawberries.
>
> *H* 152–53

This bizarre image of a Lot-like world of salt unfolds into a series of assertions about desire and its creative fulfillment, asserting the self-sufficiency of perfect reciprocity, merging need with its own "compensations."

The question apparently begged by her image is why it should be "compensation" that blossoms rather than, say, fulfillment or satisfaction. Yet as Emerson elaborates in his essay "Compensation," "An inevitable dualism bisects nature, so that each thing is a half, and suggests another thing to make it whole" (*F&S* 57). That dualism results in a universal desire for reciprocity, inducing us to understand all processes, all forms, all contingencies as utterly equalized: "a certain compensation balances every gift and every defect" (*F&S* 57). Robinson seizes on Emerson's radical insight here on "the perfect compensation of the universe," not only in her balancing of Ruth against Lucille, or housekeeping against transiency, but as well in her figurative language itself, in perceiving metaphor as the very vehicle of compensation, merging seemingly dissonant elements. Yet where Emerson pursues the idea of compensation in ledgerly terms, as "the absolute balance of Give and Take . . . in all the action and reaction of nature" (66), Robinson converts the premise into an imaginative capacity, not a phenomenal state. What Emerson understands as the necessary compensations of any binary logic, balanced between opposite poles, Robinson transfigures into a cherished human faculty for adapting imaginatively, becoming adequate to alien circumstances, gaining knowledge not through an actual fulfillment of desire, but through its lack ("the very craving gives it back to us again"). And though she does not say it, the implicit claim is that an ardent desire to know another ends by creating and fulfilling that other (much as Cather has St. Peter realize in his ruminations about Tom Outland).

This helps explain Ruth's more tentative, less oracular approach: she not only learns what she thinks by teasing out possibilities through family figures, but by probing the rhetorical figures she invokes, exploring where they might lead.[12] *Housekeeping*, in fact, began more as a poem than a novel, inspired by the play of words rather than a particular setting or event or character—each of which more customarily generates plot. As Robinson later acknowledged, she had compiled "a stack of metaphors and they cohered in a way that I hadn't expected.... So I started writing *Housekeeping*, and the characters became important for me" (Fay 41). The novel itself confirms Emerson's intriguingly counter-domestic insight in "The Poet" that words respond to other words: "all language is vehicular and transitive, and is good, as ferries and horses are, for conveyance, not as farms and houses are, for homestead" (*F&S* 233).[13] Individual words themselves, that is, resist a housekeeping regimentation, leading unpredictably to connotations that surprise us by unexpected insights rather than confirming the settled convictions we had presumed. Strange as the provenance of Robinson's novel sounds, it explains characters' names themselves, which appear to dictate behavior. Ruth is Hebrew for companion, though it develops in Middle English into "sorrow, compassion, pity"; Lucille is Latin for light; and Sylvie, Latin for woods, though its Old English and German translations are *wod* and *wut,* meaning anger but also insanity. The names and derivations lend an ironic tinge to Ruth's later claim (with its Thoreauvian echoes) that "I went to the woods for the wood's own sake, while, increasingly, Lucille seemed to be enduring a banishment there" (*H* 99). Yet intriguing as these metaphorical origins of character are, more astonishing is the way the novel's theme embodies a process of identification that lies at the heart of metaphorical superimposition. Metaphor, after all, is a figure of substitution, merging boundaries between things, blurring identities, appropriately so in a narrative of a lake that regularly floods and freezes, or floods *over* its frozen surfaces—seeming to change identity with the weather, as if landscape were a metaphor made physical.

Even so, it comes as a surprise to find that a novel that grew from a stack of metaphors exhibits relatively few of them, even as instances of its rhetorical cousin, simile, prove surprisingly frequent. Unlike metaphor, simile keeps identities discrete by invoking a comparison *as* a comparison, not an identity. And in a landscape where boundaries are constantly transgressed, in which housekeeping invariably adjusts conditions against being flooded or frozen out, simile functions more effectively than metaphor to maintain the integrity of identity, making us aware that a merging might take place but hasn't quite yet. Simile teases out equivalencies just on the verge of occurring that metaphor simply erases (because they already have occurred). Sometimes, Robinson's similes oddly seem to reverse themselves: "the wind was as rank as a hunter" (*H* 88), is followed two pages later by "her net would sweep ... unremarked as wind in the grass" (91). At other times, rhetorical figures strain against the sense they strive to clarify: "our lives floated as weightless, intangible, immiscible, and inseparable as reflections in water" (*H* 41); or a vagrant's corpse in a boxcar "sailed feet first and as solemn as Lincoln" (87), or "Stone showed pink as a scar on a dog's ear" (150). The very strangeness of such figures thwarts their normal function as similes, since they do less to "extract or epitomise some particular quality of what is being described" than to bushwhack us from one conceptual realm into another.[14] Fallen leaves appear "as limp and noisome as wet leather" (*H* 199), while buffeting waves are as "insistent, intimate, insinuating, proprietary as rodents in a dark house" (164). One might argue that such unusual analogies express Ruth's psychology, "her strangeness, her singularity" (Mullan), but their collective impact reveals more notably a world in which conventional housekeeping gestures are insufficient, even at times unnecessary, since the domestic and natural often intersect in such provocative ways. Occasionally, almost ironically, housekeeping can become the basis of simile: "At last we had slid from her lap like one of those magazines full of responsible opinion about discipline and balanced meals" (*H* 110).

In the slippery world of Fingerbone, Ruth's figurative descriptions often integrate nature and culture rather than segregating them, celebrating the wild in terms of the domestic, or vice versa: "the wind in the mountains was like one long indrawn breath. Downstairs the flood bumped and fumbled like a blind man in a strange house, but outside it hissed and trickled, like the pressure of water against your eardrums, and like the sounds you hear in the moment before you faint" (*H* 65–66). Later, reversing fields, Ruth observes that "the deep woods are as dark and stiff and as full of their own odors as the parlor of an old house. We would walk among those great legs, hearing the enthralled and incessant murmurings far above our heads, like children at a funeral" (*H* 98). Ruth's style here enacts the transient ethos Sylvie lives, defying strict housekeeping logic by refusing to eliminate anomalies, revealing instead an intersection of disparate domains that enhances each to the other's benefit. "Bones, bones, I thought, in a fine sheath of flesh like Sunday gloves." (*H* 137); or, recalling her grandmother's doilies, "bristling, like cactus blossoms" (141); or "The house was as dank as the orchard, and would *not* burn" (208). Simile binds these divergent realms together, contrary to initial expectations, which speaks less to individual psychology than to larger cultural assumptions. And in this, Robinson transfigures Emerson by adjusting compensation to a purely figurative realm, refusing to address the metaphysical claims that Thoreau endorsed and Melville doubted, but instead simply shifting the conceit from a phenomenal realm to a psychological one.

III. *Transiency*

One of Ruth's more evocative similes emerges as she contemplates Sylvie: "It is, as she said, difficult to describe someone, since memories are by their nature fragmented, isolated, and arbitrary as glimpses one has at night through lighted windows" (*H* 53). This contrast between darkness and light is perhaps more suggestive than others bridged by Ruth's similes—of flooding and housekeeping, transience and permanence, past and present—if only by figuring forth understanding as an inherently flawed scenic process. Memories become *tableaux vivants* that at first appear "fragmented, isolated, . . . arbitrary" (*H* 53), but because seen in the dark as if stopped in time, they offer a context in which imagination plays out narrative possibilities. Sylvie's return to Fingerbone literalizes this conceit, with her weird notion of housekeeping that involves turning lights out, imagining life enhanced without vision. Lucille of course rejects the idea out-of-hand (her very name, after all, aligns her with lucidity, clarity, even overtness), but Ruth finds the dark offers a release from perpetual mental housekeeping, of "survivors picking among flotsam, among the small, unnoticed, unvalued clutter" (*H* 116) of the past. In that sense, darkness offers not only solace but a realm in which loss can at least appear to be imaginatively compensated, memory can seem even partially restored, pasts can be brought into a fragile, if tentatively reassuring, alignment.

This discovery initially occurs the night she and Lucille sleep in the woods along Fingerbone Lake, to wake up "in absolute darkness" (*H* 115). Like Emerson on a bare common, become a "transparent eyeball" (*E&L* 10) she and Lucille found "all our human boundaries were overrun." Yet in defiant rejection of Emerson's celebration of the visual ("Nature always wears the colors of the spirit" [*E&L* 11]), Ruth argues instead for a convergence of inner and outer darkness where "details are merely accidental." As she dismissively observes, "Everything that falls upon the eye is apparition, a sheet dropped over the world's true workings." Instead of Transcendental access to truth, we are simply "tricked" by the apparent permanence of things when "nothing is more perishable." At first, rather plaintive about this "unvalued clutter," Ruth seizes on darkness as "the only solvent," in ridding us of feelings of loss and abandonment by eliminating visible reminders of that loss: "there need not be relic, remnant, margin, residue, memento, bequest, memory, thought, track, or trace, if only the darkness could be perfect and permanent" (*H* 116). Yet that translation of Sylvie's relaxed household style into an imaginative tactic is just as fruitless as Lucille's endorsement of her grandmother's strict practice; each mode lays claim to being self-consistent and sufficient, and neither one achieves a sense of restoration or closure.

Seeming to realize this, Ruth pulls back from the desire for clean slates, perfect knowledge, or final judgments, embracing a slippery imaginative understanding that is curiously a combination of darkness and light, as she takes increasing delight in a prospect she images to herself as "glimpses . . . at night through lighted windows." Like someone in a theater staring up at a screen, she perches in a context that allows past to meld into present, that allows another more fully to manifest herself. Of course, peering in from the dark differs from looking out, as Ruth considers travelers gazing at "their own depthless images on the black glass, if they had looked" (*H* 54)—immured in mirroring self-reflection. The scene is later recalled as a provocative simile, with Ruth comparing it to sisterhood, reconfiguring the uneasy balance of visibility and obscurity: "Having a sister or a friend is like sitting at night in a lighted house. Those outside can watch you if they want, but you need not see them" (*H* 154). Here, despite what others see of sisterly ease, they will never know. Only three pages later, Ruth teases the conceit again, now in terms of a developing sense of solitude and abandonment. But the image has transmogrified, shifting from sheer light to glistening reflections off water, tilting from bright interior to the obscure outdoors. That dislodged perspective creates as well a defiance of expectations in the recognition of her solitude, alone in the dark despite what she sees. Ruth comes to realize, however insubstantially and erratically, the self-sustaining terms of her own conceit:

> When one looks from inside at a lighted window, or looks from above at the lake, one sees the image of oneself in a lighted room, the image of oneself among trees and sky—the deception is obvious, but flattering all the same. When one looks from the darkness into the light, however, one sees all the difference between here and there, this and that. Perhaps all unsheltered people are angry in their hearts, and would like to break the roof, spine, and ribs, and smash the windows and flood the floor and spindle the curtains and bloat the couch.
>
> *H* 157–58

It is as if she were meditating on the philosophical implications of being alienated from oneself, borrowing from Melville's Ishmael in "that blackness of darkness" when "I but the better saw the redness, the madness, the ghastliness of others" (476). Ruth likewise hunkers down in the dark, aware of what she does not have, alone and abandoned, and in that "unsheltered" darkness, violent feelings emerge—indeed, emerge *as* versions of natural forces disrupting shelter itself.

Yet even more revelatory is the way a simple simile becomes transformed in Ruth's wandering rumination, as a mental transiency that allows her to understand multiple and seemingly contradictory aspects of her own traumatic experience. Darkness eviscerates but also heals, as a condition for imaginatively weaving together fragments of memory, emotion, and belief into knowledge. Or as she concludes: "What are all these fragments for, if not to be knit up finally?" (*H* 92). That knowledge is partially a gift from Sylvie, who teaches how little fixed forms of housekeeping can fend off contingency, but it also owes to more conventional ideas about housekeeping, and more importantly about writing. After all, Ruth's very effort to "knit up" fragments of her past into a coherent text has been the basis of her strained narrative and stylistic efforts all along. And in doing so, ironically, she aligns herself with Lucille, since narrative reveals itself as a form of knitting and sewing that her sister valued as housekeeping ideals. Of course, her resistance to seamlessness and ordered perfection aligns her just as significantly with Sylvie, who has been guiding her all along towards a valuing of permeable boundaries that allow past and present, memory and lived reality to generate understandings worthy of being knitted together narratively.

Increasingly, Ruth entertains such cross-connections until she finally becomes aware of the resemblance between her long-lost mother and her aunt, who "began to blur the memory of my mother, and then to displace it. Soon it was Sylvie who would look up startled, regarding me from a vantage of memory in which she had no place" (*H* 53).[15] Again, Ruth's imagination crosses categories and joins personalities, initially seeming to annul Helen's memory but leading Ruth paradoxically to feel she can at last intuit her mother, reviving Helen via the "coincidence" of sisterhood with Sylvie, through recollected moments long submerged that suddenly surface into consciousness: "Sylvie's head falls to the side and we see the blades of my mother's shoulders ... Helen is the woman in the mirror, the woman in the dream, the woman remembered, the woman in the water, and her nerves guide the blind fingers that touch into place all the falling strands of Sylvie's hair" (*H* 131–32). The process of Ruth's narrative, in fact, has been to bring her to the point where she can make a perplexing admission that seems an all but direct evocation of Melville, in Ishmael's strangely hallucinogenic narrative that merges evidence of the senses with phantasmagorical possibilities: "I have never distinguished readily between thinking and dreaming. I know my life would be much different if I could ever say, This I have learned from my senses, while that I have merely imagined" (*H* 215–16). Yet just as Ishmael productively confuses intellectual and psychological insights, Ruth's transgressive meld of "thinking and dreaming" points to the prospect of emotional healing, in helping her remember the past by re-membering it. Having vowed in the closing pages that "there was an end to housekeeping," she nonetheless keeps the concept alive through figurative restorations, patchwork as ever. She holds emotional dissolution at bay via tentatively reconstructing a past that otherwise seems simply inexplicable, unaccountably having laid waste to her life and to those she loves.

IV. A Closure that Resists

Just at the point of achieving this insight, Ruth abruptly declares in deliberately flat, pedestrian tones: "All this is fact. Fact explains nothing. On the contrary, it is fact that requires explanation" (*H* 217). As if the entire narrative reconstruction she has provided were somehow deficient—a reconstruction admittedly pieced together from scenes recollected but also from hearsay and fanciful surmise—Ruth proposes now to move among epistemological categories once again to gain an "explanation" for where she is. This brings her round-circle to her opening words, imagining now a return from her subsequent life as a transient back to her house in Fingerbone. Lucille may still be there, in a scene Ruth has imagined "a thousand times" before (*H* 218). But significantly, the scene is only conditionally imagined ("*If* Lucille is there"), and envisaged once again from Ruth's favorite conceptual site, of Lucille's presumptive daughters depicted looking out "the black window," hypothetically seeing her own face imposed on their reflections as she looks in from outside. The moment embodies a Chinese-box conjunction of fantasy *within* fantasy, of the daughters' imagined thoughts (unguessed at) within Ruth's imagined scene.

Then suddenly in the novel's final paragraph, the setting alters—"Or imagine Lucille in Boston, at a table in a restaurant." Unlike everything before, Ruth offers now not a scene of what is or might have been, but of what clearly is not, in a series of denials that appear to undo the memories that have been pieced together, the past that has been stitched whole: "Sylvie and I do not flounce . . . We do not sit down . . . My mother, likewise, is not there . . . and my grandfather . . . does not examine the menu." The final negation, however, trumps all the preceding: "We are nowhere in Boston." This is a description not only odd in itself—denying everything that had been construed as possible—but odd as well in contrast to Ruth's own gradually maturing voice, which has gently merged prospects into a compelling narrative that defies us to tell where real and imagined are entwined. Paradoxically, that repeated negation only inflates possibilities, making them more irresistible, as if Ruth were aware of the neurolinguistic axiom that the brain cannot automatically process negatives—that any statement with "don't" is initially processed in the positive. Sentences banning the thought of pink elephants require us to do just that to parse their meaning—a mental reversal Ruth deliberately performs at the end:

> We are nowhere in Boston. However Lucille may look, she will never find us there, or any trace or sign. We pause nowhere in Boston, even to admire a store window, and the perimeters of our wandering are nowhere. No one watching this woman smear her initials in the steam on her water glass with her first finger, or slip cellophane packets of oyster crackers in to her handbag for the sea gulls, could know how her thoughts are thronged by our absence, or know how

she does not watch, does not listen, does not wait, does not hope, and always for me and Sylvie.

H 218–19

All builds to a sense of closure that refuses quite to close, just as Lucille leaves a curved watermark only two-thirds rounded, though "she works at completing the circle with her thumbnail."[16] It is as if Ruth's envisioned efforts have fallen short, for all the detail that accrues in her lovingly imagined scene, leaving her and us with a sense of ambivalence that actually accords with her unstable style throughout. That ambivalence emerges in the curious tension here at the end, established by the claim that "No one watching" even imaginatively (presumably including Ruth as well) could know what Lucille was thinking. And the tension is sustained in the rest of the sentence, that no one could "know how her thoughts are thronged by our absence."

Counter-intuitively, Ruth elaborates this apparent contradiction between absence and crowding that forces us to ponder how Lucille's thoughts could be so "thronged" (thronged, that is, by absence). At last, the sentence builds to a series of five, liltingly rhythmic clauses, ratcheting up in succession negations that, for all their cumulative weight, cannot quite topple the sisterly affection Ruth imputes to Lucille: "she does not watch, does not listen, does not wait, does not hope, and always for me and Sylvie." Here again, the negations are surprisingly evocative, presenting what they still deny, before folding to the novel's final paradoxical words. Do those words deny the claims immediately preceding, the negation of all that Lucille is doing, or do they confirm them? We never know. As in earlier scenes, Ruth seems to imitate Lucille's voice, yet without quite gaining access to her sister's consciousness as she has earlier (e.g. when Ruth and Lucille differ about Helen's car, her hair, her reasons for suicide).

Still, Ruth expresses compassion for Lucille, even a desire for that feeling to be reciprocated, though she voices this not as felt reality but as a dream inverted. She keeps ever before us—in the "Imagine" and "say"—an awareness that this is not fact but only something conjured up, to be realized as we will. Ruth ends as we might have expected, with her life still not sorted in regimented "housekeeping" terms—past from present, trauma from relief, all properly parsed and arranged. The figurative transiency of her narrative has lent her a tentative sense of comprehension, but by its very nature that understanding can never be final nor otherwise offer a firm resolution. All the conclusion attests is that we always live in an indeterminate realm of conjecture and possibility.[17] Narratively, what comes through most pointedly is the way in which absence itself calls forth a lyric voice in the novel—prominently in the evocative reconstruction of others, who resonate most as they seem most lost to us. Still, it is a voice that resides at ease with other, far from lyrical moments, offering altogether a more adequate expression of the diversity of experience. And in evoking that voice, Robinson once again looks back to a long American tradition that has tried to sort out life's ostensible compensations, and narrative's more obvious ones. Her debt to Emerson, Thoreau, and Melville is clear in the revision she offers by way of Ruth's wary engagements with her own past. But as well, Robinson's testament to Faulkner and Cather is just as clear, in opening once again the prospect of visionary insight that ensues from the more hospitable gestures of housekeeping. We understand the rationale behind her insertion into a strong, if largely male canon: as a means of accommodating a distinctively pragmatist yet visionary mode, turning it to her own ends, revealing once again what writers long before had essayed, finding an ordered style adequate to the compensatory gestures that transiency seems to fulfill.

The novel ends by making us aware of its imaginative accommodations, allowing us through a mixture of memories, dreams, and fantasy, through rhetorical mergings and imaginative border-crossings, to conjure up narratives that at least in the moment can assuage a sense of loss. Yet in doing so, such narratives remind us of the felt reality of loss, if only because writing must always represent the absence of a spoken voice. Ruth's lyric modulations can only develop in the absence of those she loves. And like housekeeping, her narrative cannot tender a permanent resolution, any more than she can ever be at peace with her traumatic past. In learning to resist the inclination for faultless housekeeping or measured control, she and we resist as well "the sad tendency of domesticity—as of piety—to contract, and of grace to decay into rigor." The paradox is that we cannot know how to read the effect of Ruth's hard-won insights—whether they assuage her sense of loss or not. What we *can* grasp is that despite failing to "put an end to all anomaly" her narrative net has revealed the shape of a life in which adversity no longer seems quite so inexplicable, if only because she gives play to conflicting desires, contradictory possibilities, incompatible scenes. Striving to be at once ordered yet hospitable, comprehensive yet flexible, Ruth transfigures the normally disparaged practice of housekeeping into a decisive perspective on life's disorders—disorders that nonetheless must remain partly inexplicable and elusive.

Notes

1   Well before Robinson's figurative reinterpretation of "housekeeping," the
    anthropologist Mary Douglas had essayed her own structuralist version of
    such ordering impulses in *Purity and Danger* (1966). Noting that "concepts
    of pollution and taboo" are universal, with different meanings across
    cultures, she concluded that dirt is simply "matter out of place" (weeds as
    such do not exist, just undesirable plants). That helps explain Jewish kosher
    laws, Japanese tatami mats, even formal French gardens versus the unruly
    English variety. From this perspective, even culture emerges as a form of
    housekeeping, of discriminations distinguishing us from a more natural
    state of dirt and noise. Yet Robinson's novel challenges Douglas' imposed
    scheme by extending the figurative implications of housekeeping not
    simply to characters (who come to appreciate being "out of place"
    psychologically), but to the novel's very expression, which resists settling
    into a predictable order, either narrative or stylistic.
2   Here, Harold Bloom's *Anxiety of Influence* (1973) is central, in speaking of
    the "strong poet" who revises her predecessors. It was Martha Ravits who
    first observed that "Robinson consciously sets her novel against the great
    texts of the American tradition" (644). Tace Hedrick discusses the influence
    of Emerson and Thoreau more fully (138–42). See also Smyth (286).
3   As Hutcheon states in terms particularly apt for addressing Robinson's
    novel, "Postmodern parody is both deconstructively critical and
    constructively creative, paradoxically making us aware of both the limits
    and the powers of representation" (98). It should be clear that Hutcheon's
    use of "parody" is meant (contrary to Fredric Jameson's view of
    postmodernism) not in a particularly humorous or comic (or even
    nostalgic) fashion, but as a means of reintegrating present representational
    possibilities with past conventions, "using parody as a means to connect the
    present to the past without positing the transparency of representation"
    (98).
4   Kristin King "find[s] Ruth's voice a powerful tribute to her subjectivity,
    especially at the end. Her many acts of merging and crossing serve as much
    to make boundaries visible (thus transgressible) as to dissolve them" (579).
    Elizabeth A. Meese observes that "The text's action is as much vertical as
    horizontal, built by layering and accretion—a piling up of stories analogous
    to Sylvie's housekeeping and her discursive practices. The mood of the
    piece is that of a vision just beyond consciousness, of figures seen below the
    surface of the water with blurred vision ... Perhaps it derives from the way
    the elements merge in Fingerbone—earth and sky are watery substances,
    indistinct from the lake itself ... Or perhaps it is that Sylvie's character
    verges in and out of the conscious present, mixing with those blurred
    elements ..." (62). William H. Burke claims that "the novel might be
    fruitfully understood as an unconventional primer on the mystical life, in

which the basic accomplishments for both the protagonist, Ruth, and the reader is the expansion of consciousness through a process of border crossings—social, geographic, and perceptual. These crossings, in turn, are developed through the novel's central metaphor of transience" (717).

5 This scene echoes Melville's scene of Abab addressing a whale's head: "'Speak, thou vast and venerable head,' muttered Ahab, 'which, though ungarnished with a beard, yet here and there lookest hoary with mosses; speak, mighty head, and tell us the secret thing that is in thee. Of all divers, thou hast dived the deepest. That head upon which the upper sun now gleams, has moved amid this world's foundations. Where unrecorded names and navies rust, and untold hopes and anchors rot; where in her murderous hold this frigate earth is ballasted with bones of millions of the drowned; there, in that awful water-land, there was thy most familiar home. Thou hast been where bell or diver never went; hast slept by many a sailor's side, where sleepless mothers would give their lives to lay them down.... O head! thou hast seen enough to split the planets and make an infidel of Abraham, and not one syllable is thine!'" (339).

6 Melville later adds, of the Pacific: "There is, one knows not what sweet mystery about this sea, whose gently awful stirrings seems to speak of some hidden soul beneath; like those fabled undulations of the Ephesian sod over the buried Evangelist St. John. And meet it is, that over these sea-pastures, wide-rolling watery prairies and Potters' Fields of all four continents, the waves should rise and fall, and ebb and flow unceasingly; for here, millions of mixed shades and shadows, drowned dreams, somnambulisms, reveries; all that we call lives and souls, lie dreaming, dreaming, still; tossing like slumberers in their beds; the ever-rolling waves but made so by their restlessness" (538).

7 On transiency in the novel, see Galehouse (123–24), Geyh (112–13), Hedrick (141), and McDermott (268).

8 Relying on Svetlana Boym's study of nostalgia, Sinead McDermott has observed: "The contrast here suggests Lucille's more pragmatic usage of the past, in a manner that suits the needs of the present: she remembers the mother she should have had." As she continues, "Boym has argued that reflective nostalgia treats the past differently: rather than viewing it simply as the forerunner to the present, or as a place of stasis, the past is seen as a source of unrealised possibilities" (265). See also Meese (60–61).

9 It is hard to imagine a sharper contrast with Mary Douglas's perspective: "I believe that ideas about separating, purifying, demarcating and punishing transgressions have as their main function to impose system on an inherently untidy experience. It is only by exaggerating the difference between within and without, above and below, male and female, with and against, that a semblance of order is created" (4). In her very expression, Douglas' confidence in what constitutes cultural order could hardly differ more from Sylvie's transience or Ruth's hesitant, self-circling narrative voice.

10 As Carolina Alvarado has observed in private correspondence, Tom Outland and Roddy Blake anticipate the Foster sisters and aunt Sylvie in their own thoughtful "housekeeping" efforts (189), excavating the ruins, building shelves, ordering and cataloguing native objects while making room for themselves. Like Ruth, they recreate the past so as to understand it, and understand themselves through origins.

11 Ruth offers late in the novel an extraordinary description of Helen, "the waves in the crown of her hair, the square shoulders of her good gray dress, her long hands at the top of the steering wheel, the nails gleaming a deep red. I was struck by her calm, by the elegant competence of her slightest gesture" (*H* 196). Sinead McDermott notes: "Whereas earlier in the novel Ruth could not even remember the colour of her mother's car, she now describes her mother in vividly nostalgic and lovingly detailed terms. . . . [T]he passage functions as a form of consolation, reconciling Ruth to her mother's death" (266).

12 In his earlier essay, "Nature," Emerson wrote analogously: "The sensual man conforms thoughts to things; the poet conforms things to his thoughts. The one esteems nature as rooted and fast; the other, as fluid, and impresses his being thereon" (*E&L* 34).

13 Interestingly, in the same essay Emerson made an observation that anticipates Robinson's initial process: "Bare lists of words are found suggestive, to an imaginative and excited mind . . . Every word was once a poem. Every new relation is a new word" (*F&S* 321).

14 To be fair, John Mullan's description is occasionally true, though only to the extent that simile usually operates that way, and only for Robinson's more benign examples: "the dear ordinary had healed as seamlessly as an image on water" (15), or a cloud "like a long-legged insect bracing itself out of its chrysalis" (147). For comment on Ruth's unusual (often synesthetic) descriptions, see Stefan Mattessich (65–66).

15 Caver anticipates this argument of figures "merging" (126). See also Meese (62–63).

16 Maggie Galehouse interprets this scene more affirmatively (135). See also Mattessich (80), Geyh (119), Hedrick (150).

17 Thomas Foster reads the ending as opening the possibility that Ruth may be dead, speaking from beyond: "This undecidability that holds together two apparently mutually exclusive possibilities underscores what Meese calls the 'double gesture,' the 'negation of certainty and affirmation of possibility' that ends the novel" (97). Perhaps the best assessment is Robinson's own, that "For all that people know at the end of the book, the worst possible thing might have happened" (Fay 3–4).

Chapter 4

VIOLENCE IN *BLOOD MERIDIAN* (1985)

The red tide now poured from all sides of the monster like brooks down a hill. His tormented body rolled not in brine but in blood, which bubbled and seethed for furlongs behind in their wake. The slanting sun playing upon this crimson pond in the sea, sent back its reflection into every face, so that they all glowed to each other like red men. And all the while, jet after jet of white smoke was agonizingly shot from the spiracle of the whale, and vehement puff after puff from the mouth of the excited headsman.

—Herman Melville, *Moby-Dick* (311)

That's like saying the carpenter is obsessed with his hammer. Violence is simply one of the carpenter's tools. The writer can no more build with one tool than the carpenter can.

—William Faulkner ("Interviews") in response to allegedly being "obsessed with violence"

If we used a different vocabulary or if we spoke a different language, we would perceive a somewhat different world.

—Misattributed to Ludwig Wittgenstein (Crafts 396)

Few novels question so persistently the relation between words and phenomena, interpretive style and physical presence, as Cormac McCarthy's *Blood Meridian*. Start with the fact that much of this grotesque account is verifiable, as close to history as novels get, drawn in sometimes verbatim tones from memoirs, chronicles, eye-witness testimony, all ably documented by John Sepich. Then acknowledge how little it is driven by plot, accompanying two central characters (the kid, Judge Holden) but otherwise offered as mere peregrinations stitched together by the phrase "they rode on"—as if "plot" were less pressing for McCarthy than isolated events and the language describing them. Finally, consider quicksilver vacillations in that language itself, swerving between rudimentary realist prose and an otherwise ostentatious voice that revels in strange arabesques. The novel everywhere announces its stylistic bona fides, especially at indelible moments when symbolic constructs might seem irrelevant alongside the grim history they represent.

It comes as little surprise, then, that McCarthy's critics so often focus on the schism between the novel's gruesome subject matter and its often visionary style—a style that tests assumptions by leveling the human to the minimally animate, and animate life to no greater moment than inert rocks and insensate shrubs. Readings of *Blood Meridian* regularly celebrate this apparent challenge to anthropomorphism, which seems most vivid in its scenes of ghastly violence. Yet however singular McCarthy's vision, it emerges from a distinguished tradition in which physical violence is transmuted by rhetorical style—indeed, in which depictions seem as violent in their formal solicitations as in the physical realm they invoke. McCarthy may exceed his predecessors in the abandon with which characters destroy one another but he, no less than they, creates a verbal realm in which the humanizing discriminations quashed by his characters are restored by his narrative—a narrative whose violent rhythmic displacements confirm paradoxically the prospect of seeing anew, the very basis for ethical and aesthetic discernment. The disruptions of his prose, alternately lavish and tight-lipped, induce capacities in readers for judgment and valuation (tinged by astonishment and woe) that otherwise seem drained away by the scenes he describes.

In short, the triumph of McCarthy's novel emerges from its formal maneuvers, in the tension sustained by prose whose shape-shifting construction alerts us to its self-transforming capacity. "The language of *Blood Meridian*," Steven Shaviro observes, "is rather continually outside itself, in intimate contact with the world in a powerfully nonrepresentational way" (153). That paradox (of "intimate contact" yet in a "nonrepresentational way") testifies to the novel's uncanny power, achieving a verisimilitude that seems to value everything equally, in photographic impartiality, even as it celebrates the craft behind that illusion of verisimilitude. McCarthy here confirms a need for renewed attention to formal features rather than simply accepting scenes as readily paraphrasable. In fact, *Blood Meridian* appeared in 1985, just when deconstruction (the heir to formalism) was folding its cards to New Historicism and cultural studies. If the novel seemed implicitly to defy this critical turn, that defiance was expressed even more forcefully by McCarthy himself when reminded of his ostensible debt to Faulkner: "The ugly fact is books are made out of books. The novel depends for its life on the novels that have been written" (Woodward). Acerbic as this acknowledgment sounds, it testifies to his novel's claim on our attention as part of an inimitable literary tradition, which (especially for someone so committed to history) need not represent a retreat to sterile aesthetic considerations. But the fact that fictional "books are made out of books" only seems "ugly" because it reminds us that whatever larger social meanings ensue from a novel are dictated first by luminous details and evocative narrative configurations. That understanding constitutes perhaps the chief conclusion drawn by Marjorie Levinson in her recent survey of "the new formalism" (or as she cites Richard Strier, "formal features of a text, matters of style, can be indices to large intellectual and cultural matters" [565]).

McCarthy reminds us how to read *Blood Meridian*, neither as report from the past nor as manifesto against anthropomorphism, but at least initially as verbal artifact, demanding attention to its prose rhythms, and thereby its placement as part of tradition of other such books. If what first seems troubling about the novel is its depicted violence, what becomes gradually clear is that McCarthy transforms a narrative legacy of such depictions idiosyncratically, at once registering the dehumanizing effect of bodily evisceration in a prose that otherwise proclaims how stylistic violence (of diction, syntax, figuration) can on the contrary be redemptive. We need now to register the dilemma posed by human violence, which tends to destabilize descriptive meaning and narrative sequence, before turning to the literary tradition McCarthy inherits and transfigures. For, contrary to the assertion that *Blood Meridian*'s "odd power derives from its treating everything and everybody with absolute equanimity" (Phillips 37), the book's achievement resides instead in its alternately agitated and exhausted registers, its uneasy stylistic suasions that confirm a humanist premise at the level of description itself. As Vereen Bell observes, "*Blood Meridian* is haunted by the mystery that its own language challenges the very nihilistic logic that it gives representation to" (128). McCarthy takes the debased facts of history and transforms them through a narrative eye that selects, disposes, excludes, embellishes—in short, that registers a rhetorical violence everywhere contesting the barbarism so variously depicted, and thereby enhances ethical and aesthetic possibilities that otherwise seem flattened out.

I. Defying Expression

Scenes of brutality severely test our capacity for representation, seemingly more so than other intense experiences (say, madness or religious ecstasy or erotic pleasure), since these latter tend to induce in readers a commensurate response, while violent reactions evoked by violent scenes are rare, even sociopathic. When bodies themselves are destroyed, any affective relationship the reader might have to fictional consciousness is extinguished, as if the very capacity of language to render such events were vitiated. The novelist W. G. Sebald observed this psychological effect in accounts of the devastation inflicted on German cities at the close of World War II. Survivors of fire bombings rarely ventured accounts, Sebald noted, and the few who did were strangely unrevealing: "The apparently unimpaired ability—shown in most of the eyewitness reports—of everyday language to go on functioning as usual raises doubts of the authenticity of the experiences they record" (Sebald 25). The sheer dreadfulness of violence debilitates language ("The death by fire within a few hours of an entire city, with all its buildings and its trees, its inhabitants, its domestic pets, its fixtures and fittings of every kind"), rendering survivors incapable of words at all. And those who did succeed did so only by breaking a kind of Orwellian covenant of language, falling into "linguistic corruption and an addiction to empty, spiraling pathos [that] are only the outward symptoms of a warped state of mind" (Sebald 124).[1]

Remarkably, *Blood Meridian* confirms Sebald's thesis in its disarmingly mixed perspectives on the brutality it represents, as if displaying scenes of destruction free of unalloyed efforts to accommodate them to conventional ethical modes. In this, McCarthy is hardly unique among American writers, though the frequency of such scenes encourages readers to wonder at his striking resistance to interpretive gestures, in offering memorable descriptions from perspectives hard to conjoin.[2] In fact, the realm into which we enter becomes increasingly horrific *because* constrained by few laws, offering little sense of reasonable anticipation, scant justification for what has ensued. Violence seems registered by an odd psychology that precludes pain or dread, with threats of cruelty evoking neither trepidation nor dismay, much less alarm or terror. Equally absent is any emotional aftermath, say of regret or relief, in a novel chock-full of mayhem and brutality. Life consists simply in stoically passing through, with mere chance the only stay against the assault of a Sadean world, and ghastly violence differing little from an explosion of inanimate objects. The question tacitly raised by the novel is one Sebald suggests is unanswerable: how to depict violence in language that does not distort or sentimentalize. How, in short, does rhetorical violence differ from a rhetorical question?[3]

At a minimum, the novel's violence defies narrative progress, occasioning no emotional release and thwarting any plot resolution, with bodies simply piling up, maimed and butchered, all to no end. Or at least, that seems correct at first, before it becomes apparent that depictions of violence emerge differently, in contrasting registers. Early on, the prolonged account of a bar fight ends as the kid "backhanded the second bottle across the barman's skull and crammed the jagged remnant into his eye as he went down" (*BM* 25). Days later, a similar death occurs in a Laredito cantina, this time from a more distanced perspective, as if deadly brutality revealed close-up at Bexar were now envisioned from an angle of abstract impersonality: "How these things end. In confusion and curses and blood. They drank on and the wind blew in the streets and the stars that had been overhead lay low in the west and these young men fell afoul of others and words were said that could not be put right again and in the dawn the kid and the second corporal knelt over the boy from Missouri who had been named Earl and they spoke his name but he never spoke back" (*BM* 40). The very structure of juxtaposed clauses, linked by polysyndeton, confirms the initial sentence fragment that explains generically what has happened before action ensues ("In confusion and curses and blood"). And here, the passage's skeletal structure clarifies larger natural patterns that lend to the death an impersonal touch ("They drank on . . . the wind blew . . . the stars . . . lay low"), as if a boy "named Earl" were merely a passing figure subject to an indifferent fate. Days later, a more gruesome postlude to these depictions occurs, as riders "came to a bush that was hung with dead babies. . . . Bald and pale and bloated, larval to some unreckonable being" (*BM* 57). Each of these scenes—from eviscerating violence displayed close up, to casually elided murder presumed from afar, to haunting aftermath projected at some unfathomable purview—presses us from a disparate perspective to contemplate what the body is prone to, as mere animate object a breath away from inanimate.

And other violent moments likewise diverge from these and from each other, not in bodies defiled so much as their representations. Perspectives are cobbled together through rhetorical techniques that seem violent themselves, as when a black rider named Jackson suddenly beheads his white namesake:

Two thick ropes of dark blood and two slender rose like snakes from the stump of his neck and arched hissing into the fire. The head rolled to the left and came to rest at the expriest's feet where it lay with eyes aghast.... The fire steamed and blackened and a gray cloud of smoke rose and the columnar arches of blood slowly subsided until just the neck bubbled gently like a stew and then that too was stilled. He was sat as before save headless, drenched in blood, the cigarillo still between his fingers, leaning toward the dark and smoking grotto in the flames where his life had gone.

BM 107

The scene initially seems coldly descriptive, in language as easily evoking flowers on a table or a fountain in the square as the dead Jackson's bubbling neck. The head rolling, "eyes aghast," momentarily conjures a Medusan tableau before the scene is reduced to a simmering stew, then "stilled." Yet the phrasing shifts in the final sentence from flatly mimetic to a strange locution ("He was sat ...") that leans the corpse hesitantly backward to "where his life had gone." Description here becomes arrestingly speculative, as if the lifeless body had grown momentarily reanimated, but more importantly as if the narrator were quietly affirming his own artifice, establishing through this weird point of view an intersection of animate and inanimate dependent as much on words as on blood.

That sort of deft verbal modulation occurs as the narrator grows alternately more and less self-conscious. Consider again a very different stylization of violence, when Tigua women return at night to an encampment where Glanton's men have massacred their husbands and children. They "wandered howling through the ruins" as the narrative voice slowly surveys:

the dead lay with their peeled skulls like polyps bluely wet or luminescent melons cooling on some mesa of the moon. In the days to come the frail black rebuses of blood in those sands would crack and break and drift away so that in the circuit of few suns all trace of the destruction of these people would be erased. The desert wind would salt their ruins and there would be nothing, nor ghost nor scribe, to tell to any pilgrim in his passing how it was that people had lived in this place and in this place died.

BM 174

Of course, the "nothing" allegedly left behind is belied by the description itself, which etches its memento for later generations. Yet dramatically, style transfigures the scene, resonating in the oddly lush simile ("skulls like polyps bluely wet or luminescent melons cooling on some mesa of the moon"), or the ironic salted curing of corpses, preserved briefly by "desert wind," before fading away. As if to confound this tension between evanescence and memorial is the weird allusion to sanguinary pictograms, "the frail black rebuses of blood" that form at once tangible evidence and symbolic (all but written) testament to the massacre. Violence receding in time paradoxically endures for posterity in the scene's phrasing itself.

That oscillation between neutral chronicle and well-wrought artifact makes it seem as if the novel were unsure how to progress, which could be construed as testament to the larger problem of representing violence even as it illustrates the effects of violence as stylistic rather than phenomenological effect. The reader's eye is recurrently diverted from prose narrative to poetic surface, in a textual violence that variously, inventively eclipses the banal violence of scenes represented. That is, the very differences among violent depictions destabilizes narrative development, even as those differences display the work that style performs on bodies. In fact, the effort to find an appropriate perspective begins with the oddly-phrased, opening invocation, which foregrounds style itself as an issue: "See the child" (*BM* 4). Immediately, the paragraph turns to the elementary anaphora of "He is . . . he wears . . . He stokes . . . He lies . . . he quotes . . .," forming the most rudimentary means of advancing information. The next brief paragraph, all but entirely sentence fragments, turns to a strange addressee ("Night of *your* birth."), as if the child himself were being addressed, before switching immediately to "I looked for blackness." This disorienting shift of voice, from third- to second- to first-person, seems inexplicable until the page ends with a summary claim, "All history present in that visage, the child the father of the man." The opening imperative, the fragmentary syntax, the wobbling instability of voice, the odd use of narrative present tense (rather than conventional past), the strange intertextual invocations (Wordsworth, Pope): variously, the novel is testing out possibilities for its own expression, which will in fact become its ongoing agenda in the violent scenes that ensue.

Before this is apparent, however, the description continues in broken English, with the kid's early years reported in austere syntax, punctuated by sentence fragments: "Forty-two days on the river." Then "All races, all breeds. Men whose speech sounds like the grunting of apes." Then "Gray seabirds gawking. Flights of pelicans coastwise above the gray swells." Then "Earthen causeways across the marshland. Egrets in their rookeries white as candles among the moss" (*BM* 4–5). A chapter that cannot quite take off in its opening invocation shuttles over the kid's inarticulate life, echoing his desultory chronicle in its own incomplete sentences.

That fragmented, paratactic rhythm persists until the judge enters the novel, announcing himself at a revival meeting with deft rhetorical flourishes that signal a change in narrative style itself. The stumbling chapter almost seems to require his entrance, with its enviable energy, introducing a momentarily coherent plot of brash allegations and baseless innuendos. Claiming the preacher has had sex with a girl and "congress with a goat" (*BM* 7), he thrusts us (and his listeners) into emotional tumult as well as into a stylized realm that exists on its own terms. Of course, that realm is only fleetingly viable, as if to confirm how language creates narratives that can hold together only so long as belief can be sustained, however illegitimately, however spurious the alleged facts. In that respect, the judge prepares the way for narrative pyrotechnics yet to come, anticipating the novel's own ingenious transmutation of crude and drab materials into freshly engraved, ever diverse possibilities.

II. "Language Usurps Things"

The opening vacillations of *Blood Meridian* speak to a persistent strain in McCarthy's writing, of skepticism about realist verisimilitude itself. The violent scenes of the novel most obviously illustrate this debilitating effect (of behavior that seems beyond words to express) just as they also offer a testament to the self-sustaining capacity of prose style. Yet if actual violence tends to destabilize representation, that is only a more extreme version of the larger problem of verbal expression, articulated long after McCarthy had completed the novel by a character he created, who believes that "language was a thing corrupted by its own successes. What had begun as a system for identifying and ordering the phenomena of the world had become a system for replacing those phenomena" (Lilley 57). As the character concludes, "Language usurps things," having become "an aberration by which we had come to lose the world."[4] Whether or not this character speaks for his author, the notion that "language usurps things" offers a compelling perspective on the disruptive style of *Blood Meridian*, alternating as it does in a range between flatly descriptive and elaborately baroque. At one point, we are summarily informed that "They rode five days through desert and mountain and through dusty pueblos" (*BM* 71); at another, we amble past a seep of "vadose water dripping down the slick black rock and monkeyflower and deathcamas hanging in a small and perilous garden" (57). This shape-shifting instability of style disorients us, making our experience of the novel as unsettling as the kid's experience of the West itself. For all the depicted violence, once again, it is not the brutality *within* scenes that dislocates so much as shifting discursive registers *between* scenes structuring a volatile narrative.

That helps explain the frequency of the novel's most common locution, "they rode on," repeated endlessly from scene to scene, serving as at once the most gently paratactic of narrative spurs and a suturing phrase stitching together otherwise disparate moments and modes. "Riding on" becomes a familiar rhetorical transit over unfamiliar terrain, one that dampens emotional tension and otherwise curbs plot development. All we do is move forward in time, with experience marked simply as the sum of scenes ostensibly valued equivalently. Yet any supposed tedium to narrative that "riding on" might induce is offset by the prose itself, whose alternating style alerts us to the way the world can be "replaced" by words (as McCarthy's fictional character observes). Minimal initial descriptions, like "Catching up their mounts they rode on" (*BM* 47), become somewhat later: "They rode on through sandstone cities in the dusk of that day, past castle and keep and windfashioned watchtower and stone granaries in sun and in shadow. They rode through marl and terracotta and rifts of copper shale and they rode through a wooded swag and out upon a promontory overlooking a bleak and barren caldera" (*BM* 113). The rich alliteration—of "castle and keep," "windfashioned watchtower," "stone . . . in sun and in shadow"— draws attention away from the world described in the passage, while the nuanced distinction of "marl and terracotta and rifts of copper shale" focus us as much on sound as on sense. We may "ride on," but it is clear we are no longer cantering through a physically imagined landscape so much as ambling in a verbally resonant terrain, one where poetic pleasure has displaced narrative curiosity.

However regrettable that "language usurps things" or that words become "an aberration," *Blood Meridian* abates that knowledge by delighting in a symbolic realm agleam with archaic diction drawn from a weird lexicon. "The night sky lies so sprent with stars" (*BM* 15), we are informed, or "sun-cracked felloes" (45) appear along with "some great balden archimandrite" (273): the words seem odd, affronting even an erudite reader's sense of vocabulary. But they also serve as enticements to style itself, evident in a listing of other recondite words shorn of context: argosy, ciborium, ossuary, thaumaturge, ristras, devonian, chartvail, catafalque, surbated, tonkawa, thews, pauldron, merestone, baldric, katabasis, karankawa, esker, demiculverin, coyame, blasarius, quena, anareta, apishamore, noctambulants, chartvail, arcature, whang.

It is as if McCarthy were not simply trying to baffle the reader, but deliberately invoking diction as at once exacting descriptor and self-contained ornament with an aural and semantic life all its own, as in "patched argonauts ... Goldseekers. Itinerant degenerates bleeding westward like some heliotropic plague" (*BM* 78). Later, the kid spies an "incinerated shape" on the trail, the burned remains of scalps and peppers, of which "nothing remained of the poblanos save this charred coagulate of their preterite lives" (*BM* 216).

Such straining the limits of description dislocates language from the scenes it describes, in the process straining as well against conventional wisdom. After all, "This charred coagulate of their preterite lives" is not simply strange but abstruse, as if McCarthy were exploring via tautened rhetorical efforts larger philosophical quandaries of time, loss, and memorial. In this, like Faulkner, he indulges in an expansive syntax, in enigmatic phrasing and recursive grammar that hazard the margins of expression itself ("We endow things with names and then carry the names away with us"). More profoundly than idiosyncratic words, such passages challenge interpretation by essaying to name the inexpressible through sheer figurative excess. After the judge has saved the magician's wife from Glanton's murderous impulse, they watch a camp fire: "the ragged flames fled down the wind as if sucked by some maelstrom out there in the void, some vortex in that waste apposite to which man's transit and his reckoning alike lay abrogate. As if beyond will or fate he and his beasts and his trappings moved both in card and in substance under consignment to some third and other destiny" (*BM* 96). The struggle to sort out a logic to this intricately crafted scene is complicated by the two hypothetical similes ("as if") that shift the focus beyond an immediate depiction, invoking via analogy meanings that arise not from plausible observation but from impassioned contemplation that allows figurative language to resonate.[5] The point seems to be that the violence the magician's wife has escaped is irrelevant to any ethical considerations, and simply a happenstance effect of the unwilled effort of the judge ("he"). But the invocation of certain aureate terms (apposite, abrogate, consignment) in conjunction with a discussion of "destiny" inflates the experience beyond the characters themselves.

Even casual moments seem exalted through verbal flourishes, which can occur unexpectedly, only moments after the most elementary descriptions of riding onward: "Spectre horsemen, pale with dust, anonymous in the crenellated heat. Above all else they appeared wholly at venture, primal, provisional, devoid of order. Like beings provoked out of the absolute rock and set nameless and at no remove from their own loomings to wander ravenous and doomed and mute as gorgons" (*BM* 172). This seems a far cry from McCarthy's periodically broken syntax, depicting riders as dull, illiterate horsemen; here, they emerge as numinous, tutelary figures. The point is that both versions serve as rhetorical vehicles that reveal not only different versions of experience but different latent experiences in the same version. And in that, we withdraw from an imagined phenomenal realm in preference for transformations enacted by language. The eerily patched-together style of the novel seems inspired by *Moby-Dick*, which ranges through varied registers in an even more pronounced farrago of literary techniques. But in a novel that opens with references to Pope ("See the child") and Wordsworth ("the child the father of the man"), one would be hard-pressed to ignore such influences, the most obvious of which is Hemingway (and through him, Crane and Twain), as when McCarthy's prose patiently enacts what it describes: "They rode for days through the rain and they rode through rain and hail and rain again" (*BM* 186). More commonly, Hemingway's influence is revealed in the novel's simple lists of objects linked by conjunctions ("He'd put the bottle under his saddle and he found it and held it up and shook it and drew the cork and drank. He sat with his eyes closed, the sweat beaded on his forehead. Then he opened his eyes and drank again" (*BM* 26)). Occasionally, this pattern occurs as simple polysyndeton ("and he saw a man who sat charging his rifle . . . and he saw men with their revolvers . . . and he saw men kneeling . . . and he saw men lanced . . . and he saw the horses" (*BM* 53)). The effect of this is analogous to McCarthy's archaic diction and his Faulknerian convolutions, deliberately distancing the reader from the scene described, compelling us to pause before its distinctly verbal tenor. And in what Denis Donoghue has termed the novel's paratactic "reign of 'and,'" we as readers find ourselves swayed by the arbitrariness of any given word, which takes precedence over the referent it signifies.[6] Even in minimalist moments (or perhaps, especially then), *Blood Meridian* deliberately pushes language "at one remove from itself." Of course, all literature strives for this, but McCarthy resembles Nabokov in particular, in transforming subject matter that is resolutely depraved, gruesome, or otherwise vile into something aesthetically enchanting, putting us on notice of the way words split from the world (the way signifiers detach from signifieds). Nothing can be done about the demeaning violence of human behavior, but the figurative violence of prose descriptions has a counter-effect, paradoxically helping redeem the initially unsavory fact that "language usurps things" in the realization that things are not all we have—and that our very expression of them releases them and us to more exalted possibilities.

III. The Failed Promise of "Optical Democracy"

Late in *Blood Meridian* as Glanton's gang rides on, the narrator pauses to consider the landscape in a rumination that seems inadvertently to elucidate McCarthy's style itself: "In the neuter austerity of that terrain all phenomena were bequeathed a strange equality and no one thing nor spider nor stone nor blade of grass could put forth claim to precedence." As the narrator adds, "in the optical democracy of such landscapes all preference is made whimsical and a man and a rock become endowed with unguessed kinships" (*BM* 247). That defiance of anthropomorphism in stressing "a strange equality" of man and rock has often been taken to explain McCarthy's agenda. Provisionally, Vereen Bell first observed that "The not-human world in this novel seems to be competing on every page in every natural detail for a standing equivalent to the human" (129)—an observation subsequent critics have hardened into an agenda for McCarthy that is actively anti-humanist. David Holloway most energetically argues this for *Blood Meridian*: that "anything beyond the uniform facticity of the moment is crowded from view. Optical democracy is a kind of writing that verges on deep ecology in its reduction of all that is animate and inanimate to a dead level of equivalence" (Holloway 135). The narrative provides "an agglomeration of matter, a superabundance of material objects assembled together in a world where there are only objects to be found" (Holloway 135).[7] Not only descriptions of objects but actual objects themselves as well as characters and events are all vouchsafed an equal valance, as the Glanton gang moves cross-country over terrain no more (if no less) distinctive than themselves.

It may well be that "optical democracy" seems most persuasive at moments of vivid violence, if only because a process of stylistic selection appears then less likely—indeed, the very intensity of such scenes rests on the supposedly disordered mayhem of imagery itself. Yet what undermines the assumption is the realization that any presentation of barbarous behavior need not itself be unenlightened or anti-humanist. Holloway's claim for a stylistic leveling of human and inorganic can only be disproved, however, by attending to scenes as McCarthy presents them. Take a group of scalp hunters who attack Comanches driving a herd of ponies, only to be stunned in a reversal that seems as much verbal as phenomenal. Two long sentences extend for a page, the first of which depicts simply the approaching herd, as details accumulate, of "painted chevrons and the hands and rising suns and birds and fish of every device." Then, a horde emerges through dust in full rhetorical flourish: "A legion of horribles, hundreds in number, half naked or clad in costumes attic or biblical or wardrobed out of a fevered dream ..." Finally, the scene closes with three striking similes:

> like a company of mounted clowns, death hilarious, all howling in a barbarous tongue and riding down upon them like a horde from a hell more horrible yet than the brimstone land of christian reckoning, screeching and yammering and clothed in smoke like those vaporous beings in regions beyond right knowing where the eye wanders and the lip jerks and drools. Oh my god, said the sergeant.
>
> *BM* 53

It is as if the disconnected prose leading up to this passage, of slowly measured sentences, had been supplanted not in the depicted horror of the scene nor even in the emotional outburst but in a transformed prose style itself, the breathless accumulation of conjunctions, the alliterative "h"s ("a legion of horribles, hundreds ... half-naked" or "howling ... like a horde from a hell more horrible"), the grammatical precision and inventiveness of expression. And that reiterated "h" comes to evoke as much a horrified heaving of breath, gasped in full-throated, full-throttled explosives, as in any descriptive tone. The scene, moreover, brakes temporally, as poetic flourishes alter the violence into kaleidoscopic sequences that seem to occur in slow motion, inviting us to linger over small, seemingly irrelevant details. In this, parataxis again makes a series of observations (of "painted chevrons," "unshod hooves," naked warriors and breastplates) perfectly arbitrary and unordered, subject to nothing more than the tyrannical "reign of 'and.'" The violence of the scene, in short, is mirrored in the way that disconnected images and sudden sounds disrupt our normal interpretive skills, which matches (at a safe remove) that of the woefully beleaguered regiment.

Yet even at these perfervid moments, the ghastliness of such scenes ensues not from any "optical democracy" that successfully reduces "animate and inanimate to a dead level of equivalence" but from the opposite—from the dramatic failure to shield individuals in peril and from the sympathy unavoidably evoked by such failure.[8] Whatever aspiration for "neuter austerity" in description, for a supposed verisimilitude that frustrates an anthropomorphic bias, the rhythms of McCarthy's prose themselves defy that aspiration, enforcing a key structuralist premise that writing always displays patterns of preference, discrimination, exclusion. "Optical democracy" is unrealizable even in the passage that momentarily suggests it, not just because people are never simply things, however described, but because the narrative cannot help but focus on some things rather than others, doing so in its own stylistic choices, putting forth "a claim to precedence" in the very act of representation. Readers' expectations are shaped by a style that makes things distinctly unequal, either with other things or with humans. Even more critically, plausibility in narrative can only be achieved in the presence of inessential details, as Roland Barthes reminds us. Narrative itself defies democratic equivalence; the verisimilitude of *l'effet du réel* depends entirely on "'futile' details" notable only for their irrelevance, thus creating the "referential illusion" essential to realist representation.[9]

Further challenging a premise of "optical democracy," the novel registers violence differently throughout, as if to unsettle the reader by altering stylistically the forms of human brutality that otherwise always end the same. At one point, a boy appears, only to have his neck unaccountably broken; later, the judge indulges an Apache youth, only to inexplicably kill and scalp him. Violence, at other times represented mythically, here becomes unadorned murder, coldly uninflected, altering the effect emotionally, aesthetically, morally. On occasion, savagery is evoked comically, as when the judge creates a gunpowder amalgam with the gang's urgently implored urine: "piss, man, piss for your very souls" (*BM* 132). That scene also ends with bloodthirsty slaughter, though from a bizarrely idiosyncratic perspective once again. In short, massacres, murders, ambushes, genocide, eviscerations, scalpings, knifings all recur, but rarely in quite the same style, rarely assimilated to what has gone before. As if the myriad ways of dying are matched by myriad ways of death represented, the reader's accession to a stable discursive realm is unsettled much as the violence represented by that discourse. And just as disconcerting as McCarthy's variety of verbal depictions are his sonic tonalities, which foreground words as audible things in the world, much like the things they represent. We listen as well as read, hearing the jarring, declamatory, rasping tones of words that have "a peculiar music," as Terri Witek observes (81).[10]

Strikingly, those convinced by McCarthy's alleged "optical democracy" pay little heed to the authorial legacy he inherits. After all,

American literature embodies a tradition of imaginative violence that extends from Melville to Brett Easton Ellis, of fiction both about brutality and itself brutally baffling in its stylistic disruptions. And that tradition offers a vivid riposte to Steven Shaviro's claim: "What is most disturbing about the orgies of violence that punctuate *Blood Meridian* is that they fail to constitute a pattern, to unveil a mystery or to serve any comprehensible purpose. Instead, the book suggests that 'a taste for mindless violence' is as ubiquitous—and as banal—as any other form of 'common sense'" (149). On the contrary, the violence of the novel is as exhilarating as it is disgusting, as transcendent as it is vile, and in that very alternation becomes far from "banal." Partly, this reflects McCarthy's admission that violence is inextricable from life, that "There's no such thing as life without bloodshed" (Ellis 168). Whether the claim is true or not, violence provides the kind of conflict structuring much realist prose, and McCarthy follows in a long line of writers fully aware of this.

Michael Kowalewski argues that scenes of physical violence form a benchmark for authorial style in American literature, ranging from transparent realist efforts to more dazzling modernist depictions. The abrupt juxtaposition of stylistic transparency and opaque representation in McCarthy's prose corresponds to an oscillating pattern among discursive registers that is just as true of other savage moments in American literature: the appalling, fragmentation of "On the Quai of Smyrna" in *In Our Time*; or the hysterical scenes of Henry Fleming's reckless battlefield encounters in *Red Badge of Courage*; or Joe Christmas's vicious castration in *Light in August*. Like these, the mayhem McCarthy offers up assumes multiple shapes, ever invoking our imaginative presence as readers capable of quite different appraisals. And such wildly varying modes turns us back to the shifting suasions of language itself, as mercurial in its effects as the world it apprehends, drawing varying degrees of attention to its own inventive verbal hierarchies, its optical discriminations.

IV. Violations of Simile

The very disruptions of McCarthy's style upend familiar reading habits, sometimes violently, much as characters are violated in more scabrous ways. Yet such disruptions lead to renewed discriminations in which conventional assumptions are adjusted rather than cast aside. Perhaps the most wrenching of these occur in McCarthy's weirdly strained similes, which form the salient figure of speech in *Blood Meridian* and the clearest challenge to a stylistic reading of "optical democracy." Consider the odd effect of McCarthy's figuration in the massacring Comanches cited above, who seem "like a company of mounted clowns, death hilarious, all howling in a barbarous tongue and riding down upon them like a horde from a hell more horrible yet." Twice more, the paragraph shifts from an actual scene as envisioned by mimetic descriptors in order to contemplate the whole from another skewed analogy. And that very skewing reminds us not of similarities but of differences, of juxtaposed images and meanings "more than itself," as Vereen Bell observes (131). Or as he adds, capturing the role of simile in *Blood Meridian*: "That action in the style is like a separate story going on." However "whimsical" such figurative "preference" may be, a choice has clearly been made, so that the idea that "a man and a rock become endowed with unguessed kinships" also signals that man and rock differ in significant ways. That is the difference on which analogy hangs, elaborated variously in McCarthy's descriptions that regularly distance us from the scene itself, establishing a hierarchy of implications.

The effect of similes in *Blood Meridian* can best be measured by comparing their use in *The Red Badge of Courage*, if only because no other American author indulges the figure of speech so persistently, so inventively, so perversely as Stephen Crane. The "eyelike gleam of hostile camp-fires" (Crane 3) opens a novel punctuated by a consistently strange array, as in this sample from the opening chapters: the "wet grass, marched upon, rustled like silk" (15); "insects, nodding upon their perches, crooned like old women" (21); "the colonel . . . began to scold like a wet parrot" (32); "guns squatted in a row like savage chiefs" (36). The most notorious sentence of the novel is exemplary: "The red sun was pasted in the sky like a wafer" (Crane 56). That stylistic predilection has an apparitional effect, as if actual scenes had become somehow dream-like, transmogrified from the mimetic realism of war into another imagined realm where wet parrots, savage chiefs, and crooning old women wander through, walking on silk. Crane achieves a vision of narrative action, often violently inflected, that defines as much an interpretive lens (the lens of "like" or "as") as it does a phenomenal sequence.[11]

McCarthy is hardly unique, then, even in the frequency of similes, though it is worth pausing here to address the distinction from its figurative ally, metaphor. Consider this prospect of dawn in *Blood Meridian*, lushly evocative, highly metaphorical: "Out there dark little archipelagos of cloud and the vast world of sand and scrub shearing upward into the shoreless void where those blue islands trembled and the earth grew uncertain, gravely canted and veering out through tinctures of rose and the dark beyond the dawn to the uttermost rebate of space" (*BM* 50). Then compare a similar depiction of dawn some days earlier:

> They rode on and the sun in the east flushed pale streaks of light and then a deeper run of color like blood seeping up in sudden reaches flaring planewise and where the earth drained up in to the sky at the edge of creation the top of the sun rose out of nothing like the head of a great red phallus until it cleared the unseen rim and sat squat and pulsing and malevolent behind them. The shadows of the smallest stones lay like pencil lines across the sand and the shapes of the men and their mounts advanced elongate before them like strands of the night from which they'd ridden, like tentacles to bind them to the darkness yet to come. They rode with their heads down, faceless under their hats, like an army asleep on the march.
>
> BM 44–45

Again, McCarthy offers in two scenes alternate depictions of habitual experiences, of similar moments in disparate styles. Yet while the metaphors of the first passage weave a coherent depiction (as the earth veers among islands of clouds into space), the similes of the second wrench it apart. In just three sentences, six analogies press abruptly against one another, five strange enough to match the conceit of a Metaphysical poem. First, sunlight is "like blood seeping up," then the sun is "like the head of a great red phallus," followed by shadows that "lay like pencil lines," as men's shapes seem "like strands of the night" before the figure switches to "like tentacles to bind them," when finally the group moves "like an army asleep."

The second description disarms, if only because similes customarily alert us to similarities, rendering analogy explicit in the verbal imposition of "like" or "as." Yet simile is at the same time a figure for speculative conversion, for imagined transmutation, for potential transfer by association in yoking dissimilar entities. By stopping just shy of superimposition, however, simile keeps incipient violation in abeyance, ever just about to happen. Where the mergings of metaphor offer a merely suggestive relationship, simile tends toward the literal, clearly identifying common features between disparate nouns (Metaphysical conceits offer an extreme version of such conflation as a trope of violation).[12] That helps explain why simile forms the perfect rhetorical figure for McCarthy, since far from enforcing an egalitarian vision of either phenomena or language itself, it establishes a persistently unstable, differentiated presence. Moreover, the rhythm of similes in the passage above persists through much of the novel, characteristically rising and falling, moving from straightforward to bizarre and back—in this case, swelling from the sheerly colorful (blood-red sunrise) to the grotesque (malevolent phallus of a sun), then collapsing in the mundane ("army asleep on the march"). Strangely, in a novel so rife with similes they sometimes seem to cancel each other, this passage is the first full-fledged display of the figure, in Chapter 4. It is as if the novel needed to wait until the kid joined Captain White's regiment, settling into a characteristic forward rhythm (in this first invocation of "they rode on") before the narrative could explode with similes in a characteristic pattern. This occurs, in other words, just as the narrative shifts from the shared perspective of the kid to that of the regiment more inclusively, as if the narrator were now freeing himself to ruminations prompted by his own stylistic violence.

Curiously, the most convincing case for "optical democracy" has been advanced by those who argue McCarthy frequently deploys "similes that fail to do the work of similes" (Holloway 159). That is, since simile requires something like a hierarchy of meaning between subject and invoked analogy (comparable to the tenor and vehicle of metaphors), the absence of clear subordination levels the scene. So, David Holloway argues, evocative analogies often leave the reader wondering what is being compared: "there are simply objects and the concrete qualities of objects, arranged before us in a more or less nonhierarchical spread of language" (159). But even despite the questionable claim that McCarthy's analogies are so perversely strained that readers regularly cannot understand them, it is hardly clear why we are then left with a "superabundance of objects on view," or why some scenic details are thereby made "more contingent" (Holloway 159). On the contrary, as with Crane's similes, readers become aware of the interpretive effort generated by a narrative presence, attuned to effects of style and language on an otherwise mimetically rendered scene. The most peculiar similes seize on specific objects to mark them as special, worthy of a strained style. In that sense, though meanings are multiplied, and scenes made to resonate, meaning itself is hardly dispersed.[13]

Of course, McCarthy's similes function no more alike than Crane's do. Sometimes, they are casual ("rolled in it like dogs" (*BM* 54); "slept like dogs" (65)), or otherwise predictable ("like the spume from sea swells," (175); "squatting there like some deserter" (60)). But these moments fade against conceits that sprout up elsewhere, in an alternation that alerts us once again to the violence enacted by similes. Consider, for one more example, a suffering snake-bit horse whose "skin had split open along the bridge of its nose and the bone shone through pinkish white and its small ears looked like paper spills twisted into either side of a hairy loaf of dough" (*BM* 115). Baking and snake-bite, cuisine and death, are united momentarily before similes disappear for pages from the text, as the narrative becomes flatly descriptive, uninflected, with rare figures of speech. In this, McCarthy is unique, seeming to draw attention to his stylistic pyrotechnics through the more flatly mimetic passages that serve as contrast.[14]

The intensity of similes is achieved, then, by contrast with other kinds of description into which the narrative regularly shifts, as if in deliberate defiance of any attempt to treat "everything and everybody with absolute equanimity," and instead as a means of enhancing stylistic oscillations and shifting registers. After all, if everything were treated with equal aplomb, why would descriptions vary so much at syntactic and figurative levels? The answer seems to be that we are not meant to settle into a customary pattern. Landscapes may recur, violence be repeated, familiar figures come and go, seemingly similar in a narrative in which the repetition "they rode on" confirms the habitual residue of daily life. Yet the forms of hypotyposis keep shifting vertiginously, unpredictably. Occasionally, landscapes give off a pictorial glow captured poetically, alliteratively, with once again a distended simile: "The sun was just down and to the west lay reefs of bloodred clouds up out of which rose little desert nighthawks like fugitives from some great fire at the earth's end" (*BM* 21–22). Just as often, however, flat unmodified description suffices: "They sat side by side among the rocks and watched the day lengthen on the plain below" (*BM* 56). So eccentrically does style shift through the novel that part of the experience of reading is simply an alertness to contingency, in a growing expectancy for the unexpected, at least descriptively speaking, to see how radiantly language can transmogrify experience. Still, nothing in the "unguessed kinships" of McCarthy's depictions differs from similar efforts of authors like Crane or Melville, or suggests the irrelevance of a humanizing narrative perspective.

Consider this revelatory moment, in which the novel's most violent character encounters one of its most ravishing settings: "fallen leaves lay like golden disclets in the damp black trail. The leaves shifted in a million spangles down the pale corridors and Glanton took one and turned it like a tiny fan by its stem and held it and let it fall and its perfection was not lost on him" (*BM* 136). There is no ethics to the

scene, no sense of transfiguration through landscape, no link at all
between observer and observed. "Perfection" for Glanton is simply a
fleeting view soon forgotten, hardly adumbrated in the narrative (that
is, his perception fails to tally with the reader's). The "perfection" that
exists for the reader occurs not in nature but in the lyricism of the
passage, its balanced appositions and alliterations, its slightly disjunctive
clauses and unfolding syntactical rhythm that seem to match Glanton's
ride up switchbacks, until the final sentence, bound together in
polysyndeton that links a series of discrete moments from "the leaves"
to "its perfection." That everything in the passage has been chosen as
part of an evocative scene, constructed as a verbal concoction, confirms
how fully discriminations and exclusions direct our imaginative eye
and entertain our poetic ears in flat defiance of any "optical democracy"
that exists before the narrator intervenes. And that creative interloper
leaves as he came, signaled by a waning of such descriptions late in the
novel as the kid escapes harm and the narrative slides forward thirty
years to his death. Ending as it began, at least descriptively, the narrative
achieves a similarly flat pace that offers a cryptic scene of dancing judge
that matches the opening mystery of fighting kid.

V. *Savagery and Transfiguration*

Blood Meridian is a strange historical novel, in relying so thoroughly on
authentic records of actual events even as it transforms them through a
narrative that everywhere disrupts conventional assumptions. The
appalling violence of the documented past would seem to silence any
account, and yet that violence is matched by a different kind of narrative
and stylistic disorder that has paradoxically the opposite effect. For far
from confirming through its peripatetic subject matter some radical
dehumanization, some flattening out of ethical discernment into
"optical democracy," McCarthy instead suggests via skewed prose
registers the possibility of ever greater moral discriminations, ever more
humanly distinctive modes of sympathy and appreciation. If that lesson
can never be fully learned, it always presents itself, as Judge Holden
suggests in responding to a rider's question "as to whether there were on
Mars or other planets in the void men or creatures like them." The Judge
denies there are, but offers a salutary view:

> The truth about the world, he said, is that anything is possible. Had
> you not seen it all from birth and thereby bled it of its strangeness it

would appear to you for what it is, a hat trick in a medicine show, a fevered dream, a trance bepopulate with chimeras having neither analogue nor precedent, an itinerant carnival, a migratory tentshow whose ultimate destination after many a pitch in many a mudded field is unspeakable and calamitous beyond reckoning.

BM 245

The Judge's own flamboyant rhetorical style echoes parts of the narrative, in his medley of strange images, his fleetingly odd diction ("trance bepopulate with chimeras"), his Faulknerian claims just shy of pretentious ("neither analogue nor precedent"; "calamitous beyond reckoning"). But his central point of a "truth about the world" is that conventional ways of viewing "from birth" have gradually diminished experience, "bled it of its strangeness." And to restore a sense of possibility is first to set aside blinkering assumptions about how life is or ought to be, and thereby to foreswear *a priori* epistemological categories.

The "fevered dream" of *Blood Meridian* reminds us of something part of our earliest knowledge: that violence, human or inanimate, is an ineradicable condition of life. Banal as this seems, our central narratives recall that knowledge to us, from Faulkner, Crane, and Melville back through Shakespeare to classical texts (*Beowulf, The Aeneid, The Iliad*), where dubious varieties of human savagery are ever on display. Yet in each of these cases, it is the transformations performed by language that matter, anticipating the way McCarthy regularly puts words to the test, making readers cringe at depictions of inhuman depravity, then delighting in the way words create their own world, in which images shift iridescently and meanings effloresce. *Blood Meridian* makes us aware of a drive toward meaning and yet of meaning's persistent dispersal, in scenes at once grotesque yet resplendent, viscerally excruciating yet meticulously crafted. Stephen Tatum has broadly declared that "What counts in McCarthy's fiction is the necessity of confronting the *real*, which is to say the world as it is, as it presents itself rudely and mysteriously and contingently to human consciousness" (476). Yet given the mediated state of our relation to the world, it might be more accurate to invert this claim, countering that the response of human consciousness to the rude, mysterious, and contingent itself transforms "the real" into one of myriad forms it can take.

McCarthy's fictional character deplored the notion that "language usurps things," taking us out of "the world as given" to leave us with a "secondhandedness" of nomenclature in which "we experience nothing."

Yet this regret is no more reliable a guide to *Blood Meridian* than the novel's own passing assertion of "optical democracy." On the contrary, a disruptive style makes some things more luminous than others, some things less enshadowed. The invariable secondhandedness of language is after all its singular virtue, where meanings reside. And McCarthy's triumph is to take the grubby, violent, agreed-upon facts of history and transform them through a narrative eye that selects, disposes, excludes, embellishes. Offering no final resolution (no literary text can), his novel nonetheless is hardly "self-cancelling" (Holloway 16). Quite the contrary, his landscape is at once radically transfigured and determinate ground, if of an entirely symbolic variety. In this, McCarthy's Southwest is strangely akin to Flaubert's Rouen (as described by Barthes): "only a sort of setting meant to receive the jewels of a number of rare metaphors, the neutral, prosaic excipient which swathes the precious symbolic substance, as if, in Rouen, all that mattered were the figures of rhetoric to which the sight of the city lends itself—as if Rouen were notable only by its substitutions" ("Reality" 144). That perfectly evokes the strange fashion by which place can be known, by which history can be trumped in the narrative perspectives that re-create it.

Lyrical at times, at others simply archaic and recondite, at still others barely literate: the dissociative style of *Blood Meridian* defies accommodation to conventional assumptions. And that's the point. For in making the world once again new, free of readerly accommodations, no longer bled "of its strangeness," the novel's disruptions themselves explain why it ends by not showing the presumed death of the kid in the outhouse at Fort Griffin, when we've already been exposed to so much. It is as if, after being presented throughout with brutality, in often brutal stylistic forms, we are now left to our own imaginative devices. The novel may once again be giving back to us a sense of strangeness and wonder, even though we know (as the judge reminds us) that all will recur endlessly: "do you not think that this will be again? Aye. And again. With other people, with other sons" (*BM* 147).

Notes

1   Elaine Scarry has argued: "Physical pain does not simply resist language but actively destroys it, bringing about an immediate reversion to a state anterior to language" (*Body in Pain* 4). Paul Fussell, from a more historical perspective, observes: "The problem for the writer trying to describe elements of the Great War was its utter incredibility, and thus its incommunicability in its own terms" (139). As he adds: "the war was much

worse than any description of it possible in the twenties or thirties could suggest" (174). Perhaps McCarthy writes at a historical moment when language is at last adequate to its brutal subject. Coincidentally, Elaine Scarry's study of the inexpressibility of violence against the body and McCarthy's unblinkingly violent novel both appeared in 1985.

2   Vereen Bell has observed, "One strength of McCarthy's novels is that they resist the imposition of theses from the outside, especially conventional ones, and that they seem finally to call all theses into question" (xiii). Still, as Michael Kowalewski warns of his own study: "One of the pitfalls awaiting a study like this is the temptation inadvertently to romanticize scenes of violence by taking a sort of bleak pride in their recalcitrance to moralizing" (15).

3   Saidiya Hartman's study of accounts of slavery questions the reader's participation in "black suffering. What interests me are the ways we are called upon to participate in such scenes. Are we witnesses . . . ? Or are we voyeurs fascinated . . . ? What does the exposure of the violated body yield?" (3). Her book excludes such scenes for "exacerbating the indifference to suffering that is the consequence of the benumbing spectacle" (4).

4   The conception of language as "aberration" has a long history, notably expressed by George Puttenham in 1589: "As figures be the instruments of ornament in euery language, so be they also in a sorte abuses or rather trespasses in speach, because they passe the ordinary limits of common vtterance, and be occupied of purpose to deceiue the eare and also the minde, drawing it from plainnesse and simplicitie to a certaine doublenesse, whereby our talke is the more guilefull & abusing, for what els is your Metaphor but an inuersion of sence by transport; your allegorie by a duplicitie of meaning or dissimulation vnder couert and darke intendments" (128).

5   As Stephen Tatum remarks, McCarthy's characters traverse "a liminal world 'between' . . . This nevertheless 'open' world is beautifully rendered through one of McCarthy's trademark syntactical strategies: his serial presentation of sentence fragments introduced by the subjunctive expression 'as if,' each fragment provisionally venturing a different interpretation of whatever action inaugurated the sequence" (479–80). For other examples of "as if," see 14, 146, 243. This habit is more pronounced in the later Border Trilogy than in *Blood Meridian*, though it seems to anticipate the pattern.

6   Donoghue more fully states: "No relation of cause and consequence is proposed: no article requires more attention than another. The effect of this writing is to nullify the force of successiveness and to make the details appear to compose themselves as a picture. Even the words that stand out as fancy writing . . . allow themselves to be assimilated without fuss to the parataxis. They are subdued to the reign of 'and'" ("Teaching *BM*" 275).

7   See also Kreml, Lilley (158), Phillips (28, 33), and Witek.

8   Holloway claims, "The ghastliness of this scene, and its sheer amorality, is not conveyed by the relentlessness of the sentence alone, but also by the

way McCarthy diverts the eye of the reader into what, in the context of such carnage, seem like absurd contingencies: the way light reflects off shields, the way heels hang, the way bows flex, what the necks of ponies are doing" (136). Yet this alleged "ghastliness" would seem to contradict his claim for the "facticity of the moment" in which moral or emotional "preferences" are made simply "whimsical." Why should McCarthy's style make the scene seem ghastly rather than beautiful?

9 Barthes adds: "Flaubert's barometer, Michelet's little door finally say nothing but this: *we are the real*; it is the category of 'the real' (and not its contingent contents) which is then signified; in other words, the very absence of the signified, to the advantage of the referent alone, becomes the very signifier of realism" ("Reality" 148). Fredric Jameson argues against "Barthes' conception of an empty sign—a passage which would function as pure connotation without any denotative content" ("Realist" 376).

10 See also Nancy Kreml on McCarthy's sonic qualities as contributing to "a different kind of speech" (142); and Holloway on the "materiality" of McCarthy's language (85-7).

11 Frank Bergon states that "at their most extreme, Crane's scenes seem not so much observed reality as reality metamorphosed.... A world in which occult and demonic forces move in and out of things and people is best represented through abrupt hallucinatory details. Images overlap, details of the most ordinary perceptions fuse with images of man's deepest obsessions and fears (31, 147).

12 Helen Gardner's classic definition is apropos: "a conceit is a comparison whose ingenuity is more striking than its justness," and further, that "a comparison becomes a conceit when we are made to concede likeness while being strongly conscious of unlikeness" (xxiii).

13 Stephen Tatum describes McCarthy's "world of possibility" by aptly assessing the effect of a rhetorical habit more common to his other novels: "This nevertheless 'open' world is beautifully rendered through one of McCarthy's trademark syntactical strategies: his serial presentation of sentence fragments introduced by the subjunctive expression 'as if,' each fragment provisionally venturing a different interpretation of whatever action inaugurated the sequence" (480).

14 Still, Crane offers an instructive pattern, as Frank Bergon observes: "So Crane's fiction is filled with what Yeats would call 'numb lines,' lines which may be unexceptional in themselves but which, by contrast, heighten the lines before or after" (9). McCarthy takes this alternation from the level of sentences to paragraphs and pages.

Chapter 5

TALK IN *THE ROAD* (2006)

If you stand right fronting and face to face to a fact, you will see the sun glimmer on both its surfaces, as if it were a cimeter, and feel its sweet edge dividing you through the heart and marrow, and so you will happily conclude your mortal career. Be it life or death, we crave only reality. If we are really dying, let us hear the rattle in our throats and feel cold in the extremities; if we are alive, let us go about our business.

—Henry David Thoreau (400)

The novel is significant, therefore, not because it presents someone else's fate to us, perhaps didactically, but because this stranger's fate by virtue of the flame which consumes it yields us the warmth which we never draw from our own fate. What draws the reader to the novel is the hope of warming his shivering life with a death he reads about.

—Walter Benjamin (101)

Early in Cormac McCarthy's *The Road*, the unnamed father falls asleep beside his son near a campfire:

He woke toward the morning ... and walked out to the road. Everything was alight. As if the lost sun were returning at last. The snow orange and quivering. A forest fire was making its way along the tinderbox ridges above them, flaring and shimmering against the overcast like the northern lights. Cold as it was he stood there a long time. The color of it moved something in him long forgotten. Make a list. Recite a litany. Remember.

31

This scene of calm retrospection, which leaves the father moved by "something in him long forgotten," shifts abruptly from third- to second-person in the injunction (as clipped triple imperative) to "Make a list. Recite a litany. Remember." It is as if the father, having recalled so stirring a moment, needed to admonish himself to summon up other such memories and transfigure them verbally—in short, to become fully alive to the "flaring and shimmering" across faraway ridges. Yet more compelling than this thematic testament to memory is the passage's seamless formal slippage, of omniscient narrator suddenly allying himself with the father, who is speaking either to himself or directly to the reader—as if the obliquities of narrative itself were tested in this perspectival adjustment, reminding us of how literature itself aspires to reorient consciousness.

Further enriching the passage is McCarthy's memory of the novel's conception in just such a scene, of himself as anxious parent hovering over his son in an El Paso hotel not long after September 11th, 2001:

> John was asleep. It wasn't night, it was probably about 2 or 3 o'clock in the morning. And I went over and I just stood by the window looking at this town. There was nothing moving, but I could hear the trains going through, a very lonesome sound. And I just had this image of what this town might look like in 50 or 100 years. I just had this image of these fires up on the hill and everything being laid waste, and I thought a lot about my little boy.
>
> Winfrey

Musing about "my boy," McCarthy hastily scribbled two pages that night evoking a world dimmed, radically diminished, pages that grew into a novel mixing autobiographical fact with fiction to become something of a secret letter to his son, but that more ambitiously aspires to reconfigure narrative possibilities for a future "laid waste."[1] Just as *The Road* depicts the tenuous survival of an environment against odds, it registers the triumph of narrative as a sustaining endeavor at the end of a post-modern era, evoking the mystery of words that in fragile formulations and equivocal evocations keep alive the possibilities of stories themselves. The novel confirms that the world we know hangs in the balance of linguistic continuance, and that only via such narrative strategies do we share even a hope of recovering some sense of humanist regeneration.[2]

McCarthy is among our most accomplished novelists, confirmed in part via his command of a long literary tradition, in part via his relentless refashioning of the novel form in an era uncertain about how to restore resonance to words long worn, or how to renew narrative's strained ethical role. *The Road* at first hardly seems to fulfill that promise in its truncated pedestrian mode, which seems as void of elaboration as its bleakly exhausted subject. But then unobtrusively, an array of inchoate sketches takes on a tenuous structure that emerges through a series of crucial rhythms, beginning with a thematic alternation of fear and relief, of looming threat and narrow escape from danger. Narratively this rhythm is echoed in a temporal ebb and flow, from present consciousness back through flashbacks and dreams, corresponding in turn to stylistic swings amid prose registers, of fragmentary exposition sliding into rich lyrical outbursts.[3] Gradually, what had seemed a simple fable of survival becomes a sophisticated meditation on the intersection of past and present, the relation between language and experience, the give-and-take between narrative and a tradition of literary expression, and perhaps most prominently a mystery that remains unresolved in the slippage among these pairings. If global catastrophe has led to irreversible environmental collapse and chilling human depravity, what distinguishes father and son is less any skill at survival than their conjoint effort to talk, to sustain a dialogue that defies their brutish isolation, with the father invoking a power of words to recast the "long forgotten" into living possibilities for his son.

The Road echoes that invocation in its self-consciously belated status as narrative in a tradition now exhausted, seemingly irrelevant. For by closing on "they hummed of mystery" (R 287), the novel reminds us how enigmatic the survival of language itself has been. We are left with the most tantalizing of questions: who has in fact told this story of the death of possibility in a fable that at once invokes and rejects literary tradition? After all, McCarthy's version of wasteland—a common trope of modernism from the beginning—defies not only modernist techniques or the notion of a personal voice but any accompanying assurances about fragments "shored against my ruins." The world McCarthy delineates is clearly seeping away, and yet against that loss the novel celebrates what Lydia Cooper describes as "the creative force of language as a prophetic 'fathering' of humanity" (139). At the end of an era, McCarthy silently joins forces with other late modernist novelists (Jonathan Saffron Foer, Richard Ford, Jonathan Franzen, Philip Roth, David Foster Wallace, among others) in returning us to a long-valued humanist role for literature, even if his narrative landscape is distinctively less salubrious than theirs.[4] Turning back from the experimental borders traversed in *Blood Meridian*, McCarthy reasserts the centrality of certain older narrative practices that have weathered the assaults of postmodernism. And with an eye slightly jaded but nonetheless directed toward a son whose life has yet to be lived, he looks back to the past as a means of crafting redemptive narrative possibilities. The argument that follows is meant to be similarly recuperative, in the close attention paid to McCarthy's deliberately strange, often unsettling stylistic choices. For the sustaining value of *The Road* lies in its insistence that words themselves, as part of both a continuing domestic dialogue and an enduring cultural legacy, become a necessary if hardly sufficient stay against dissolution.[5]

I. Dead Landscapes, Strange Words

The Road is as disorienting a novel as any McCarthy has written, beginning with confusion about where it takes place. All that is initially clear is the anonymous father's need to protect his son as they scavenge for food and clothing in an anonymous wasteland. The first hint of actual danger is the father's realization that "This was not a safe place" (*R* 5), followed by the claim that "No godspoke men" were on the road (32). Soon, death seems ubiquitous: "A corpse in a doorway dried to leather" (*R* 12); "Three bodies hanging from rafters" (17); "mummified dead everywhere" in the first city they pass (24). The man's friends are dead; his wife a suicide; the cause of catastrophe beside the point since consequences are all, with "Everything dead to the root" on land they pass: "No sign of life" (*R* 21). Flora and fauna have both been extinct for years, so long that a bird tattoo on a man they meet is described as having been "done by someone with an illformed notion of their appearance" (*R* 63). Indeed, nature's demise has withered language itself, evidenced by the figure of speech "as the crow flies" (156), which simply bewilders the boy in a world without crows. And part of what terrifies father and son in the figures they encounter is their inarticulate silence: "They neither spoke nor called to each other, the more sinister for that" (*R* 67). Antecedents and motivations shrivel in the shriveling of language itself, confirming how fully history itself is now defunct, with geography soon a casualty as well (signaled in their "tattered oilcompany map" (*R* 42)).[6]

Pervading the novel is an abiding sense of loss, not only the loss of things themselves or even of words to express them but the loss of any anxiety about loss itself as an otherwise "troubling issue." Early on, the father ruminates on this sense of emotional obsolescence as he thinks back to "those first years" after the disaster, wondering at what is left:

Creedless shells of men tottering down the causeways like migrants in a feverland. The frailty of everything revealed at last. Old and troubling issues resolved into nothingness and night. The last instance of a thing takes the class with it. Turns out the light and is gone. Look around you. Ever is a long time. But the boy knew what he knew. That ever is no time at all.

R 28

The paratactic exposition here defies connecting links that might turn the experience around, evoking a luminous meaning from simple scattered shards. After capturing inimitably the image of feeble vagrants, themselves emblematic of the land through which father and son "totter," the flashback shifts to review the effects of this disappearance of all once held dear. Whole categories of thought almost whimsically erode with the extinction of "the last instance of a thing"—it simply "Turns out the light and is gone." Yet the loss of any anxiety about not only those lost things but such "old and troubling issues" seems to abrogate time itself, to collapse it into sheer disconnected bestial moments, turning "ever" into "no time at all." Only the father resists this slide into animal acceptance, persistently speculating at what has passed irrevocably, both in the world and in the words embodying it:

He tried to think of something to say but he could not. He'd had this feeling before, beyond the numbness and the dull despair. The world shrinking down about a raw core of parsible entities. The names of things following those things into oblivion. Colors. The names of birds. Things to eat. Finally the names of things one believed to be true. More fragile than he would have thought. How much was gone already? The sacred idiom shorn of its referents and so of its reality. Drawing down like something trying to preserve heat. In time to wink out forever.

R 88–89

Here the rhetorical question, "How much was gone already?" itself implies unspeakable amounts beyond recovery, with the novel itself testament to a before-and-after of loss in its teetering between long stripped-down passages of paratactic simplicity and occasional bursts of lyric delight, verbal eruptions of rich imagery. Yet mostly, all that remains is "a raw core of parsible entities," with words and idioms revealed in their dependent fragility, and only the father's powers of recollection left as repository for what once was. Moreover, not just colors and names have ebbed away but with them the very "things one believed to be true," like loyalty or honor or self-restraint, all about to "wink out forever." The sole breakwater against such erosive currents is memory, flimsily shielding a revered past against the tide unloosed by those who value nothing more than survival, horrifying transients first encountered "shuffling through the ash casting their hooded heads from side to side . . . Slouching along with clubs in their hands, lengths of pipe" (*R* 60).

Yet even as words disappear with their referents, or otherwise die out from disuse, the narrative pulse of the novel resurrects possibilities. Murderousness and cannibalism may accumulate as memories, but the cadence of terror and violence is itself punctuated by scenes of mitigating renewal in a rhythm of systole and diastole that becomes part of what it means to be more than minimally alive. Horrifying encounters are intersected by days of miraculous restoration, first when father and son stumble upon a seemingly enchanted house to discover a packet of grape drink mix, a cistern of fresh water, an orchard of long-forgotten apples: "Nothing in his memory anywhere of anything so good" (*R* 123). Simple pleasures take on a lustrous glow when framed against privation, both in the actual experience and in its representation for us as readers. A second magical house has an underground bomb shelter with "Crate upon crate of canned goods. Tomatoes, peaches, beans, apricots. Canned hams. Corned beef" (*R* 138). As the man wonderingly muses, this "richness of a vanished world" (*R* 139) restores them briefly to wholeness and health in delicious food, warm water, deep sleep, but as well in the enriched vocabulary (forgotten until now) used simply to depict their good fortune. Later, they cook dinner in a "grand house" with chandeliers and china bowls (*R* 208). The last of these enchanted places is the foundered Spanish sailboat, from which they salvage food and supplies to find respite once again. All these are part of what seems like the mystery of life's renewal, matched at other brief moments by tantalizing signs of hope: when they hear a dog, despite believing the species has died out; when they smell the scent of cows in a barn, though "they were extinct" (*R* 120); when they discover morels on which to feast; when apple trees still blossom (proverbially, the only fruit forbidden in Eden; now the only hope for some Edenic rebirth of fruit, at last).

These fleeting moments, which remind the man of a "vanished world" fading from memory, occur in an ashen landscape evoked by an ostensibly rudimentary style. Yet even as the style seems aptly commensurate with its subject, it also has a transfigurative effect in its burnished diction and precise perspective, redeeming a world descriptively that seems otherwise void of value. Words not only matter, then—in a fashion familiar from McCarthy's earlier novels, where baroque descriptions often transmute otherwise banal scenes—but they matter self-consciously, as if evidence of a larger effort to resist an easy slide into authorial stammering. Near the end, the man feels forlorn:

> The days sloughed past uncounted and uncalendared. Along the interstate in the distance long lines of charred and rusting cars. The raw rims of the wheels sitting in a stiff gray sludge of melted rubber, in blackened rings of wire. The incinerate corpses shrunk to the size of a child and propped on the bare springs of the seats. Ten thousand dreams ensepulchred within their crozzled hearts. They went on. Treading the dead world under like rats on a wheel. The nights dead still and deader black. So cold. They talked hardly at all … Slumping along. Filthy, ragged, hopeless.
>
> *R 273*

Despite a claim for being "uncounted and uncalendared," the description itself stories their days, capturing the inimitable gruesomeness of experience in the simple elision from "raw rims" to "incinerate corpses shrunk to the size of a child." That eery equivalence between innocence and "melted rubber" blends into a bizarre evocation of dreams somehow congealed in hearts burnt crispy. Then, the vivid imagery subsides much as it intensified, in an alternating rhythm that releases us from a grotesquely vivid realm in which we were immured, paradoxically signaling the death of variety in a landscape momentarily enlivened by the richness of imagined transmutations.

The solitary paragraphs of the novel, moreover, isolated by borders of white space, compel the pauses, reversals, and shifts in direction that reinforce this general discontinuity—indeed, that make reading the novel similar to reading a poem, asking the reader to pause and reflect, to slow the tempo, to contemplate silences in the text as moments when language itself prepares to continue (as if absolving narrative of the undue pressure to hurry plot along). In a wasteland where things are left out, having evanesced or become extinct, McCarthy's very style tends towards the fragmentary, with normal parts of speech dropped, other usage distorted, lending to sentences a bizarre cadence and immediacy, sometimes generating strangely gnarled meanings.[7] Scenes appear unencumbered by verbs, simply shimmering as a series of nouns that make us hesitate, in realizing that syntax itself has come to embody the isolation it depicts. Far from "[e]verything paling away into the murk" (4), details glow in a dazzling verbal matrix.

McCarthy is an unusual claimant to the late modernist mantle, perhaps especially in this transfiguring of wasteland imagery into dazzling descriptions, as if language itself might offer a humanist stay against chaos. Yet coming at the end of a tradition, he is no less inventive than his predecessors (including his own earlier self as stylist) at capturing the fragmentation of time and consciousness, memory and dream. Immediately, in the novel's opening paragraph, we are paradoxically made aware of the humanizing capacity of language in the refusal to concede to the scene an erasure of values that the scene would seem to demand. The man sightlessly awakens "in the woods in the dark and the cold of night" (3), reaching for his son before recalling the dream from which he has awoken. And the dream's very elaboration, in the triplet similes of this first paragraph ("Like the onset of some cold glaucoma . . . Like pilgrims in a fable swallowed up . . . sightless as the eggs of spiders") disorients us even as it establishes the larger dissociative aura experienced by man and child confronted by a nightmarish world. Moreover, the repeated reliance on "w" ("When he woke in the woods," "wakened," "wandered," "wet," "swallowed," "inward," "swung," "water," "bowels" and so on) has itself an odd sonic effect, enhanced by the very slippage of "w" from consonance to assonance (as a labiolized velar consonant, it can be a vowel as well). It is almost as if the dream signaled a release from pedestrian prose, from the simple diction of a paratactic style to a richer, more evocative and elaborate, even distinctly human (because embellished and man-made) realm. The narrative voice asserts itself as salient as anything it represents, gradually revealing to us the capacity to recall a past and sustain it into the future. Partly this is achieved directly through the disconcerting breaks themselves in narrative time and consciousness— the alternation between present and past, reality and dream, dread and desire. The novel, that is, disrupts chronology in a way at once confusing yet enabling, even familiar, attesting again to McCarthy's debt to modernism but also turning the screw, collapsing perspectives as well as transforming conventionally sequestered scenes of consciousness.

But if memory seems to defy the evidence of one's senses, it also confirms the possibility of reconstructing a verbal past that might illuminate the darkened vista of the present. Words, after all, are the shapers of recollection, and their very disposition alters understanding. Consider the father's recollection of spending a day with his uncle on a lake, where nothing special occurs except calm effort and repose, all suitably reflected in a crystalline prose:

They tied the rope to a cleat at the rear of the boat and rowed back across the lake, jerking the stump slowly behind them. By then it was already evening. Just the slow periodic rack and shuffle of the oarlocks. The lake dark glass and windowlights coming on along the shore. A radio somewhere. Neither of them had spoken a word. This was the perfect day of his childhood. This the day to shape the days upon.

R 13

Here, "the perfect day" comes as flashback interposed in the narrative of a gruesome trek south (between the son having just seen a corpse and both about to head through "raw hill country" (*R* 14)). The scene not only defies present circumstances, it also contravenes the father's insistence that "you remember what you want to forget." That contradiction, however, cannot disguise his tacit wish for the bond with his uncle to match what he hopes for his son. Later, he brings the boy to his childhood home to share just such exalted recollections, of Christmas stockings and winter storms with his sisters near the fire: "The boy watched him. Watched shapes claiming him he could not see. We should go, Papa, he said. Yes, the man said. But he didnt" (*R* 26). Against the boy's fear, the father evokes the power of memory, keeping the past alive in an effort—central to all cultured belief—to revive the dead, to sustain the value of former lives as part of a distinctly human, and harmonizing, currency. "This is where I used to sleep. My cot was against this wall. In the nights in their thousands to dream the dreams of a child's imaginings, worlds rich or fearful such as might offer themselves but never the one to be" (*R* 27). Again, the boy begs to leave, as apparently "scared" of the unsettling reach of such memories as of present threats. And in that sense, his fears are sound, since the call of the past reminds us not only of the death of what no longer is, but the death of the present moment as that nostalgic past is being recalled.

Flashbacks, memories, dreams: all regularly disrupt the narrative flow in a fashion that nonetheless makes the narrative come alive, forcing us to concentrate on sounds and images that reflect the man's mood of puzzlement, anxiety, disjointedness. But they also help defy the abysmal present, offering a rear-guard defense of a vivid, humanizing past that everywhere else—in the landscape, in encounters with cannibals and psychopaths—is being obliterated. Even more than memory, dreams bring an iridescence to an otherwise ash-gray setting: "And the dreams so rich in color. How else would death call you? Waking in the cold dawn it all turned to ash instantly. Like certain ancient frescoes entombed for centuries suddenly exposed to the day" (*R* 21). As the man considers this otherwise "colorless world of wire and crepe" (*R* 116), he finds habitual comfort in "Rich dreams now which he was loath to wake from. Things no longer known in the world" (131). This explains the tonalities in his reverie of the wife he still mourns: "In dreams his pale bride came to him out of a green and leafy canopy" (*R* 18). So rich are these dreams that he distrusts their effect, as if they should become a Scylla-like lure, distracting him from his paternal responsibilities. As McCarthy suggests, dreams have a humanizing power by not allowing the vitality of the past, the drama of one's earlier efforts, to die off in the sepulchral present. The dislocations of consciousness that otherwise seem so disorienting in the here and now are registered as either memorable or distracting. At some points, pleasurable dreams are rejected altogether: "He mistrusted all of that. He said the right dreams for a man in peril were dreams of peril and all else was the call of languor and of death. He slept little and he slept poorly" (*R* 18; also 32). But when he is wakened by nightmares, they seem no more useful or life-enhancing than his conscious, day-light hours.

Instead, what is signaled by the man's dreams is release from the present, granting him thereby access to the dreamlike *in* the present. Strikingly, dreams and memories become buoyant experiences, unlike the looming psychological wastelands of high modernists like Eliot and Hemingway for whom disruptive fragments of the past keep threatening the present, needing to be kept at bay. A gray silt of recollection everywhere dulls and drains their characters' immediate landscapes, keeping them unceasingly on edge, with no way or where to escape. By contrast, the father regularly finds reprieve in conscious retreat to recollected scenes paradoxically more vivid, more life-like and flourishing: "Do you think there could be fish in the lake? No. There's nothing in the lake. In that long ago somewhere very near this place he'd watched a falcon fall down the long blue wall of the mountain and break with the keel of its breastbone the midmost from a flight of cranes and take it to the river below all gangly and wrecked and trailing its loose and blowsy plumage in the still autumn air" (*R* 20). Here, in defiance of the stark "nothing in the lake," his flashback juxtaposes not only a dazzling scene of falcon diving but dazzling language itself, in the startling invocation of Gerard Manley Hopkins' favorite sonnet, "The Windhover," with its "dapple-dawn-drawn Falcon, in his riding ... the achieve of, the mastery of the thing!" Granted, the allusion to a Christ-like savior might seem a vain gesture, in the post-apocalyptic absence of any religious salvation or present model for Hopkins' "hurl and gliding [that] Rebuffed the big wind" of adversity. Yet in Hopkins' alchemy of poetic language,

McCarthy finds a secular redemption that restores the mystery of language itself as testament to human endeavor, transforming the present into something transcendent, with the self-sustaining capacity of words transmuting austerity into poetry: "The land was gullied and eroded and barren. The bones of dead creatures sprawled in the washes. Middens of anonymous trash. Farmhouses in the fields scoured of their paint and the clapboards spooned and sprung from the wall-studs" (R 177). It is as if, in this barren wasteland, what testifies to human resilience and command is the capacity not simply to see the world anew, but to express it anew, in vividly resonant verbal configurations—to experience it in less impoverished terms than it minimally evokes. And the early allusion to Hopkins' masterpiece alerts us at moments like this to McCarthy's evocative diction (the Middle-English "middens" for refuse heap) and his taut alliterations ("barren. The bones"; "Farmhouses in the fields"; "spooned and sprung ... studs"), but especially to what seems like Hopkins'"sprung rhythm" as an imitation of natural speech. The sentence fragments themselves, here as elsewhere, tend to shift focus back to individual words, working in tandem as sheer description.

That is again reminiscent of a distinctly modernist gesture, transforming a diminished present via the "one true sentence" Hemingway had invoked as entry into any imagined world. Such attention to the simplest verbal dictate is evident everywhere in *The Road*, beginning with the narrator's stunningly abstruse diction.[8] Consider these strangely placed words: "slutlamp" (R 7), "gryke" (11), "riprap" (13), "vestibular" (15), "discalced" (24), "firedrake" (31), "rachitic" (63), "claggy" (75), "woad" (90), "accure" (116), "chary" (116), "illucid" (116), "churt" (129), "middens" (177), "isocline" (222), "bollards" (262), "bindle" (236), "salitter" (261), "dolmen" (261), and "loess" (280). Each quite precise, each equally evocative in sound itself, the words collectively defy the leveling effect of an otherwise deadened terrain.[9] And the frequently odd similes function likewise (seen in the opening paragraph), crossing psychological and linguistic realms as the narrator seizes rhetorically an ostensible meaning out of a world devoid of meaning, sometimes darkening the present scene but also attesting to the enduring capacity for humanizing discriminations. A snowflake melts "like the last host of christendom" (R 16), while "[b]y day the banished sun circles the earth like a grieving mother with a lamp" (32). Trout, now a vanished species, are recalled "as they turned on their sides to feed. Reflecting back the sun deep in the darkness like a flash of knives in a cave" (R 42). Here, it is as if the fleeting allusions—to Hemingway's stylistic revival, to the *ichthys* of Christian resurrection—were captured in the analogy to light glimpsed in the cave that opens and closes the novel. Alternatively, collapsing just such hope, the threatening man from the truck appeared "[l]ike an animal inside a skull looking out the eyeholes" (R 63). From another, strangely comic perspective, father and son are depicted as having "wandered through the rooms like skeptical housebuyers" (R 206), caught in a comparison now lost with all the other banalities of pre-apocalypse life. And in a telling analogy (half-Poe, half-Department of Transportation) that conceives the dying father as a corpse revived and reburied, "he woke coughing . . . Like a man waking in a grave. Like those disinterred dead from his childhood that had been relocated to accommodate a highway" (R 213). As in other similes throughout, the narrator here strains at descriptive inventiveness, turning the visible world at a deliberately odd angle, making us understand the father's vitiated existence as zombie-like resurrection, brought back to life to accommodate a novel intent on keeping language alive.[10] By allowing alien vistas to collide with the one he describes, the narrator's similes transfigure a series of ostensibly thin scenes into linguistically complex ruminations.

This helps explain the father's dismay at language itself, in its capacity to transform experience and expectations, having now realized how little of what he read as a child has prepared him for the world he inhabits. In this, he seems to speak authorially for literature in a postlapsarian era. Searching a house with his son, lingering over illegible, water-drenched books, he considers the very soddenness of the world as having smothered out viable hopes, in a passage as notable for the understanding it evinces as for the way it expresses such knowledge:

> Soggy volumes in a bookcase. He took one down and opened it and then put it back. Everything damp. Rotting. In a drawer he found a candle. No way to light it. He put it in his pocket. He walked out in the gray light and stood and he saw for a brief moment the absolute truth of the world. The cold relentless circling of the intestate earth. Darkness implacable. The blind dogs of the sun in their running. The crushing black vacuum of the universe. And somewhere two hunted animals trembling like ground-foxes in their cover. Borrowed time and borrowed world and borrowed eyes with which to sorrow it.
>
> R 130

Somehow, the soggy meagerness of books gives him, if only by contrast, a fleeting insight into "the absolute truth of the world." But the passage can stand for many others in its fragmentary broken syntax, which helps us concentrate on disconnected moments and objects. And the whole confirms father and son by the end (along with the reader) as the hunted animals invoked by the passage. In a novel that offers itself as a latecomer, offering as well a retrenchment from McCarthy's earlier modernist triumphs, the father despairs of any transcendent insight, even as that expressed despair is for an earth described as "intestate," dead without hope for future generations. This invocation recalls Stephen Crane's own bleak view of earth as "a whirling, fire-smote, ice-locked, disease-stricken, space-lost bulb" (348). Crane's perspective is ironic, however, offered at a second remove from his character's consciousness, while McCarthy's father realizes fully just where he is. Father and son are left "trembling" in a simile so weak it seems a tautology (of animals become simply animals), no longer capable of acknowledging that language *might* transform a view of conditions.

The passage nonetheless ends with a final, all but desperate gesture—"Borrowed time and borrowed world and borrowed eyes with which to sorrow it"—as if the conceit of father and son as hunted animals itself were a stay against expiration and loss, even though the eyes to view this lost world must be "borrowed" from some condition of recollected time, of past certainty. The line itself, moreover, awakens us poetically (in its triple iteration) and sonically (in its half-rhyme of "borrowed" and "tomorrow") to a culmination of literary expression in one of Shakespeare's more famous soliloquys, Macbeth's lament over his wife's death: "There would have been a time for such a word. Tomorrow and tomorrow and tomorrow creeps . . ." (V.i.). In short, even in the midst of a dead landscape, with human prospects radically foreshortened, with language itself come to seem unavailing, the very sounds and rhythms of words invoke the redemptive possibilities of expression. The problem for the father *within* the novel has become how to revitalize words so that they no longer seem deceptive, so that they can give direction and solace to a new generation. But the problem for McCarthy *of the novel* is commensurate, in seeking to forge a transition in late modernism that might auger a prospect for literature itself. Though these two are connected, it may be appropriate to address the second problem first.

II. *Legacies*

The Road's careful attention to language—in its often strained verbal resonances and surprising poetic effects—raises a larger thematic consideration about the role of legacies, not only in the fictional father's worries about what to pass on to his son but in McCarthy's own self-consciousness about his literary forebears. Perhaps inadvertently, the father's pointed encounters with books introduce, if inadvertently, the question of the novel's own *bona fides*, its credentials as part of an ongoing tradition. And few other recent entries have been so mindful of their place in literary history, drawing on a radically diminished thematic content to recall the myriad possibilities of late modernist narrative exposition. The father alerts us to that tradition in the passage above, but also in the anger he later feels in his fevered state at the distortions of literature, as he recollects having once been in the:

> charred ruins of a library where blackened books lay in pools of water. Shelves tipped over. Some rage at the lies arranged in their thousands row on row. He picked up one of the books and thumbed through the heavy bloated pages. He'd not have thought the value of the smallest thing predicated on a world to come. It surprised him. That the space which these things occupied was itself an expectation. He let the book fall and took a last look around and made his way out into the cold gray light.
>
> R 187

The very capacity to believe verbal fabrications in their prompting of hope seems to him a treacherous deceit in view of the state of the world. The "lies arranged in their thousands" have created "an expectation" out of nothing but words, or rather the ostensible "space which these things occupied."

Given such expressed skepticism about the status of books themselves, it seems surprising to find how often *The Road* registers its tribute to a range of classical authors. Or as McCarthy himself acknowledged in a rare interview: "The ugly fact is that books are made out of books. The novel depends for its life on the novels that have been written" (Woodward 30). Obvious signs of indebtedness occur in the scene of footprints on hot macadam, recalling Daniel Defoe's *Robinson Crusoe* in the heart-stopping glimpse of Friday's footsteps on sand. Similarly, the opening deforms Emerson's "transparent eyeball" in the "cold glaucoma" (*E&L* 10) of the world, just as the paragraph more generally echoes classics from *Beowulf* to *The Faerie Queene*, introducing a nightmarish monster as emblem for monstrous times. Elsewhere, the Bible and Ovid are invoked, as is Arthurian literature, with grail imagery repeatedly cited to evoke the son's hallowed importance.[11] And the very topos of the world as wasteland extends from Eliot and Fitzgerald forward, though *The Road* once again transforms that now traditional setting as itself the place of transfiguration. It is Hemingway, however, whose adoption of the topos most prominently engages McCarthy, in his self-conscious revision of the Nick Adams stories with their focus on the relationship of father and son; as well, the novel's thrice-fold reference to trout points specifically to "Big Two-Hearted River," while the stories' notably paratactic style defines McCarthy's own dominant register, at least in this novel. As if inescapably, the novel extends and transforms the very tradition the father abjures, if in a distinctly darkened mode.

All of which is to say that rhetorical figures and literary echoes effectively transpose the impoverished thematic experience of *The Road* into a more generative, prolific, and finally mysterious realm. Perhaps the most enigmatic aspect of such transposition involves the novel's telling itself, of an unidentified narrator offering a conventional third-person perspective, frequently in free indirect discourse aligned with the father's perspective (termed by Genette a heterodiegetic mode). In a post-apocalyptic world, the very role of narrator seems suspect, excluded by default, as if narrative and language itself were effectively annulled by global conditions. How can that perspective have survived, we wonder. Yet the seamlessness of that perspective, which tellingly engages a reader's sympathy, is itself abruptly ruptured on nearly a dozen occasions when the narrator shifts to second-person, compounding the mystery. It is as if the dissociative effects of the novel's use of simile at a figurative level were being echoed at the metaleptic level of voice, in the mercurial shifts among perspectives. Consider the description of the man's fear of wearing out the past by recalling it:

> Memory of her crossing the lawn toward the house in the early morning in a thin rose gown that clung to her breasts. He thought each memory recalled must do some violence to its origins. As in a party game. Say the word and pass it on. So be sparing. What you alter in the remembering has yet a reality, known or not.
>
> R 131

Why does the narrative here suddenly abandon the third-person voice, and to whom is the imperative, "So be sparing," directed? It comes immediately after another cited imperative ("Say the word and pass it on"), meant as conventional instruction in a projected "party game." Yet the cautionary entreaty that follows suddenly shifts perspective, imagined by the narrator as he actually inhabits the father's consciousness, however fleetingly, in a moment of identification with the man's need to warn himself about a reality beyond memory, beyond discourse, as if the entire enterprise of recalling the past in any words at all were a dangerous practice to which he needed to steel himself. Again, the mystery of the moment occurs in our wondering why this warning needs to be given here, and from this vantage.

One explanation for McCarthy having the father invoke the second person is precisely that it is "an extremely protean form," as Brian Richardson observes: "The 'you' ... threatens the ontological stability of the fictional world, insofar as it necessarily addresses the reader as well as the central character. ... This 'you' is inherently unstable, constantly threatening to merge with another character, with the reader, or even with another grammatical person" (311–12). The possibility that the father is speaking to himself, *sota voce*, never quite excludes an equally probable explanation that he is addressing the reader.[12] Or as Richardson teases out the multiple implications of such usage in general:

> The nature and identity of the narrator becomes itself a miniature drama as a familiar narrating situation is established throughout the text only to be utterly transformed at the end. The heterodiegetic narrator outside the story turns out to have been in there all along; the seemingly daring narrative 'you' is instead a more conventional apostrophe, the story of another is revealed to be the story of oneself. The conventional practice is deployed until it is turned inside out, revealing the artificiality of a perspective, whether designated 'third person' or 'heterodiegetic,' that can be so easily inverted. And it will be noted that the move is always away from traditional objectivity and omniscience, from the third person to the first.
>
> 312

The very instability of the second person means that its occurrence always makes the reader wonder at the possibility of breaking the fourth wall, having a character turn to the audience.

Yet even more dramatic shifts in voice occur in those handful of moments when the narrator himself adopts a first-person "I," which intimates an identification with the father that goes well beyond conventional free indirect discourse. The most vivid of these instances occurs after a dog is heard barking (the only sign of canine life) and the boy sees another "little boy" whom the father refuses to help.[13] As his disconsolate son weeps, then falls asleep in his arms, the father starts to justify himself in a passage whose opening sentence shifts abruptly from third- to first-person, and whose closing two sentences shift as abruptly back:

> The dog that he remembers followed us for two days. I tried to coax it to come but it would not. I made a noose of wire to catch it. There were three cartridges in the pistol. None to spare. She walked away down the road. The boy looked after her and then he looked at me and then he looked at the dog and he began to cry and to beg for the dog's life and I promised I would not hurt the dog. A trellis of a dog with the hide stretched over it. The next day it was gone. That is the dog he remembers. He doesnt remember any little boys.
>
> R 87

The narrator here inhabits the man's consciousness for the entire paragraph as he recollects a moment well after the global disaster when the family was still intact, with the son's empathy blending into the present in the desire to care for not only both dogs (past and present) but for the little boy as well. Still, the man's final assurance to himself—"He doesnt remember any little boys"—oddly suggests that his son has imagined the entire present scene, of a dog they only think they heard, and of a boy whom the man has not seen at all. Either that, or he feels guiltily driven to deny his son's experience. Either way, the leap into first-person voice intimates once again a strange collapsing of boundaries, not only of past and present, of real and imagined, but of sympathetic narrator and contrite father. And the father's regret at denying his son, even if out of pragmatic necessity, seems to have spurred the narrator here into a kind of rapport, identifying with the father's quandary.[14]

The novel leaves the question disturbingly open, compounding its otherwise fractured style in dislocations of consciousness, asking what to make of lost worlds, of fading memories, of lost humanity itself. The mystery that lingers over much of the novel (where? when? to what end?) culminates here in the largest enigma of all, of who is telling the story. Admittedly, third-person accounts often leave us in doubt about narrators who seem more puppet-masters than players, pulling strings we never notice, shifting views without explanation, remaining solidly anonymous and unforthcoming about themselves. But in a post-apocalyptic setting, where literate humanity itself seems to have all but disappeared, the very ability to have a hearing, to tell a story, to give an account, seems forfeit. And our question about the novel's narrator comes to rest (as intimated above) on the attention to precise diction in a frequently vivid style, suggesting the father himself is somehow serving as an author-figure, keeping literary tradition alive. This is never made explicit, in a narrative so often stripped to essentials of walking a road that goes nowhere, with perspectives dislocated, with strained figures of speech, with language inventively caressed in the effort to keep horror at bay and to make sense of what is left. Whatever the enigma behind its telling, the novel brings narrator and man (and occasionally a directed reader) together in their intersecting efforts, each wanting to make sense of ways in which experience can still be justified, narrated, negotiated in recognizably humane terms, even when all else seems lost.

In this, once again, McCarthy is emulating literary tradition itself, with the conjunction of his novel and those others on which it builds embodied in the relationship between father and son, transmitting a heritage, committing oneself to renewed forms of past practice.[15] The paradox of that commitment is that the father feels intensely the effect of narratives gone awry, so much so that after dreaming of his dead son, he refuses to fall back asleep in fear of a narrative drive he cannot control: "What he could bear in the waking world he could not by night and he sat awake for fear the dream would return" (*R* 130). This comes to seem akin to McCarthy's own destabilizing of narrative sequence, devising a novel that is simply peripatetic, seemingly free of plot. And the father's ambivalence about nightmarish narratives corresponds to an ambivalence he feels about the boy's chances, embodied in the contrast of two remarkable similes that identify the boy with the very rhythm of the novel itself. Hobbling on, coughing, the man sees his son looking "back at him from some unimaginable future, glowing in that waste like a tabernacle" (*R* 273). Yet little more than a page later, "He turned and looked at the boy. Standing with his suitcase like an orphan waiting for a bus" (*R* 275). From divine tabernacle, the portable house of God, to parentless waif, the father's view of his son alternates between hope and despair, confident the boy can carry on yet fearful at leaving him without guidance, exposed to the road. Or as he earlier expresses his ambivalence, stroking his son's hair: "Golden chalice, good to house a god. Please dont tell me how the story ends" (*R* 75). That deeply divided feeling is based on simply the strength of his love, as his wife long ago discerned: "The boy was all that stood between him and death ... you wont survive for yourself" (*R* 29, 57). And the plea to be left in suspense establishes his own commitment to narrative uncertainty and mystery itself, in the playing out of renewed possibility over time.

From this perspective, the novel's dramatic oscillation between danger and release—a rhythm clearly beyond one's control, invariably exceeding expectations—is supplanted by a more deeply affecting cadence of ordinary exchanges as the father fondly holds the boy or quietly watches him sleep. Early on, he amuses his son as they bobsled over snow in a cart: "the first he'd seen the boy smile in a long time" (*R* 19). He gives him a rare can of Coca Cola or a packet of grape drink, or shows him his childhood home before they finally summit the pass, completely a paternal cycle: "The boy stood beside him. Where he'd stood once with his own father in a winter long ago" (*R* 33). Wanting himself to pass things on—memories, knowledge, history—the father "told the boy stories. Old stories of courage and justice as he remembered them" (*R* 41). Teaching him Whist and Old Maid, he makes sure the boy knows the alphabet, but as well in the process of teaching also learns about himself: "Sometimes the child would ask him questions about the world that for him was not even a memory. He thought hard how to answer. There is no past. What would you like? But he stopped making things up because those things were not true either and the telling made him feel bad" (*R* 53–54). The death of the past seems to lead to infinite possibilities for "making things up," but the man realizes the son holds him to a certain accountability, a principle of historical truth that precludes simple invention. In this, the son represents not simply his progeny but a standard against which his own and others' lives might be measured, in place long before the boy came into that life. His sadness at the prospect of his son's demise results not simply from personal feelings, so he thinks, but something larger: "it wasnt about death. He wasnt sure what it was about but he thought it was about beauty or goodness. Things that he'd no longer any way to think about at all" (*R* 129). The boy becomes the figure for thinking about such possibilities, fresh and uncontaminated, linking the father's past with humanity's future. Of course, we realize the father himself has no future, since his death by lung disease is confirmed early on, "coughing … a fine mist of blood" (*R* 30). That hacking cough is the novel's most repeated activity, worsening progressively, though it looms less importantly as end to the narrative than in signaling what can be done in the interim. And less troubling than knowledge of his own death is the fear that he will be unable to respond persuasively to his son's inquiries. At a minimum, he wants to give the boy reason to carry on, which explains his retort when the boy despondently admits "I wish I was with my mom": "Dont say that" (*R* 55). Repeatedly, he addresses his son's question, "Are we going to die?," with a cautious optimism meant to inject self-confidence in the boy's capacity to survive on his own (*R* 10, 94, 100).

The relationship of father and son embodies a tension between pragmatic self-preservation and innocent morality, keeping alive for both a fear of what they may be becoming. The father's shrewd sense of risk is repeatedly provoked by events on the road that prompt his son's compassionate willingness *to* risk. Yet gradually, each schools the other, with filial compassion balanced by paternal anxiety until finally the boy protests killing a thief who has stolen their gear: "Just help him, Papa. Just help him. . . . He's so scared, Papa" (*R* 259). Significantly, the father's compliance itself confirms the son's ability to sustain their humanity, lending an unmistakable religious tone to the son's summary claim, "I am the one." (*R* 259). Or as the father admits early on, "He knew only that the child was his warrant. He said: If he is not the word of God God never spoke" (*R* 5). The mystery of parenthood, no less than other mysteries in the novel, consists not only in the capacity of children to teach their elders, but for them to become like language itself in revealingly symbolic ways, individual signifiers of multiple humanizing possibilities. And in this, again, the novel's plot embodies its style (and vice versa) by offering a reflection upon the resources still available to confront a diminished world, both physical and symbolic.

Even more basic than any lesson of compassion or vigilance is simply the need to converse, to defy a natural inclination to fall back on the isolate self, and in so doing to keep alive the habit of narrative as a distinctively transfiguring human activity. For every occasion in which the son's anger leads him to tight-lipped silence, the father enjoins him against it: "You have to talk to me" (*R* 77).[16] The very condition of speech, of mutual verbal exchange, becomes as central to their relationship as to the novel's language itself. This helps explain by contrast the horror of the father's bizarre nightmare of aliens who "did not speak . . . and then had skulked away" (*R* 153)—a nightmare from which he awakens only to intuit that his son may feel similarly about him: "to the boy he was himself an alien. A being from a planet that no longer existed." Whatever his grief at the world he has lost, its memory matters less than simply convincing his son to speak, since that is the lost world's true legacy, in fostering an ongoing conversation. This helps explain the odd iteration of "okay" in their dialogue, the most frequent word in the novel. Serving as phatic discourse more than actual exchange of information, "okay" becomes an intermediate term, resonating as neither right nor wrong. As Dawn Saliba observes, "The word itself carries different connotations. At times it's a questing for permission, at other times it's a pressing of

will, but most often it's a pleading call for existential reassurance—
another ritualistic call and response that serves to reassure that the two
are physically and psychically safe" (*R* 146). Depending on context, the
word shelters layers of implication yet always expresses a determination
of father and son to negotiate, to agree to disagree. In its primitive
articulation, it confirms that articulation itself is worth the effort. And
in this, McCarthy again reveals a deep engagement with Hemingway,
whose "iceberg theory" of writing relied on omitting superfluous details
so as to capture nuances of understanding communicated just beneath
the level of spoken discourse. Father and son exchange "okay"s as a
means of cementing their relationship, building on the very desire to
maintain a verbal link that always gestures to something more than just
keeping the conversation alive. And the novel itself, it should be clear,
aspires to something like the same condition, of translating a heritage
into the future, conveying a set of narrative dynamics into new territory,
thematic and formal.

III. Sustaining the Mysteries

The Road distinguishes itself from McCarthy's earlier fiction perhaps no
more distinctively than in its thematizing the need to teach a younger
generation of pleasures to be realized in diminished times. Those
pleasures are obviously verbal, involving the reader's engagement with
the novel itself, but they also encompass more conventional virtues
having to do with conversing and negotiating, listening and persuading,
which may be the more important lessons the father struggles to convey
to his son. Indeed, even less pressing concerns are voiced, of passing on
knowledge and competency, sometimes simply defined as an acquired
precision in craft itself. The narrator enacts this in the painstaking
exactness with which he describes the man repairing a cart: "He pulled
the bolt and bored out the collet with a hand drill and resleeved it with
a section of pipe he'd cut to length with a hacksaw. Then he bolted it all
back together and stood the cart upright and wheeled it around the
floor. It ran fairly true. The boy sat watching everything" (*R* 16–17).[17]
Later, the father will make sweeps for the cart out of broomsticks,
though along with handiness he is equally savvy about bullet trajectories
and brain parts, "things with names like colliculus and temporal gyrus"
(*R* 64). These sporadic lessons match the son's growing expertise, who
by the end can trace their stolen cart himself through a sand trail left
behind: "Here it is, Papa" (*R* 254). As importantly, the father imparts a

general appreciation for what still abides, even in the midst of suffering, though this is sometimes conveyed indirectly: "No lists of things to be done. The day providential to itself. The hour. There is no later. This is later. All things of grace and beauty such that one holds them to one's heart have a common provenance in pain. Their birth in grief and ashes. So, he whispered to the sleeping boy, I have you" (*R* 54). This corresponds to the kind of nurturing his wife had commended even in her despair, offering fleeting hope for their isolate state: "A person who had no one would be well advised to cobble together some passable ghost. Breathe it into being and coax it along with words of love. Offer it each phantom crumb and shield it from harm with your body" (*R* 57). That "passable ghost" she proposes is of course their boy, beguilingly breathed into being through the father's patient words. And the paradox is that words themselves come to seem superfluous at moments of sheer contentment, shared in gratification, as confirmed in one of the novel's more satisfying lines: "They spent the day eating and sleeping" (*R* 155), an experience that matches the "perfect" silent day the father had spent with his uncle in childhood.

In contrast to all the dismissive reasons for not continuing—all justifications for escaping the bleak synesthesia of a "blackness to hurt your ears with listening"—the father seizes hope in an arbitrary choice void of rationale or advantage. That hope is partly constructed on what he recalls of the past, of culture and human variety in a pre-holocaust world, brought to life in the useless brass sextant he recovers from the ironically named sailboat, *Pájaro de Esperanza*: "It was the first thing he'd seen in a long time that stirred him" (*R* 228). Like the forest fire that had earlier "moved something in him long forgotten," the sextant reminds him of a cultural context in which humane values wove through things and events. That context still exists as imagined possibility, and father and son hold to convictions that seem unwarranted, even dangerous, precisely because they "carry the fire"—a phrase the son repeats as a mantra (*R* 83, 129, 216, 278, 279, 283). Partly, the phrase suggests that being human means passing on knowledge *of* the human, refusing to let it die. That includes even carving a flute for the boy, who plays "[a] formless music for the age to come. Or perhaps the last music on earth called up from out of the ashes of its ruin" (*R* 77). That his son soon discards the flute confirms nothing more than the absence of any guarantees, just as the father's losing their lighter seems little more than ironic, a literal but hardly figurative failure to "carry the fire" (*R* 126). Unlike those they encounter, however, the father nurtures esteem for a past that seems erased by the present, even as the "whited out" billboards they occasionally pass reveal old advertisements re-emerging as "a pale palimpsest" (*R* 127). The process is worth emulating, and the welcome prospect of a vital past leeching into the present comes to seem akin to the likelihood of people elsewhere, here *in* the present, acting like them. The boy first broaches this possibility in wondering whether "on the other side" (*R* 216) of the ocean a father and son are doing the same as they are, recalled by the father later that night as he sits on the beach and contemplates others carrying "the fire":

> Too black to see. Taste of salt on his lips. Waiting. Waiting. Then the slow boom falling downshore. The seething hiss of it washing over the beach and drawing away again. He thought there could be deathships out there yet, drifting with their lolling rags of sail. Or life in the deep. Great squid propelling themselves over the floor of the sea in the cold darkness. Shuttling past like trains, eyes the size of saucers. And perhaps beyond those shrouded swells another man did walk with another child on the dead gray sands. Slept but a sea apart on another beach among the bitter ashes of the world or stood in their rags lost to the same indifferent sun.
>
> *R* 218–19

This rumination in pitch dark, of spectral life in the deep sea and then of humans somewhere beyond, wonderfully transforms a temporal image into a physical one—not of the past emerging but of existing possibilities multiplied, as others confront the same obscure present with similar imaginative power. And the very rhythm of the passage conveys an emergent hope, in the shift from broken English into compound constructions, as the sibilance of "seething hiss" seems to unlock the man's imagination not only to the "cold darkness" that has drained both literal and figurative light, but to "another man ... with another child" resisting the demise of all they hold dear.

"Carrying the fire," in short, requires not simply a nuts-and-bolts Mr. Fixit with inventive engineering skills, nor even a quick-triggered guardian ready to defend his child. What is crucial is a figure of imaginative, even poetic capacities, able to construct in narrative a kind of tapestry for lives under duress. This is what the dying father means near the end in encouraging his son to tell his own stories, though the son responds that he has no "happy" stories like his father's to tell (*R* 268). Dismissively, he rejects his father's inventions of "helping people" as not "like real life," since the two of them clearly do not aid those they meet. As the father ponders his son's words, he comes to feel a sense of self-division between his private despair and his expressed paternal hope, his inner feeling of devastation yet of generation as well. Only a few days earlier, he had given way to cynicism about the value of writing at all, imagining death as the demise of articulate sound:

> He walked out into the road and stood. The silence. The salitter drying from the earth. The mudstained shapes of flooded cities burned to the waterline. At a crossroads a ground set with dolmen stones where the spoken bones of oracles lay moldering. No sound but the wind. What will you say? A living man spoke these lines? He sharpened a quill with his small pen knife to scribe these things in sloe or lampblack? At some reckonable and entabled moment? He is coming to steal my eyes. To seal my mouth with dirt.
>
> R 261

Yet even in a globe contracting inexorably with cold, he refuses to capitulate to so bleak a vision of eternal silence, which alternates with his encouragement of the need for speech: "Talk to me." Against all that reason dictates, he realizes how much "carrying the fire" is always a venture against odds, defined not as unthinking faith but as stalwart, imaginative sustaining of efforts against the dark. This is part of what he had earlier meant in embracing the uncertainty of his son's fate ("Please don't tell me how the story ends") as a gesture at once of fragile hope and enduring mystery. The fact that he conceives that mystery as a "story," moreover, confirms once again his own identification with the narrator's efforts.

With the death of the father at the end of *The Road*, we realize "the fire" *has* been carried via a son prepared for what will ensue, by now having internalized certain hard-earned virtues. As the father enjoined midway through: "Okay. This is what the good guys do. They keep trying. They dont give up" (*R* 137). That initial "Okay," moreover, is as prominent a part of the lesson as the drive to persevere, since it points to a verbal agreement later defined as simply to "talk to me." Just prior to his father's death, the son rehears that lesson translated into otherworldly terms, but also conveyed to us in a language no less moving for being simple, even banal:

> You said you wouldnt ever leave me.
> I know. I'm sorry. You have my whole heart. You always did. You're the best guy. You always were. If I'm not here you can still talk to me. You can talk to me and I'll talk to you. You'll see.

Will I hear you?

Yes. You will. You have to make it like talk that you imagine. And you'll hear me. You have to practice. Just don't give up. Okay?

Okay.

Okay.

I'm really scared Papa.

I know. But you'll be okay.

R 279

Some pages prior, the narrative perspective had fluctuated ambiguously between the two, as the boy's consciousness looms larger and the man's becomes ever more fragile. That ongoing oscillation extends the effect introduced by the second- and first-person slippage earlier, compounding the process of cultural transmission for characters as well as readers. "The lack of speaker differentiation," Dawn Saliba again observes, "also causes an interesting confusion in the minds of the reader. It is very likely that McCarthy purposefully renders the speaker unclear in order to highlight the childlike qualities of the father and the sometimes-mature qualities of the son" (145). Then, just prior to his father's death, the boy "closed his eyes and talked to him and he kept his eyes closed and listened. Then he tried again" (*R* 280). This effort at "prayer" fails, though the narrative dips briefly once more into the man's consciousness before finally identifying with the son's perspective (the father having passed away). Still, the boy's narrative gesture registers the rebirth of literary possibility, of talk as the most rudimentary form of storytelling.

The transfer from father to son has occurred, with the arrival of the stranger in a "gray and yellow ski parka" signaling, if somewhat miraculously, the promise of more colorfully sustaining possibilities (*R* 281).[18] The world is no less threatening, but risks can be hazarded in the knowledge of a larger community of veritable humans. What ensues will necessarily remain a "mystery," as the novel's last word intones, with even the closing paragraph of brook trout stippled with "maps of the world in its becoming" offering a strangely detached, if mildly reassuring perspective. And the very uncertainty about whose voice this could be (not the father's, since now dead; not the son's, since speaking of knowledge he could not have) incites the reader to confront once again the transformative power of narrative in the midst of dissolution. As Allen Josephs inquires of "that stunning and cryptic last paragraph":

Is the narrator addressing the reader directly when he says: 'Once there were brook trout in the streams in the mountains. You could see them standing in the amber current where the white edges of their fins wimpled softly in the flow. They smelled of moss in your hand'? Or is that second-person pronoun directed at the narrator himself, as a rhetorical question? Or is there an intentional conflation of narrator and reader and even ghosts? The man who remembered the trout in the early mountain section of the novel is dead. But you, the reader, cannot help associating the trout here with those remembered trout. They are as iconic as Hemingway's trout, or more so, as they are intentionally evocative, both early in the novel and intensely so now in this echoing vision of them, shared in the foreground between the complicit narrator and the willing reader and in the background with Hemingway and the deceased father. . . . It is no coincidence that the final word of the novel is "mystery."

141–42

Given a novel that paradoxically proclaims it cannot exist ("What will you say? A living man spoke these lines?"), the narrative is still forthcoming. "The impossibility of the novel being written ultimately fails to prevent it from being written," observes Matthew Brailas, teasing out the paradox:

> The narrator denies his own hopelessness in the very act of articulating hopelessness through the spoken word. . . . This contradiction seems to go hand in hand with another, related paradox: that a novel about the death of all beauty in the world is itself incredibly beautiful and incredibly poignant. That a novel about the collapse of human civilization and human goodness revolves around a story of deep and unconditional love.

We end with this conundrum of narrative voice that reinforces a larger sense of mystery in *The Road*, which comes as close to being a fable as any major recent novel.[19] Characters lack names; events are unidentifiable as historical episodes; plot is all but nonexistent. Yet anonymity need not mean impersonality; quite the contrary, the whole achieves greater intensity this way in a novel that paradoxically confirms its late modernist credentials in perhaps the least modernist of forms. And despite the father's repeated despair at the inadequacy of books, the literary does live on; like father and son falling back on what they have known, McCarthy himself reverts to an earlier mode to keep innovative expression alive. Returning this way to older forms, he makes us newly aware of certain tested literary insights. The past may flare and shimmer across faraway ridges, but this letter of a novel reminds us that literature keeps that past alive and thereby aids the present in its own search for meaning. Describing a journey through despair to a tenuous, fragile hope of endurance, *The Road* effectively reinforces a set of rudimentary truths—about the need for love and community, about the saving capacity of memory, about the mysteriously transformative effects of story-telling. Beginning with the father's dark dream of "a cave where the child led him by the hand" (*R* 3), the novel ends by closing the circle, as the dying father believes he is there once again: "The dripping was in the cave" (3, 280). He may himself never find the light, but he dies with the knowledge that his son carries it onward, still on the road, having promised in tears to "talk to you every day" (*R* 286). And that talk, "like talk that you imagine," becomes a humanizing prayer simply by being overheard.

Notes

1 The road that initially appears in some indeterminate landscape becomes identifiable as a trail cutting through McCarthy's childhood roots, with the opening quest from river to bridge identifiable as Henry Street in Knoxville, leading to an abandoned trailer park near the Cumberland Gap that then traverses Norris Dam and the Newfound Gap in the Smokies. Wesley Morgan offers a clear mapping of the novel, identifying McCarthy's unnamed city as Knoxville (40), and the fictional house of Christmas memories as the one he himself grew up in.

2 This directly contradicts Andrew Hoberek's recent reading, which aligns the novel's thematic "affect of exhaustion" with his assessment of its enervation "at the level of style itself" (486–97); it is hardly clear that *The Road* "abandons *Blood Meridian*'s residual suspicion of style" (495), however less obviously flamboyant or baroque. Ashley Kunsa comes closer to anticipating my argument in her reading of McCarthy's late style, though her enthusiasm seems at times unearned: "it is precisely in *The Road*'s language that we discover the seeds of the work's unexpectedly optimistic worldview." To agree with her that "the language of *The Road* begins to set both characters and readers free from the ruin" (65) does not finally underwrite so confident a judgment of its purported optimism.

3 McCarthy had invoked such narrative and syntactical innovations in many of his earlier novels, nearly all set on the road in often alien landscapes. As Allen Josephs rightly observes: "Virtually all of Cormac McCarthy's fragmentary, often picaresque, novels are road or trail novels involving walking, riding, driving, rowing, or some combination thereof, and all of his characters are indeed *hombres del camino* or men of the road. . . . Father

and son, carrying the fire, in all that dark and all that cold: Which novel are
we in? We are in all of them—they are all one long variously fabled
story—and we have come to the end of the road. What is there? What is at
the end of *The Road*, at the end of '[t]he immappable world of our journey,'
to purloin a phrase from *Cities of the Plain*?" (133). Likewise, Dianne C.
Luce has assessed "the role or function of story" as a self-conscious concern
of McCarthy's fiction throughout (195).

4 For a discussion of modernist and late modernist configurations in terms
specifically of McCarthy, see Phillip A. Snyder and Delys W. Snyder
(28–29).

5 The *Gospel According to John* establishes the mystery of language itself as
central to not simply belief, but existence: "In the beginning was the word,
and the word was with God, and the word was God."

6 Rune Grauland argues that *The Road* is not only McCarthy's only novel
"detached entirely from history, it also breaks with his famous attention to
place . . . [T]he characters of *The Road* are facing a landscape so vague it
almost is not there, yet consequently also a landscape that comes to mean
everything" (59–60).

7 Sally Butler notes McCarthy's deliberate violation of common usage of the
preposition "in" (rather than "on") through the novel, always in reference to
the floor (e.g., "Trash in the floor, old newsprint" [*R* 21]; "He lifted out the
tray and set it in the floor" [122]; "he turned on the flashlight and laid it in
the floor" [147]; "the lid snapped off and fell in the floor" [209]; "The boy
was crouching in the floor" [266]). Butler ventures that "one explanation
could be that McCarthy . . . is attempting to amend the definition of 'floor'
. . . as something more than just a surface, to imagine instead an enclosed
space. . . . Thus, the floor becomes more than a surface upon which all
things—living and nonliving—exist. It becomes instead a sort of repository
for all things left on Earth, absorbing them rather than simply resting
beneath them." Whether or not this is the reason, the weird usage certainly
exemplifies McCarthy's skewed effort and evocative results.

8 According to Dawn Saliba, "Neologisms and kennings are dotted
throughout, formed out of the need to illustrate the vast and sullen
deafening chaos that subsumes the duo" (147). As she adds, "all sorts of
kennings from 'feverland' (28) to 'lampblack' (244) to 'deathships' (218)
abound. This embodies the new lyricism that emerges from a fallen and
forlorn world. . . . But as verdant as McCarthy's prose is, it is all in an ironic
service of the portrayal of a world where words die" (147–48).

9 Michael Kowaleski has written of Stephen Crane in ways evocative for
McCarthy: "Reading Crane is a bit like wearing glasses in a cold climate;
there is a continuous fogging and clearing of your vision as you enter and
leave heated buildings. Yet to put the matter this way is misleading, for the
verbal action that works against his realism is felt not as a failed attempt at
realistic imagining but as part of an entirely different perceptual mode, one
in which we are made aware of the sounded presence of words. When we

are not seeing through language to imagined life in Crane's fiction, we are listening to an authorial voice fashioning a conceit, stiffening its syntax, mimicking a literary convention, or employing a purposefully audacious word" (112).

More simply, Nancy Kreml has remarked of *All the Pretty Horses*: "Finally the opaque style is marked by the foregrounding of sound through repetition" (142). And Terry Witek offers a close reading of *Suttree*, stating: "McCarthy is a master of such minute calculations, his word choice not only particular in meaning but particular in sound as well, bringing our attention to the individual properties of words and then drawing them into a peculiar music" (81).

10 Some similes seem less effective: "Like certain ancient frescoes" (*R* 21); "The fireblackened boulders like the shapes of bears on the starkly wooded slopes" (30); they walk "in their rags like mendicant friars sent forth to find their keep" (126); "They went on. Treading the dead world under like rats on a wheel" (273).

11 Allen Josephs confirms that the working title of the novel's earliest draft was "The Grail," and argues for the uncertainty of the novel's religious imagery by claiming that "from the very beginning that ambivalence about God was to form a central theme of *The Road*" (134). Josephs later adds, "the combination of the *grail* and the *blessed child* in the early drafts clearly conveys McCarthy's sense of the boy's role in unmistakably Christ-like iconography" (139). For a review of larger literary influences on McCarthy, see Steven Frye (6–7).

12 Lydia Cooper observes that "there are eleven sections where the text is technically narrated in the first person but there is no 'I' narrator ... Instead, these passages are in the imperative mood, indicating that the reader is being allowed to overhear the father talking to himself" (146). According to her, "the father's imperative mood drives the oracular rhythms of the text" (159).

This may be true, though commentators generally find the second person an oddly indeterminate voice. As Helmut Bonheim asserts: "Just as the narrator's 'I' often has an oddly double status in that we cannot tell whether it refers to a narrator within the fiction or also to an author in outside reality, the 'you' is often ambiguous in its reference. The linguists speak in such cases of 'sloppy identity' or of 'referential slither'" (76). The fact that boundaries are blurred between an observer and the person addressed is precisely the point of such narration. As David Holloway has claimed of McCarthy's earlier fiction: "these novels commit the reader to what looks like a permanent condition, a static or timeless order of things where the act of representing the world presents writer and reader with contradictions and conflicts that cannot be reconciled or overcome" (44). This effect is compounded by *The Road*.

13 Cameron Platt observes that this scene uncannily anticipates the novel's conclusion, when a stranger appears as if to satisfy the boy's earlier distress

at having abandoned a dog and boy: "his arrival uncannily answers the question, 'Who will find the little boy?' The father's final promise reads like a moral, and the coordination of the boy's earlier concerns with his final condition—coupled with the deus-ex-machina quality of the stranger's arrival—almost suggest that the boy conjures the goodness of the stranger by the hope of goodness that he holds for the other little boy." Platt then continues to contemplate the boy's final choice, invoking the father's earlier admonition: "'When your dreams are of some world that never was or of some world that never will be and you are happy again then you will have given up. Do you understand? And you cant give up. I wont let you' (189). Human choice may be most meaningful and powerful, by this vision, when it acknowledges its limitations and wrestles honestly with the constraints and contingencies of the present world. The possibilities that the boy imagines do not align perfectly with the realities he encounters, but he adapts his expectations, measures the relative risks of his options, and chooses to trust a man he does not know." As Platt argues, "in a narrative landscape that appears inhospitable to human agency, the novel closes on a moment of choice."

14 Tellingly, other modernist texts replicate this merging of narrative voice and subject. Marilynne Robinson's *Housekeeping* (1980) has the narrator, Ruth Stone, imagine becoming her own grandmother (*H* 16); Philip Roth's *American Pastoral* (1997) has Nathan Zuckerman break into his construction of Swede Levov's Marine experiences in WWII, actually becoming the Swede (210–11).

15 Arguing against this position, Richard Gray asserts: "If any of the old narratives that used to make sense of people's lives are recalled in *The Road* at all, they are recalled only to be subverted, flattened out into an absence of meaning" (263).

16 For repetitions of this injunction, see *The Road* 79, 93, 103, 129, 140, 184, 246, 261, 267, 283-84. Still, as Dawn Saliba observes, "the father can do little to pull the boy out of his selective mutism" (150).

17 John Cant observes of this passage, "The care with which the actions are described matches the care taken over the actions themselves, a characteristic matching of style and meaning. The wording is technical and accurate; there are no missing verbs. The effect of the passage is to divert the reader's mind from the anxiety generated through the identification with the protagonists in the extremity of their plight, just as it diverts the minds of the characters themselves to be absorbed in practical activity" (275). Richard Gray, using identical language, compares this with similar moments in *Heart of Darkness* and *In Our Time* (268).

18 According to Lydia Cooper, "The slow flush of color spreading through the grim darkness of the novel likewise seems to counter the father's increasingly despairing interior world, suggesting that the son may possibly succeed in bringing the 'fire' of sacred meaning back to the emptied vessels of his universe" (149). Shelly Rambo has observed that "Reviews of the

book diverge greatly in their reading of the final two paragraphs" (100). Richard Gray, deeply skeptical of the ending, declares: "It is as if, at this moment, McCarthy has withdrawn into the sheltering confines of American myth ... If this is an act of recuperation, and it certainly appears to be, then it does not work. On the contrary it is deeply unconvincing— not least, because it is at odds with just about everything that has occurred in the novel before" (271). Andrew Hoberek claims that *The Road* "abandons *Blood Meridian*'s residual suspicion of style and instead embraces it as the site of the world's imaginative reconstruction. Hence the novel's final paragraph, which in elegiacally mourning the lost world of nature, seems to undercut any hopefulness evoked by the boy's discovery of a new family" (497). Dana Philips likewise argues that the closing paragraph is beautiful but "the most damning" (186). See also Saliba (153).

19 Michael Chabon argues that identifying *The Road* as a fable is itself a sign of "anti-science fiction prejudice" (108), though his own identification of it "as a lyrical epic of horror" seems less instructive.

Chapter 6

BELATEDNESS IN *THE BRIEF WONDROUS LIFE OF OSCAR WAO* (2007)

... the mingled, mingling threads of life are woven by warp and woof: calms crossed by storms, a storm for every calm. There is no steady unretracing progress in this life; we do not advance through fixed gradations, and at the last one pause: —through infancy's unconscious spell, boyhood's thoughtless faith, adolescence's doubt (the common doom), then scepticism, then disbelief, resting at last in manhood's pondering repose of If. But once gone through, we trace the round again; and are infants, boys, and men, and Ifs eternally. Where lies the final harbor, whence we unmoor no more? In what rapt ether sails the world, of which the weariest will never weary? Where is the foundling's father hidden? Our souls are like those orphans whose unwedded mothers die in bearing them; the secret of our paternity lies in their grave, and we must there to learn it.

—Herman Melville, *Moby-Dick* (535)

The spotted hawk swoops by and accuses me,
   he complains of my gab and my loitering.

I too am not a bit tamed, I too am untranslatable,
I sound my barbaric yawp over the roofs of the world.

The last scud of day holds back for me,
It flings my likeness after the rest and true as any on the
   shadow'd wilds,
It coaxes me to the vapor and the dusk.

I depart as air, I shake my white locks at the runaway sun,
I effuse my flesh in eddies, and drift it in lacy jags.

—Walt Whitman, *Song of Myself*

One death is a tragedy; one million is a statistic.

—Attributed to Joseph Stalin (1958)

Junot Díaz's *The Brief Wondrous Life of Oscar Wao* is an explosive, frenzied, unstable novel as different from *The Road* as one might imagine, though it also regularly defies its status *as* a novel. Consider how its title gives its ending away before we actually begin; how often multiple footnotes erase the conventional distinction between text and context; how often myriad intertextual references interrupt our reading, in charged allusions to anime, fairy tales, science fiction, canonical novels and comics that collectively dismantle any consistent mood; how often professions of anxiety about literary influence surface throughout; and of course, how often pointed historical judgments punctuate a fiction that never troubles to assure us of its historical authenticity. It is as if Díaz, like McCarthy and Robinson before him, were discovering in the very writing how to create a novel in the late modernist period, though in his case by fleshing out the ghostly appurtenances of narrative structure itself. A decade earlier, Gérard Genette had theorized that literary status occurs in terms of palimpsests revealing a set of ur-texts, as aspects marginal to a text that weave familiar references together, making a plot resonate. And it is as if Díaz deliberately took this premise to an extreme, embracing every instance Genette invokes to define "the more distant relationship that binds the text ... to what can be called its paratext: a title, a subtitle, intertitles; prefaces, postfaces, notices, forewords, etc.; marginal, infrapaginal, terminal notes; epigraphs; illustrations; blurbs, book covers, dust jackets, and many other kinds of secondary signals, whether allographic or autographic" (*Palimpsests* 3). All these presumed background ingredients emerge in Díaz's novel as foreground, including enigmatic illustrations, blank pages, even a strangely exorbitant list of acknowledgments at the end. Given the helter-skelter, sometimes repetitive, often feverishly corybantic rhythm of the whole, the question that arises is: Why take this form? What is gained by so frenetic a turn to the self-conscious margins as displacement for a central narrative line?

And the explanation for this multiplication of plot inversions, which disrupts character development and confuses narrative sequence, is as a metaphor for the displacements wrenched into shape by diaspora. In a species of higgledy-piggledy haphazardness, the novel embodies its theme of a Dominican-American writer grappling with the voices that inspired him, the history that created him, the literary influences that enabled him. In the following, I build on the work of critics intrigued by this ethnic, national, and gendered mix, though my argument assertively focuses on the novel's aesthetic rather than its cultural components.[1] Rather than reading *The Brief Wondrous Life* as a supposedly accurate mirror of Dominican-American experience, or even as a riotous celebration of characters conventionally excluded from the American novel, I want to explore its centrifugal structure, its persistent displacement of otherwise familiar narrative elements to the margins in formal maneuvers that have more generally come to characterize late modernism. Some of these effects have been anticipated by David Foster Wallace's *Infinite Jest* (1996) and Dave Eggers's *A Staggering Work of Heart-Breaking Genius* (2000), but Díaz exceeds them both in the ambition of his meta-referential pyrotechnics as well as the renewed vision of authenticity to which he aspires. His novel relies on various postmodern techniques, but only to embrace a genuine subjectivity at odds with postmodernist irony, and it does so from the outset, beginning with its title. After all, invoking Hemingway's story ("The Short Happy Life of Francis Macomber"), Díaz not only renders Oscar de León's death a forgone conclusion but effectively undoes linearity in an inversion of beginning and end, establishing how fully the echoes that occur beyond the novel's margins will reshape our understanding. Regularly disrupting the narrative are other peripheral interventions from every available phantom corner (memory, history, popular culture, family rumors, ethnic and gendered stereotypes) that speak to the supposedly central account of diasporic survivors. And by repeatedly establishing the periphery as taking precedence over a coherent central narrative, the novel stands expectations on their head. That reversal continues variously, beginning with footnotes that invert the local and the historical, or intertitles that dice and slice to inform us tersely what to infer from an adventure yet to ensue. No sooner does the narrative gain traction, moreover, than it suddenly brakes, starting over, retreating backwards generationally, compounding a series of other strange peripheral moments.

These formal gymnastics succeed by transgressing boundaries crossed by other neo-realist novelists, though it is worth stressing that Díaz flouts these borders more zealously, and collapses narrative breaches into a more defiant kaleidoscope of a novel. The narrator's exposure of his involvement in writing, breaking the fourth wall; the accumulation of supposedly authoritative sources, placed in historical footnotes; the lapse into fantasy or memory or casually irrelevant personal comments; the circularity of narratives that seem to have little to do with one another; the lurch between languages, along with a cavalier invocation of popular cultural references: all these define strategies now familiar to readers accustomed to the lingering effect of postmodern play.[2] But like other late modernists, Díaz invariably pulls back from the edge of postmodernism's ontological doubts, its immersion in a sheerly textual realm. For his central focus lies in giving fervent voice to Oscar and Yunior de Las Casas as well as to Oscar's sister, Lola, and their mother, Beli Cabral. Embracing these four in their stumblingly quirky expression, moreover, he establishes narrative progression as a series of hiccupping, hyphenated, unruly interruptions, linking outsider status with structural disruption itself.

From the beginning, it is clear that *The Brief Wondrous Life* involves the problem (and challenge) of achieving a distinctive voice. But Díaz nicely formalizes that challenge in the textual confusion of inside and out, establishing an intersection of separate and shared identities as a way revealing how rarely identity is ever one's own alone. Voices exist fully, distinctively, only as they reveal themselves interconnected with others, a premise that precludes any straightforward chronology as well as any conventionally separable sequence of cause and effect. Yunior discovers in the process of writing that no adequate order emerges from his diasporic materials, and that the only narrative corresponding to his life must bow to the clash of history, popular culture, sexual role-playing, vernacular speech, and silence. That intermixing of compelling and seemingly inappropriate materials is as much a part of the reader's experience as Yunior's, helping to explain why the novel seems not to know how to begin, even as it gradually teaches new ways of unfolding that make narrative conventions themselves seem less tyrannical, less single-minded, more evocative than we had imagined.

If we regularly feel adrift in a novel that turns things upside down, disrupting not only temporal and spatial coordinates but readerly expectations as well, it only reminds us of the satisfying jolt that can accompany expectations abruptly gainsaid. Consider the moment when Lola learns that her former Dominican lover Max has died in a car crash, spurring her to leave the island:

> It was only when I got on the plane that I started crying. I know this sounds ridiculous but I don't think I really stopped until I met you. I know I didn't stop atoning. The other passengers must have thought I was crazy. I kept expecting my mother to hit me, to call me an idiota, a bruta, a fea, a malcriada, to change seats, but she didn't. She put her hand on mine and left it there.
>
> *BWL* 210

That "you"—"until I met you"—surprises us as we pause before realizing she is addressing Yunior, the philandering narrator himself, wholly unable to confess his love for Lola.[3] And here lies the crux of the novel, written entirely by Yunior, inhabiting a series of characters to report serendipitously what he has learned. For we remain unsure about what to make of this evocation of Lola's feelings for him, as he incorporates and internalizes her voice, then ventriloquizes her, expressing his love for her through hers here for him.[4] The moment collapses not only their mutual compassion but also, in this context, her mother's affection for Lola ("her hand on mine"), suddenly allowing us to appreciate the novel's disruptive momentum. Elsewhere, lines of consciousness and voice have seemed momentarily confused, inside melding with out—as here, even as the novel's strangely recessive structure will regularly surprise us by the insights achieved via its unexpected turn backward.

That is simply one of many borders breached—sometimes substantive, at others formal—which as we read begin to suggest the ghostly presence of other worlds, figurative as well as historical. At their most obvious, such suggestions occur to characters themselves, as when Oscar experiences "girl-friend problems" in high school, and happens to learn his mother also had a difficult love-life: "now it seemed that it was Oscar's turn. *Welcome to the family*, his sister said in a dream. *The real family*" (*BWL* 45). The moment crystallizes the novel's belated rhythm as well as its ventriloquizing of others, more generally underscoring a realization that only another's experience can contextualize our own, with a parent adumbrating why a child is here, suffering, succeeding, persevering anew. These transpositions among the Cabral generations are linked to the larger diaspora from Santo Domingo to the United States, as both familial succession and cultural dispersion map each other via formal shifts in the novel. But even as *The Brief Wondrous Life* declares itself a novel of diaspora, its ambitions emerge as more than merely political, social, or cultural, revealed in a disruptive narrative arrangement that forces the reader off-balance to endorse a vision of voices interconnected across family, ethnic, racial, gendered and generational lines. And that vision begins with the problem of simply beginning, of knowing which voice to start with, and why. For Díaz, despite the sometimes ironic tone of the novel and Yunior's pervasively arch tone, resembles all the writers of this study in defying a postmodern vision. The heart of his novel is a persistent striving for authentic presence, for a sustaining voice amid all the structural and ideological forces that would deny its expression. Part of this enlivening paradox is that the traditional humanizing virtues of genuine communication and personal transformation, so often celebrated by high modernism, emerge by formal displacements that might otherwise seem to deny them. In short, he inventively uses the meta-referential tricks of his postmodern predecessors to undermine their ironizing assumptions.

I. *"What's past is prologue." (The Tempest, II: 1: 253)*

At first glance, *The Brief Wondrous Life* confounds the reader trying to fathom links among separate parts, as if it were deliberately avoiding realistic notions of character and subjectivity, of sequence and connectedness, by shifting so disconnectedly among loose-lipped discussions of Dominican history and adolescent sexuality, popular culture and the pressures of diasporic experience. Soon it becomes apparent that the novel's initial focus at least is on the problem of simply telling a story, unraveling a chronology that organizes crucial experiences and ignores the irrelevant. This problem is characteristic of one strand of late modernism (e.g. Eggers), in the anxiety about beginning at all. Díaz's initial sentence ("They say it came first" (*BWL* 1)) establishes a self-declared curse as the initiating moment of the whole, with *Fukú americanus* announced as a hemispheric gesture that still perseveres. At which point the narrator's strangely self-divided voice takes over: "But now that I know how it all turns out . . ." (*BWL* 6). And in the eight sequestered sections of the novel, each inaugurates a singular temporal architecture as if to affirm anew the priority of a moment when plot then ensues. Yet by starting over and over again, Díaz establishes an unstable frame unusual even among contemporary novels, in which supposedly legitimate claims are unsettled, allowing diverse interruptions and assorted textual ruptures to complicate the narrative.

Repeatedly, a nostalgic gesture encourages the hope that plot might unfold predictably, simply by virtue of having proceeded straightforwardly from an antecedent moment. The opening chapter speaks of the "Golden Age" of Oscar's youth (*BWL* 13), the perfect era supposedly followed by a long decline. Chapter 2 then opens with Lola's revisionary claim that "*This is how it all starts: with your mother calling you*" (*BWL* 51), an italicized section that ends only after Beli reveals her cancerous tumor, as Lola repeats, "I was waiting to begin" (75). Beli's story then abruptly breaks the rhythm in Chapter 3, which opens with a redefined priority once again: "Before there was an American Story, before Paterson spread before Oscar and Lola like a dream . . . there was their mother, Hypatía Belicia Cabral," with her "inextinguishable longing for elsewheres" (*BWL* 77). That triply iterated "before," in its adverbial slippage from temporal to spatial usage, only compounds the persistent desire of characters to be somewhere else, accentuating how fully sequence in the novel is achieved through flashbacks and displacements, reminiscences and returns—all of which the reader must construct imaginatively, retrospectively.

Confirming this pattern, Yunior opens Chapter 4 with his own claim of precedence: "It started with me. The year before Oscar fell ... I got jumped as I was walking home from the Roxy. By this mess of New Brunswick townies" (*BWL* 167). At last, the title figure is revealed as a Dominican nerd, though we linger only briefly before the sequence turns backward again, with Chapter 5 at the outset announcing another claim for precedence: "When the family talks about it at all—which is like never—they always begin in the same place: with Abelard and the Bad Thing he said about Trujillo" (*BWL* 211). The novel's obsessive concern with beginnings, even more with priority, repeatedly proclaims itself in the overriding desire for finding prior causes for current effects. And only in the sixth chapter is the narrative turned the other way, launching itself more conventionally with "After," no longer driven by an insistent pressing backward in time: "After graduation Oscar moved back home. Left a virgin, returned one" (*BWL* 263). The short final two chapters then settle into a more familiar chronological pattern in "brief" testament to the life that can at last be known, beginning to end.

The novel's structure, in short, seems oriented deliberately around an inability to structure the novel, in failing to find a satisfactory form adequate to events that require being narrated. We keep wondering at the interlocking significance of different temporal sequences, even as the process of starting over, then starting over once again causes us to lose sight of the novel's multiple repetitions. Regularly characters suspect something is about to begin anew, or change, or otherwise reveal itself, as Lola declares in addressing Yunior: "But that's not what I wanted to tell you. It's about that crazy feeling that started this whole mess, the bruja feeling that comes singing out of my bones, that takes hold of me the way blood seizes cotton. The feeling that tells me that everything in my life is about to change" (*BWL* 72). Yet nearly everyone else likewise feels temporal hiccups, the sense that experience has suddenly been either jump-started or disabled at some critical moment. Incorporating this as a structural premise in the novel, Yunior identifies "the Bad Thing Abelard Said" as the moment invariably singled out by the de Leóns' to explain their bad fortune: "There are other beginnings, certainly, better ones, to be sure—if you ask me I would have started when the Spaniards 'discovered' the New World—or when the U.S. invaded Santo Domingo in 1916—but if this was the opening that the de Leóns chose for themselves, then who am I to question their historiography?" (*BWL* 211). As ever in this novel, beginnings are arbitrary and fully conceded as such, flatly stated as if no other introduction had ever been declared. What distinguishes the gesture here, however, is Yunior's focus on the de Leóns' power of selection, suggesting how fully choice of antecedent, of initiating facts for the stories we tell, helps to define us and in the process grants us some autonomy.

For all the importance attributed to priority, however, the premise is paradoxically subverted in Yunior's opening description of *Fukú americanus*. After all, by performatively creating what it describes, the curse actively begins a process that has no beginning itself. Columbus becomes both creator of fukú and its earliest victim, with the supposed malediction setting all in motion despite no prior cause, at least that we are aware of. Fukú lends to this novel of recurrent beginnings a perplexing sense that beginnings may not matter at all, since a curse is always already in place. And compounding the paradox, Yunior's actual discovery of the concept of fukú occurs late in his own chronology (after Oscar's beating by the capitán's goons, when he returns to Patterson). Though he opens the novel with a curse, then, Yunior's delay in understanding its function suggests at last the fragility of sequence itself; the weight placed upon time in the novel always unsettles time's role in events. Why else does Yunior pay such attention to accidental belatedness or the need to be on time? "Each morning, before Jackie started her studies, she wrote on a clean piece of paper: *Tarde venientibus ossa*. To the latecomers are left the bones" (*BWL* 219). Is that in fact true, or simply something a character believes in sorting out her life? Later, her father will offer an alternative sequence, to his regret: "But alas, instead of making his move Abelard fretted and temporized and despaired" (*BWL* 230). Abelard fails to follow Lydia's advice to flee to Cuba, and the repetition of "*Tarde venientibus ossa*" (231) suggests at once how important delay retrospectively seems and how uncertain it is as explanation of what ensues. In his last Saturday night tryst with his mistress Lydia, Abelard is simply caught in disbelief:

> Can you believe how long it's been? He asked her in amazement during their last Saturday-night tryst. I can believe it, she said sadly, pulling at the flesh of her stomach. We're clocks, Abelard. Nothing

more. Abelard shook his head. We're more than that. We're marvels,
mi amor. I wish I could stay in this moment, wish I could extend
Abelard's happy days, but it's impossible.

BWL 236

Yunior's very inability to "stay in this moment," characterized by his
wrenching narrative into and out of sequence, corresponds to something
of Abelard's sense of wondrous atemporality—both, in vivid contrast to
Lydia's clock-bound notion of the human machine.

Still, even the standoff between Abelard's and Lydia's conceptions of
time is defied by Yunior's narrative interruptions, his reversals and
repetitions, which have the effect at once of seeming to bind events to
an unalterable structure and of making time seem nonetheless
bridgeable and unobstructed. This helps explain Yunior's back-flipping
narrative leaps, in resisting at once those who feel unduly constrained
by time and those blithely unaware of its passing. Or as he observes, in
depicting Oscar's decision to summer in Santo Domingo: "It's strange. If
he'd said no, nigger would probably still be OK. (If you call being fukú'd,
being beyond misery, OK.) But this ain't no Marvel Comics *What if?*—
speculation will have to wait—time, as they say, is growing short" (*BWL*
270). Yunior seems able at once to anticipate alternative choices and yet
to register his deep suspicion that alternatives might ever occur in time,
explaining why the novel's presentation seems so often self-enclosing
(fn. 29 embodies this bind, opening and closing the same way, as if the
repetition foreclosed any other options (*BWL* 244)). In the end, Yunior
realizes the essential repetitiveness of all the scenes he describes, which
come to mirror each other and thereby to render characters more or less
the same, at least in terms of the events they suffer if not in their
characteristic voices.

Most obviously, violence recapitulates itself endlessly, sometimes all
but exactly. When the capitán has Oscar beaten, a strange revelation
occurs: "And yet this world seemed strangely familiar to him; he had the
overwhelming feeling that he'd been in this very place, a long time ago.
It was worse than deja vu" (*BWL* 298). That beating reminds us of others,
of both Beli and Abelard caught in their own violent encounters before
Oscar ever arrives. Almost ruthlessly, repetition enforces a notion of
family fukú that leads various generations into eerily similar narrative
traps. Beli's life becomes entangled with Trujillo's sister, much as her
father Abelard became entangled with Trujillo, who lusted after Beli's
older sisters. By Abelard's later section, the stalwart relentlessness of
repetition has become clear in the recurrent turn backwards in time,

even if characters fail to realize this as clearly as readers do. Still, the echoes occur as déja vu when Inca and Beli care for Oscar: "If they noticed the similarities between Past and Present they did not speak of it" (*BWL* 301). Yunior's musing on their silence, however, itself alerts the reader to what they may not have noticed.

As violent moments punctuate the novel in repetitive patterns across generations, so too are erotic moments reiterated in an ongoing cycle of sexual encounters: of Lola in high school with Aldo; of her mother Beli in school, first with Jack Pujols, then with the Gangster; of Beli's father Abelard with his mistress Lydia; or later, of Yunior with Lola, followed by a string of other faceless women. Whether life appears as a series of repetitions when seen from the angle of fukú, or whether the repetitions themselves encourage our belief in a long-lived curse, the point is that sameness is reiterated from great-grandparents down through the generations. And it comes as little surprise that the novel's ending therefore occurs as stuttering repetition. Part III opens with a backward-looking "This happened in January" (*BWL* 311), to date the whole, while its opening chapter then announces itself as "The End of the Story," explaining "That's pretty much it" (323). Still, Yunior cannot let go, and adds "On a Super Final Note" (*BWL* 324) that is then followed by an apologetic "It's almost done. Almost over" (329). Even here after all, Yunior cannot locate the occassion that might finally end it definitively, or otherwise settle on a conclusion adequate to the energies that have preceded, any more that he could define an initiating moment leading to all that follows. Part of his difficulty lies in the question that looms for every other character, each of whom wonders where his or her life takes the shape it does. And the novel persistently grapples with this question through its abrupt alterations in tone, diction, and subject matter, keeping before us the problem of capturing a life's arc in direct narrative sequence.

The novel's characters embody the problem of characterization in late modernism, at least as Díaz construes it: of relating events that in their ordering and duration might evoke a sense of authenticity, even subjectivity, despite the destabilizing ironies of the narrative voice, inflected by apparent postmodernist textual contingencies.[5] Beli, for instance, seems almost an allegory for finding a story too early, too late, too little known. Conceived in a prison visit her mother made to Abelard, she is then left abandoned when both parents die unexpectedly, a sister drowns, another is killed by a stray bullet, while family servants die unaccountably. She is sold, to live "anonymously among the poorest sectors on the Island, never knowing who her real people were, and subsequently she was lost from sight for a long long time" (*BWL* 253). Her refusal to speak of these years, ever "skitter[ing] away from me and my stupid questions" (*BWL* 253), testifies to the way in which victimization results so often in silence, in the breakdown of personhood itself (and Yunior's footnote here confirms that other victims were similarly close-lipped). Words simply fail, with Beli embodying the problem of finding a story, generating a narrative, that is characteristic of the entire novel.

This problem of articulation occurs in the novel's style itself, spectacularly so in the section entitled "Oscar Goes Native" that confirms his decision to stay in Santo Domingo. For three complete pages, a single sentence continues, punctuated only by the anaphora of "after ... after ... after" (*BWL* 276–78), as if all we can recover from varied events is mere sequence. Temporality resists easing into causality, chronology declines to take flesh as history, and only belatedness is affirmed by the sentence that abruptly ends: "after he caught a cold because his abuela set the air conditioner in his room so high, he decided suddenly and without warning to stay on the Island for the rest of the summer with his mother and his tío" (*BWL* 278). That first extended sentence is followed by a shorter but equally arbitrary sentence of linked events, equally expressed in the anaphora of "after" (*BWL* 279), as if the novel had now found the true *beginning* of Oscar's "*real* life" at nearly the novel's end and so might actually justify the adjective "brief" in the novel's title. As well, Ybón is described here as the "I, Shabine" of Derek Walcott's epigraph, the figure who embodies the true "nation" behind the paradise of Santo Domingo, pulling together the novel's beginning with its end.

The series of mechanically advancing mini-narratives prompted by the adverb "after" compounds the larger structural problem of narrative progression that has been apparent all along: of how to begin and how to end, but more generally how to define lives intersecting. Díaz finds ways to avoid the curse of sheer repetition by seizing on the terms of history itself, both personal and national, even as the tyranny of repetitive forms (historical, gendered, familial) refuses to loosen its hold. For the question his novel addresses is the curse of fukú, a curse Columbus first invoked in the Caribbean but one endemic to family and individual lives as well. How do we break from established or otherwise conventional frameworks to create zafas or counterspells, and in that rupture more generally to frame alternative novelistic possibilities? How do we avoid being merely repetitive, following familiar compositional patterns, assimilated despite ourselves into commonplace paradigms? As Díaz's novel intimates from the outset, *Fukú americanus* is not simply the "Great American Doom" invoked by Columbus but the larger, debilitating problem of recurrence itself. For repetition is a curse, not only for characters *in* the novel but for the novel form itself that thrives on transitions and change, development and difference.

While *The Brief Wondrous Life* seems to enforce something like a postmodern curse of sameness by revealing different lives repeating each other, affected alike, it also undoes that curse in swerving *between* lives in their anomalies and irregularities, evoked even more sharply by distinctive, self-confident voices. One voice emerges from another, son and daughter from mother, mother from father in turn, each unaware of the vibrantly singular voices that gave it life, each trying to make his or her voice vibrate uniquely. Granted, the novel gives us lives in reverse, stretching from Oscar back to Abelard, making us realize that the past does not so much create the present as simply exist prior to it, with children expressing themselves as if entirely unique, with no one appearing to feel or risk or experience something before in the same way. Yet if characters share similar urges and even replicate each other's lives, those similarities are disguised and trumped by each character's characteristic tonalities and expression. Plot is sacrificed to sound, in short, narrative to acoustics, with the past brought to life by disguising predictable patterns buried beneath fresh expressions, idiosyncratic gestures, unique styles.

II. Ventriloquisms

Ironically, the novel triumphs by revealing how little we lead isolated lives, unlistened-to or otherwise unheard, but instead invigorate our own sensibility by incorporating and transmuting the voices of others. Indeed, that is the process by which a sense of authenticity (and subjectivity) is generated against the repetitive sameness of so many repetitions in the novel. Consider Yunior describing Oscar in phrasing that echoes Oscar's own idiom: "Could write in Elvish, could speak Chakobsa, could differentiate between a Slan, a Dorsai, and a Lensman in acute detail, knew more about the Marvel Universe than Stan Lee ... Couldn't have passed for Normal if he'd wanted to" (*BWL* 21). Oscar comes to life not because of what he does but because of the way he speaks, the voice he inhabits, made intensely present for us as Yunior listens, then reproduces him on the page. More generally, the novel triumphs through the kitchen-sink approach to language at which Oscar excels, with everything thrown in: geeky cultural references and urban slang; high literary asides and profane expletives; sentimental bromides and horrific revelations. Yunior's expressive mode (which is to say Oscar's, from whom Yunior has learned) is alternately vulgar and poignant, learned and crass, superficial, callous, and flip: a riot of accents and idioms, even a strange mix of languages themselves. Of course, for anyone not bilingual, Spanglish is a disorienting experience, though perhaps no more bewildering than the immigrant experience of being thrust into a new culture, forced to learn the ropes. As Díaz has remarked:

> You can't grow up in New Jersey without encountering thirteen languages when you walk out your door. Conventionally, books act as consolation; they're more or less transparent. Yet in life we don't understand ninety percent of what's going on. Unintelligibility underpins any speech act. The Victorian novel erases this unintelligibility. But we're accustomed to dealing with worlds that are unintelligible, untranslatable, in which half of what happens may not immediately, or even ever, make sense.
>
> Díaz interview

Mistaken as Díaz is about the Victorian novel, he does accurately identify unintelligibility as a default epistemological position, and recovers that experience for the reader as immigrant.

Moreover, unlike most hyphenate novelists since the turn of the nineteenth century, Díaz refuses to have his characters be assimilated, homogenized, or otherwise erased linguistically (refuses, that is, to allow their subjectivities to be erased by conceding to postmodernism's view of inauthenticity. Partly he achieves this simply via the raw amalgamation of languages in a single text, shifting amid discourses and accents, signaling how fully the past has been casually sanctioned and incorporated, brought into the present as a hybrid that reinvigorates English and makes the novel anew. Spanish is not quarantined off by italics, identified as distinct and foreign, but is instead simply, casually endorsed. Similarly, Yunior refuses to rein himself in by codes of acceptable speech, and the vulgarity of his style is itself part of the ticket of admission in the familiar use of "nigger" or "fuck" or the reference to various terms for female and male sexuality ("tetas," "culo"). That hyperbolically rude style engages us in grasping his (and Oscar's) desire for authenticity as Dominicans in a strangely mixed world of equal-opportunity alienation.

Yet while the novel dumpster-dives into the low reaches of language—the familiar expletives and offhand slurs and easy vulgarities—it also reaches high in allusions to a broad range of canonical texts. Again, these palimpsests of cultural reference and literary knowledge turn the novel inside out, re-establishing an inversion of cause and effect that links *The Brief Wondrous Life* to an entire tradition, if via a casual borrowing from postmodern pastiche and parody.[6] The most dramatic invocation occurs in the concluding words ("The beauty! The beauty!" (*BWL* 335)), meant as refutation of Conrad's closing to *The Heart of Darkness*: "The horror! The horror!" The title commandeers Hemingway, though Díaz interestingly raises the stakes from happiness to wonder. And even the play with Oscar's nickname confirms an insider's knowledge, as Hispanic accents misshape a random reference to Oscar Wilde into a new sobriquet: "Melvin said, Oscar Wao, quién es Oscar Wao, and that was it, all of us started calling him that: Hey, Wao, what you doing?" (*BWL* 180). The name not only echoes a Chinese genocidal dictator other than Trujillo but serves as an English-language homophone for sheer amazement. High and low registers, English and Spanish, are reshaped into a revived mix from the Dominican diaspora of "DoYos." And while Yunior tells the novel, it is Oscar's nerdiness, inventiveness, and omnivorous reading that shape Yunior. Skipping among linguistic registers, he enforces a continual challenge to ways of speaking, bringing a past alive by making it different from the voice of the present, juxtaposing one discursive category against another.

Of course, an obvious challenge to comprehension, particularly odd for a novel, occurs in the thirty-three footnotes casually sprinkling the text. After all, footnotes confirm by their very inclusion a question of boundaries, of what to insert and exclude, where to begin and end, and of how much information to provide. They also introduce an academic conceit, increasingly characteristic of postmodernist and late modernist novels where boundaries themselves are brought under scrutiny (Nabokov's *Pale Fire* (1962), Ishmael Reed's *Mumbo-Jumbo* (1972), Patrick Chamoiseau's *Texaco* (1992), David Foster Wallace's *Infinite Jest* (1996)), even if Melville and James Fenimore Cooper had anticipated the practice more than a century before.[7] Yet footnotes seem particularly appropriate for a novel pitched against the curse of *fukú americanus* and its threat to silence Dominican history, since any such threat of exclusion simply drops the statement to the bottom of the page. And if the diminished font of footnotes suggests how Dominican history is being attenuated, the footnotes themselves introduce an array of perspectives, of other knowledge and more formalized voices that can annotate and comment upon the unfolding story.

Of course, the question arises as to whether the author is thus patronizing readers by presuming to know what they do not.[8] Weaving together public facts with personal memories, known political histories with entirely imagined fictional lives, Díaz's footnotes tend to warn of a desire on the part of the reader for the kind of written control that Trujillo himself represented politically. In this, they reflect the novel's larger testing of the relation between authorship and authority, between a casual writerly "dictater" and a more formidable political dictator. Yunior happens to find this unexpected brotherhood between tyrants and novelists unremarkable, even though they might otherwise seem like natural antagonists—a brotherhood he admits to, appropriately enough, in a footnote: "Dictators, in my opinion, just know competition when they see it. Same with writers. *Like, after all, recognizes life*" (*BWL* 97). It is as if Yunior here recognized his utter control over our novelistic understanding as an authorial dictator of style, confirmed by Díaz's own admission that "readers are like Dominicans under Trujillo's dictatorship: they have a longing for authority, to offer a glimpse of the real. In Santo Domingo, we loved the simple narratives that Trujillo gave us" (Interview).[9] Footnotes tend to trap the reader much as the Dominican military trapped Beli and Abelard, asserting historical truths that homogenize history, locking us into simple explanations that function as curses, much as fukú does. Of course, Yunior's unusual footnotes consist of competing voices that playfully deny or compound or contort the very history they assert, having the effect of keeping us just as off-balance as we were before our eyes were diverted.

The variety of voices that extend all the way down into footnotes underscores more than simply the novel's concern with reviving a heterogeneous Dominican-American sensibility. That variety also defines possibilities for the late modernist novel itself, in its multiplication of representations of irreducible selfhood that are not coincidental with each other, and that thereby allow us to assume experience is plural, capable of being communicated to those who do not share it. Paradoxically, the conceit of *Fukú Americanus* returns as a curse of the New World that continues to destroy not only lives but the stories that create them, by binding generations together, offering a monologic explanation for all disasters. Yet if the opening prologue plunges us into the doom-laden story "that's got its fingers around" the narrator's throat (*BWL* 6), the book itself releases us to a view of lives as different as they are alike, as idiosyncratic as they are commonplace: unique zafas to undo the evidence of fukú they represent. Díaz plays repeatedly with a notion of personalities reduced to a single curse yet freed by accounts that establish their differences. Or as Lola realizes midway through: "if these years have taught me anything it is this: you can never run away. Not ever. The only way out is in. And that's what I guess these stories are all about" (*BWL* 209). The disorienting variety of stories told in the novel (as well as the disruptive voices that compound that variety) has the effect of undoing traditional notions of authority, especially in terms of a realist novel's claim to a single imperative.

Yunior inhabits others' voices, ventriloquizing them, inventing them, often so abruptly as to render assertions or questions somehow oblique, precluding our knowledge of who has made them. Consider the moment he asks "*How had the breakup affected Olga? What he really was asking was: How had the breakup affected Oscar?*" (*BWL* 16). The "he" here is surprisingly a self-reference to Yunior himself, making us realize that he is writing, trying to inhabit Oscar's perspective, even if up to now he has presented events he could not know. Not until five pages later will he refer to himself ("if like me" (*BWL* 21)) in the first-person, which seriously delays his emergence in the novel. That destabilizing of voice is compounded by the use of the second person, addressing the reader right off by declaiming our ignorance of Dominican history. The second chapter then follows by opening again with "you" (*BWL* 51), confusing the reader initially at who exactly is meant until Lola emerges. Part II continues the ploy, opening with an unidentified first-person voice that admits "I wouldn't feel that again until I broke with you" (*BWL* 205). Lola's intonations seem clear but it remains uncertain who is speaking or to whom, even as Yunior once again ventriloquizes her voice. It is another odd projection of Yunior's desire for Lola to desire him. Elsewhere, he needs conversely to distinguish himself from another: "as though (Oscar's words now) she were some marooned alien princess ... He was in love" (*BWL* 282). That need to disentangle his own words from "Oscar's words now" attests to how fully voices meld together, compounding the slippery nature of Yunior's mixed account.

Yet reliability is everywhere thwarted, with Yunior even occasionally refuting claims he otherwise forwards, offering distinctly alternative narratives ("He didn't meet her on the street like he told you" (*BWL* 289)), or advancing versions that seem to contradict his own ("Ybón, as Recorded By Oscar" (289)). Who, we wonder, is speaking accurately? And the novel's wonderfully stuttering conclusion sustains this uncertainty, in postponing Oscar's ability finally to speak in his own actual voice, not that of his designated spokesman. "The Final Letter," as the last section is subtitled, has Yunior admit that "He managed to send mail home before the end" (*BWL* 333), though for some inexplicable reason the letter itself is deferred. A series of indirect discursive claims ("He reported that ... He wrote that ... He wrote that ..." (*BWL* 334)) keep us one remove from direct speech itself, offering Yunior's transcribed interpretation, not Oscar's own words. Only at last are we switched into a direct quote, "He wrote: ..." (*BWL* 335), as if for all his intentions to let Oscar tell his own story Yunior could not quite give over the verbal reins. Indeed, the novel becomes as much a testament to Yunior's unnoticed flowering into a novelist as to Oscar's perilous history. And while his grudging accession to Oscar's voice is a tribute to his own achieved command of a pungent cross-mix of styles, even more remarkably Yunior has learned (in a way Oscar himself never realizes) how to incorporate others' voices and sensibilities, indeed to inhabit their consciousnesses as a way of understanding his own possibilities.

Yunior's recovery of Oscar's story has necessarily involved everyone else's as well, and imagining their feelings for each other (including prominently Lola's feelings for him) has led to the novel's receding structure, its turn from character to character, unexpectedly backing its way abruptly generation by generation into the past. The lesson seems to be that only another's experience can help contextualize one's own, and that those horrible things that happen to each individual need a proximate cause, a sympathetic echo. This helps explain why Yunior imagines the tormented experience of Oscar's grandfather, Abelard Cabral—a man passionately in love with his mistress, yet unlucky enough to be blessed with daughters lusted after by Trujillo. The account is as incredible, as brutal, as any that comes after, almost as if the further back one goes the worse it becomes. More importantly, we realize that Oscar and his forbearers" experiences contribute to Yunior's transformation into the writer Oscar would have been. And in this, the persistent ventriloquizing that Yunior has practiced in unfolding the de León saga has initiated his metamorphosis into a figure at once more mature and self-integrated.

III. Postmodern Inflections

Part of Yunior's achieved maturity has to do with his willingness to suspend an unquestioning belief in authority, not only others' but his own, as if the usual calm assumptions behind presumed novelistic authenticity needed to be challenged, even undermined. That destabilizing of the late modernist novel becomes itself transposed as a feature of psychological well-being, of caution and disinterested sympathy in the face of conflicting claims. Yet if Yunior's ability to skate among multiple surfaces becomes the sign of his gradual mastery of others and himself, that skill makes it no easier for the reader caught between his flamboyant fabrications and his avowals of historical authenticity. The shifting paratexts of the novel most obviously disorient us, in the vertiginous transpositions in Spanglish, vernacular lingo, fairy tale and anime invocations, classical references, and political rants.[10] Yet the underlying narrative is just as destabilizing, leaving us never quite sure of even the fictional status of events, unlike the narratives of so many modern novels, from Humbert Humbert's photographic memory of Lolita, to Ruth Stone's unimpeded imagining of her grandmother's life, to Nathan Zuckerman's sheer invention of Swede Levov's experience. In each of these earlier novels, we may wonder at the status of fictional representations but that status is rarely a cause for consternation.

Yunior, however, leaves the reader adrift in contradictory claims for characters and events, alternating back and forth between arrogance and ignorance, assurance and uncertainty, registering an instability that corresponds to his repeated impulse to start over again. The effect of this, strangely enough, is not to lessen our sense of authentic characters lurking beneath Yunior's descriptions but to strengthen our belief, if only in matching the very indeterminacy we feel encountering those in our daily lives. Consider how often he draws attention to researching his narrative: "information on the Gangster is fragmented; I'll give you what I've managed to unearth, and the rest will have to wait" (*BWL* 119). He seems to be authenticating his account, confirmed by a later admission to having recorded conversations: "I wish I could say different but I've got it right here on tape. La Inca told you you had to leave the country and you laughed. End of story" (*BWL* 160). And that admission is confirmed by his confession to having sneaked a view of Oscar's diary: "Was I really reading my roommate's journal behind his back? Of course I was" (*BWL* 185). The point is that Yunior is relying on evidence, on documents, on taped testimony from others, even though he sprinkles his account with admissions of not knowing obvious facts he should be aware of had Oscar actually talked with him or revealed his journal. Yunior salaciously asks, "but did they ever kiss in her car? Did he ever put his hands up her skirt? Did he ever ..." (*BWL* 40), as if ignorant of Oscar's experiences, even as he claims to know all. Is this merely a rhetorical gesture, of introducing doubt into a confident narrative? Later, he will ask the same question, phrased in the same way, though this time with an answer. Subtitling the section "What Never Changes," he admits: "Oh, they got close all right, but we have to ask the hard questions again: Did they ever kiss in her Pathfinder? Did he ever put his hands up her supershort skirt? . . . Did they ever fuck? Of course not. Miracles only go so far" (*BWL* 290). The exact repetition of phrasing, though offered up as support for a different interpretation, unsettles any reading and makes one wonder about the basis on which Yunior presents his narrative.

That doubt pervades the novel, and seems part of its allure, since Yunior regularly alludes to his own inability to ground information. This might be taken as an element of postmodern play, except instead of putting historical knowledge under suspicion, the admission simply enforces a late modernist sense of authenticity, of partial knowledge as ever the human condition. As Yunior admits, "How much Beli knew about the Gangster we will never know" (*BWL* 119). And yet he then asserts that "the Gangster adored our girl and that adoration was one of the greatest gifts anybody had ever given her" (*BWL* 127). Supposedly, if we accept Yunior's account, he introduces her to sexual knowledge we have no reason to believe he has ever confirmed. In fact, Beli seems to have achieved exactly what Oscar will later desire, even though we fail to question how Yunior could have learned this information, given Beli's silence about so much in her past. Likewise, the account of Beli being advised by the Gangster is unsettling, since Yunior seems to have inhabited her memory, even though Beli has been close-lipped with everyone:

> Of those nine years (and of the Burning) Beli did not speak. . . . It says a lot about Beli that for *forty years* she never leaked word one about that period of her life: not to her madre, not to her friends, not to her lovers, not to the Gangster, not to her husband. And certainly not to her beloved children, Lola and Oscar. *Forty years.* What little anyone knows about Beli's Azua days comes exclusively from what La Inca heard the day she rescued Beli from her so-called parents.
>
> *BWL* 258

All is silence, so Yunior declares, and yet he nonetheless is able to report on scenes and feelings otherwise admittedly lost to history.

At various points, however, to our consternation, Yunior confesses to making everything up. For a late modernist novel this might well seem a surprising claim, if only by introducing serious doubt about the characters we have met, and thereby raising suspicion about his other claims as well. Consider this problematizing footnote: "In my first draft, Samaná was actually Jarabacoa, but then my girl Leonie, resident expert in all things Domo, pointed out ... but that was one detail I couldn't change, just liked the image too much. Forgive me, historians ... forgive me!" (*BWL* 132). Given how much of a novel enforced by footnotes attests to its authenticity, both fictional and historical, it comes as an unsettling surprise to realize Yunior is admittedly inventing details, and that Oscar or Lola may be mere figments of his imagination. Later, in describing the Gangster's wife as supposedly "a pro herself in the time before the rise of her brother," Trujillo, Yunior suddenly interrupts himself to admit "shit, who can keep track of what's true and what's false in a country as baká as ours" (*BWL* 139). And later again he confesses: "But hey, it's only a story, with no solid evidence, the kind of shit only a nerd could love" (*BWL* 246). Nerd or not, the boundary between fantasy and fact keeps shifting, much like that which occurs between footnotes and the main text, or between English description and interjected Spanish expressions. It is as if Yunior were taunting us with a narrator's unearned tyrannical power, recalling a postmodern hallmark only to pull back (as Nabokov did) from the edge of sheer textual invention.

Yunior's shape-shifting relation to truth is akin to much else that proves so unstable about a novel that defies novelistic expectations. Yet even admitting regularly that little upholds his claims to authenticity, that he is inventing what he reports, he still falls back on a plea that "this is supposed to be a *true* account of the Brief Wondrous Life of Oscar Wao" (*BWL* 285).[11] The misgiving might seem an unusual confession to make, especially since he just introduced a "Note from Your Author" that acknowledges dubiety: "I know what Negroes are going to say. Look, he's writing Suburban Tropical now. A puta and she's not an underage snort-addicted mess? Not believable. Should I go down to the Feria and pick me up a more representative model?" (*BWL* 284). It's clear that Yunior is thoroughly aware of the slipperiness of his writing credentials, revealing his deceptiveness right at the beginning in referring to L. Frank Baum's *The Wonderful Wizard of Oz* (1900), when he offers "one final final note, Toto, before Kansas goes bye-bye" (*BWL* 7), reminding the reader of another fictional domain presided over by an all-powerful wizard. Again, the narrative role is undermined by its own gesture of control, of sweeping us into an account that doesn't quite hold together, or otherwise wrap things up. Yet as Díaz has speculated, "we all dream that there's an authoritative voice out there that will explain things, including ourselves" (Interview), even though Yunior reveals the fallacy of any such longing. Authorship and authority are both deeply troubled, with Yunior at once enforcing his narrative will over materials, but also acknowledging the unstable aspects of such authority. Still, only by enabling others' voices, in however unstable a mix, does he gain his own.

IV. Blank Pages

Narrative is regularly brought into question in *The Brief Wondrous Life*, through temporal regressions, the shift among voices, and the multiple paratexts that proliferate throughout. But further disabling Yunior's ability to find a thread linking past and present are the frequent lapses, oversights, and omissions that occur in his efforts to understand the de León family. At times, he is reduced to simply reading Oscar's journal to fill in events, but at other moments evidence simply disappears. Does Abelard Cabral actually make the joke about Trujillo that leads to so much fukú for his descendants or not? All we have are conflicting accounts. What of Beli's vanished years, from birth to age nine when she's sold to strangers? All we know is that "she was lost from sight for a long time" (*BWL* 253) and that "Beli never thought about that life again. Embraced the amnesia that was so common throughout the Islands, five parts denial, five parts negative hallucination" (*BWL* 259). It is as if her silence attenuates her past and thereby makes it possible for her to continue untrammeled, beginning anew in a perfectly American pattern. At other points in the novel, the present itself is killed off, sometimes literally, in a process that reminds us of the reason for Yunior's desperate endeavors elsewhere to authenticate lives. Abortions, for instance, seem to signal the death of story as well as of lives: of Lola who aborts a pregnancy because Yunior cheats on her; of Beli beaten so badly she loses her child; of Ybón's reported abortions. In each case, unlived lives alert us to the link between murder and repression, silence and loss, in a pattern willfully defied by the novel's regular turn backwards to the past, and in its celebration of an acoustic medley. Perhaps nothing evokes that tension so fully as the central event for the de León's, of Abelard's tragedy and ensuing curse, since no one wants to talk about it: "there is within the family a silence that stands monument to the generations, that sphinxes all attempts at narrative reconstruction. A whisper here and there but nothing more" (*BWL* 243). The very story Yunior wants to recount seems to dissolve as mist wherever he looks, again at once invoking a singular postmodern pattern even as it defies that pattern, confirming the authenticity of his efforts: "if you're looking for a full story, I don't have it. Oscar searched for it too, in his last days, and it's not certain whether he found it either" (*BWL* 243). Narrative, at least as we expect it, always seems to fail in the gaps and silences that defiantly resist comprehension, though that failure merely leads to further, sometimes contradictory, otherwise ingenious efforts to recover the past. And those efforts themselves confirm the late modernist claims for our inadequate knowledge, our insufficient understanding, that end up finally confirming the novel's testament to authenticity, in encouraging a belief in selves that always lie slightly beyond our capacity to understand, or to represent adequately in words.

Just as powerfully, political tyranny fails in the free moments that emerge despite repressive gestures, if only because dictatorial silencing seems to inspire spoken dictation, however variously. Yunior expresses this best in a footnote devoted to the political crook Joaquin Balaguer, who succeeded Trujillo and later "claimed he knew who had done the foul deed ... and left a blank page, a *página en blanco*, in the text to be filled in with the truth upon his death" (*BWL* 90). Tyranny may temporarily erase truth but it evokes a desire for its restoration, which helps explain the recurrence of another paratext, the *página en blancos* throughout the novel, as both quoted fact and actual blank pages that seem to require inscription (*BWL* 8, 10, 76, 166, 202, 262, 308, 314, 328, 332). Characters undergo trauma so horrendous that words seem inadequate, allowing their stories to disappear as they migrate north to New Jersey, with blank pages performing that disappearance for the present. Yet Yunior's persistence at recovering and inventing the past will lead to "the day the *páginas en blanco* finally speak" (*BWL* 119), when life—or at least the record of that life and its distinctive voice— will be restored. The blank page of narrative involves everything he thinks irrecoverable, as a paradoxically mute expression of history that in turn encourages belief in his account's authenticity, resting on the tension between event and recollection, narrative and phenomenological experience. Strangely, Yunior's very ignorance is invoked as validation of his account: "Even your Watcher has his silences, his *páginas en blanco*. Beyond the Source Wall few have ventured" (*BWL* 149).[12]

Part of the rationale for the dazzling pyrotechnics of Yunior's account is to highlight by contrast the absence of so many other distinctive voices, so many reliable memories and histories. And if blank pages help alert us to that absence, even more significant in *The Brief Wondrous Life* is the disappearance of books themselves—not simply words, or casual dialogues, or unwritten events, but full and elaborate publications. Consider occasions when books are invoked but never appear. Beli's father may have written a monograph about the Trujillo regime but no sign of it ever surfaces: "The Lost Final Book of Dr. Abelard Luis Cabral. I'm sure that this is nothing more than a figment of our Island's hypertrophied voodoo imagination. And nothing less" (*BWL* 246). As Yunior adds, concerning the fact that "none of Abelard's books" survived: "You want creepy? Not one single example of his handwriting remains" (*BWL* 246). Trujillo's thoroughness at expunging traces of what he most feared contrasts again with Yunior's flamboyant inventiveness, as if in response to Trujillo. In fact, Yunior's anxiety about absent books occurs in reconstructing Oscar's beating at the hands of the capitán's goons, when Oscar supposedly has a dream: "An old man was standing before him in a ruined bailey, holding up a book for him to read . . . but then he saw that the book was blank" (*BWL* 302). And that scary prospect is repeated in Yunior's own recurrent dream of Oscar:

> in some kind of ruined bailey that's filled to the rim with old dusty books . . . Dude is holding up a book . . . I want to run from him, and for a long time that's what I do. It takes me a while before I notice that Oscar's hands are seamless and the book's pages are blank.
>
> *BWL* 325

The eeriness of Yunior inhabiting Oscar's terrified consciousness in the face of blank books has brought them together, and leads to his own concerted effort to collect all Oscar's books in hopes his niece will fill the blank pages, "add her own insights and she'll put an end to it" (*BWL* 331). Filling the pages, as Yunior himself has been doing, is the only adequate conclusion to the ravages life has visited on Oscar.

Of all the absent books, the most significant is the conspicuous volume Yunior himself is unable to finish despite writing every day. And that sense of incompletion is matched by the failure of Oscar's concluding chapters to arrive at last, when he had promised that all would be explained. The story that supposedly will drive a stake through the heart of fukú, that will "put an end to it," is held out as possibility but never represented within the novel itself. Yunior knows the contents of the letter Oscar writes to Lola and even reads chapters from Oscar's continuing account, including descriptions of his final experiences with Ybón. But the concluding summation that Oscar has promised will explain away all Yunior's questions is lost in the mail: "the fucking thing never arrived!" (*BWL* 334). All that is left is the hope for "Lola's miraculous daughter" Isis (*BWL* 330), the supposedly perfect reader, who will gather up the fragments into a coherent and understandable whole.

V. Centrifugal Narrative

The Brief Wondrous Life of Oscar Wao defies the promise of a coherent reading, as if coherence itself represented a misconceived goal, achieved only as an imperializing cultural gesture, one intended to confirm being assimilated and comfortably understood. Yet the ongoing diasporic experience of cultural disequilibrium is expressed in the novel's own polyphonic excess, its continuing disruptions that confirm the lack of resolution felt by immigrants now for decades. And that formal achievement occurs in Díaz's rejection of familiar novelistic conventions, seizing from postmodernism those disorienting aesthetic constructions intended to estrange us from characters, and reshaping them to create a sense of personal authenticity. Voices compete, fragmenting even their own expression, while marginal events and random assertions attest to how fully the center fails to hold, even as paratexts displace that center. The late modernist lesson discovered by Diáz through writing the novel is that centrifugal forces of narrative revise narrative borders themselves. Many of the novel's innovations have already been discussed, including its temporal regressions, its melding of voices, its multiple paratextual references ranging from footnotes to classical and popular allusions. Yet Genette has observed other available possibilities, and to give some sense for Diáz's exhaustive use of even odd textual diversions, consider the appearance of actual illustrations, starting with the mysterious feathered head on the book's cover. More significantly, the title page is decorated with an image of "Fat Man," the atomic bomb detonated over Nagasaki in 1945. The first of the novel's three sections offers a simple illustration of a hydrogen atom with circling electrons (*BWL* 9), followed in Part II by a line drawing of a clenched fist raised in political opposition (203); Part III delineates a more cryptic image of anchors locked within a wheel-like structure, each equidistant (309). The combination of these uncanny images remains baffling, unremarked and seemingly irrelevant to the plot, even as they inflect the novel's presentation, begging the attentive reader to register these iconic innuendos. One explanation links the images to Oscar's favorite anime film, Katsuhiro Otomo's *Akira* (1988), which is filled with apocalyptic events defining an aesthetics of violence. Thus, the laceration on Beli's back is directly invoked as "a world-scar like those of a hibakusha" (*BWL* 257), or as David Ting has written: "through this Japanese word, Beli is transformed into a post-atomic survivor. . . . Beli becomes more than a girl from Santo Domingo; in Díaz's international, historical comparisons, Beli becomes a survivor of the trauma that the world has inflicted on its citizens through violence in history." And the inscribed imagery introducing each of the book's sections silently reinforces this internationalizing gesture.

Given the cryptic nature of illustrations sprinkling the novel, perhaps there is little need to discover a rationale for its footnotes. Why are some Spanish words glossed while most are not (see fn 5, *BWL* 19)? And what justifies the commentaries of history as if in defiance of narrative requirement ("Although not essential to our tale, per se, Balaguer is essential to the Dominican one, so therefore we must mention him, even though I'd rather piss in his face" (fn 9, *BWL* 90))? Yunior acknowledges the irrelevancy of the information, which like so many other paratexts in the novel disrupts yet creates its meaning. If we never quite learn how to weave paratexts seamlessly into an overall reading, or otherwise to decipher the dislocations, marginalizations, interruptions, silences and absences, all we can do is presume and invent, encouraged by other major omissions throughout. What, for instance, do we make of actual blanks inserted for words, as in: "_____ _____ _____, said the Mongoose, and then the wind swept him back into darkness" (*BWL* 301)? Oscar is dreaming that a "mongoose was the Mongoose," as he repeats the words "less" and "more" until the Mongoose itself reiterates the sequence—though whether this is more or less is never resolved, nor is it clear what Oscar means. Strangely, moreover, at this inexplicable moment in which words fail, the three blanks seem to match Yunior's own later unspoken words that "could have saved us," him and Lola (*BWL* 327). The undisclosed words seem to be "I love you," an avowal Yunior is incapable of expressing, though again no other assurance confirms this.

The triumph of *The Brief Life of Oscar Wao* lies in its studied lack of transparency, its turbulent shifting among a series of palimpsests and narrative misdirections, among half-heard voices and misremembered memories, as readers ride the roller-coaster narrative through its neck-wrenching turns and breathtaking drops. Díaz claims he wrote *The Brief Wondrous Life* not to confirm readerly assumptions but to undermine them in the very process of pulling the disparate, peripheral parts of the novel together into a whole, however unstable and partial. And much as his ostensible subject concerns the experience of Do-Yos adrift in America, his larger goal is to rewrite the late modernist novel.[13] He too, like other major artists, wants to find newly authentic ways of giving voice to those who have been silenced, without simply replacing them with "dictaters" who tyrannically silence others in turn. In this characteristically local account, Díaz turns away from the authority of the author, whom he admits is always a tyrant, in order to return control to the reader, ever disoriented but capable of finding his way. The multiple misdirections throughout disrupt an authoritative authorial voice, revealing how fully formal issues in the novel that so often seem casual or unrelated, turning things inside out, are nonetheless the central instrument of meaning. Questions that emerge from accounts of cultural repression become formal and modernist issues: of belatedness, of ventriloquism, of serial paratexts.[14] And in its quick-silver shifts from any commanding narrative posture, the novel makes the paratextual diversions themselves part of the machinery of literary freedom.[15] If identity is revealed afresh as disrupted and destabilized for Dominican-Americans, the novel reveals more commandingly how readers everywhere live at least occasionally in states of half-knowledge, confused languages, unstable heritages, scarifying personal histories, where otherwise marginal considerations loom surprisingly large. Díaz resembles other late modernists in his iconoclastic approach to the novel, attempting to find new ways to tell familiar stories about people (in his case) deprived of a voice, and eager to grant a full sense of selfhood to those he describes. The fact that he configures character as a function of multiple intersections succeeds in releasing the reader from a more or less prescribed interpretation. And in that release, we enter into Yunior's revival of his friend Oscar, but even more into a renewed understanding of the tumultuous possibilities of narrative itself.

Notes

1   See Paul Jay, Ashley Kunsa. For an example of a more extreme such reading, see Elena Sáez: "Díaz's novel is a foundational fiction for the Dominican diaspora, an attempt to reconcile exile with belonging, diaspora with nation, marginal with mainstream. Despite '[t]he beauty' of sex that Oscar finally experiences (335), the novel's ending cannot reconcile Oscar's inauthenticity with the nation's definition of masculinity. Rather, the narrative emphasizes the structures of feeling that organize the reading experience and how much power the dictating voice and its values hold over our understanding of Truth and History" (544–45).

2   Among other late modernists, Don DeLillo, Dave Eggars, Jonathan Safran Foer, Jonathan Franzen, David Mitchell, Philip Roth, David Foster Wallace, even Art Spiegelman, have each triumphed through one or more of these disruptive strategies. For a useful recent account, see Wolfgang Funk.

3   Brian Richardson has observed that the second person is "an extremely protean form.... The 'you' ... threatens the ontological stability of the fictional world, insofar as it necessarily addresses the reader as well as the

central character. . . . This 'you' is inherently unstable, constantly threatening
  to merge with another character, with the reader, or even with another
  grammatical person" (311–12). On second-person narration, see as well
  DelConte.

4 Richard Patteson assumes that Lola tells her own section, as opposed to
  being ventriloquized (12).

5 For a shrewd assessment of the tension in late modernism between realist
  mimetic practice and postmodern play, see Irmtraud Huber (22–28).

6 Describing the Gangster's wife, Yunior observes that "if this was Dickens
  she'd have to run a brothel—but wait, she *did* run brothels!" (*BWL* 139).
  Earlier, in Lola's "Summer of Her Secondary Sex Characteristics," he slyly
  invokes Yeats's "Easter, 1916": "*a terrible beauty has been born*" (*BWL* 91).
  And *Moby-Dick* appears when "Beli returned to El Redentor from summer
  break to the alarm of faculty and students alike and set out to track down
  Jack Pujols with the great deliberation of Ahab after you-know-who. (And
  of all these things the albino boy was the symbol. Wonder ye then at the
  fiery hunt?)" (*BWL* 95). Earlier, Lola goes to Santo Domingo where she sees
  La Inca: "She stood like she was her own best thing" (*BWL* 74)—a clear
  reference to Sixo's claim in Toni Morrison's *Beloved*. Even Nabokov seems
  ever-present, in Lola's name itself (Dolores), but also in the plangent
  rhythms of Yunior's 1st-person voice.

7 Notably, Cooper himself adds footnotes abundantly throughout his
  Leatherstocking Tales, though evidence suggests he did so partly out of
  anxiety about convincing readers of the authenticity of his fictional claims.
  Catalina Rivera has observed (notably in a footnote): "In interviews, Junot
  Díaz has referenced *Texaco: A Novel*, by Patrick Chamoiseau as the
  inspiration for his intimate footnotes. Readers of Manuel Puig's *Kiss of the
  Spider Woman* (first published in Argentina in 1976) will also recognize the
  utilization of footnotes in a parallel endeavor to express the trauma of a
  story that resists traditional narrative forms" (6).

8 Díaz has claimed: "The footnotes are there for a number of reasons;
  primarily, to create a double narrative. The footnotes, which are in the lower
  frequencies, challenge the main text, which is the higher narrative. The
  footnotes are like the voice of the jester, contesting the proclamations of the
  king. In a book that's all about the dangers of dictatorship, the dangers of
  the single voice—this felt like a smart move to me" (O'Rourke 2).

9 Díaz elsewhere observed: "We all dream dreams of unity, of purity; we all
  dream that there's an authoritative voice out there that will explain things,
  including ourselves. If it wasn't for our longing for these things, I doubt the
  novel or the short story would exist in its current form. I'm not going to say
  much more on the topic. Just remember: In dictatorships, only one person
  is really allowed to speak. And when I write a book or a story, I too am
  the only one speaking, no matter how I hide behind my characters"
  (O'Rourke 2).

10 For the best account of science fiction references in the novel, see Blanco.

11 Richard Patteson notes this (10). As he points out, Yunior somehow knows of Beli's dream (*BWL* 261), though she never speaks of the nine horribly abusive years with her foster family (11). And Patteson acknowledges where Yunior admits to wanting to make things up (*BWL* 160), or where he admits to Lola withholding the truth (312).

12 Sean O'Brien has observed: "It is interesting that while the earlier *páginas en blanco* are more historical and political (Columbus's name, Balaguer's politically volatile knowledge, Abelard's moment of political damnation and missing political book), the more numerous erasures toward the end of the book are increasingly focused on the personal, dealing with relationships and personal emotions and decisions. The last erasure—Oscar's missing package that promises to explain everything—presents an intriguing question, then: just what is everything Oscar thinks we would need to understand his story?" (81–82).

13 Confronted by those confused by his novel, Díaz has claimed that "I'm especially interested in the participation of the reader (which doesn't occur in Russian novels). The kind of role-playing games Yunior loves (*Dungeons and Dragons*) require participation, and the novel is meant to replicate that feeling. One of the conceits, I love about *Oscar Wao* is the missing books in the novel. The first of these is the one Oscar mailed home, explaining so much, which is sent by Caribbean mail (an in-joke is the horrible state of mail service there). The second is the one his grandfather wrote; the third is the one Yunior cannot finish; and the fourth occurs in the final pages, in Yunior's dream. I feel that my main idea is the book itself isn't done until the reader puts it together" (Interview). Díaz added that his novel raises many questions akin to *baká*: Why is Yunior writing? Who is the man without a face? How does Isis fit into the plot? What is the mongoose? "When the reader answers these questions, he completes the novel, much like Isis putting Osiris back together from his broken fragments (Interview).

    Richard Patteson has also observed: "The dialectic of *narrative, erasure,* and counter-narrative informs *Oscar Wao* on the novel's deepest levels" (14). As he states: "*Oscar Wao* ultimately asks how the Other be encountered without resorting to assimilation—the denial of otherness altogether—or annihilation" (18).

14 Sean O'Brien has claimed: "Readers of *Oscar Wao*, in being forced to decide so frequently what knowledge they will marginalize through the decisions they make about researching or simplifying each intertextual reference, are encouraged to consider to what degree their choices reflect or differ from those that have led to the kinds of personal and political situations depicted in the novel" (89).

15 Richard Patteson argues that "Diaz, following the practice of many writers who discuss their books publicly ... attempt[s] to shape how the novel is read. He insists that 'Yunior's telling of this story and his unspoken motivations for it are at the heart of the novel' ... but it might also be said

that the interviews, and Díaz's unspoken motivations for them, are equally central. An author's compulsion to control does not necessarily end with publication. Like his narrator Yunior (and perhaps like all narrators), Díaz is torn between the competing needs to challenge authority and to exercise it. *The Brief Wondrous Life of Oscar Wao* attempts to acknowledge and incorporate this internal struggle; it incorporates the struggle's most paradoxical feature, the notion that the act of telling is itself an exercise of power, into the deepest design of the novel" (5).

EPILOGUE: RESISTING RULES

What one seems to want in art, in experiencing it, is the same thing
that is necessary for its creation, a self-forgetful, perfectly useless
concentration.

—Elizabeth Bishop (*EB* 288)

I do not know how other teachers deal with this extravagant
personal force of modern literature . . . but when the teacher has
said all that can be said about formal matters, about verse-patterns,
metrics, prose conventions, irony, tension, etc., he must confront the
necessity of bearing personal testimony.

—Lionel Trilling, *Teaching* (8)

Speed-reading was a woeful detour in my book-worming life, though it
happily left little positive imprint. Given how unsatisfactory the practice
proved from the beginning, no surprise should occur at how rapid my
flight was to the alternative, or how many remarkable moments ensued
over the course of a teaching career that repeatedly put paid to Evelyn
Woods's predictive strategy and in the process revealed engaging
dilemmas in sometimes the simplest texts. A large part of my pedagogical
strategy has been a response to that early experience, as I've simply
asked students in a variety of courses how they may have been stumped
or stymied or slowed by their reading. Time and again, the obscurity of
narrative tangles and descriptive snarls, which were occasions Evelyn
Woods strove to avoid, has proved my favorite entry into texts. And I
long ago discovered that such difficulties had little to do with style,
whether laundry lists, news reports, or self-proclaimed "literary" texts.
Difficulties emerged as often with writers like Melville or Twain or
Hemingway, who otherwise seem transparent, as they did with James
and Faulkner, whose syntactical strategies patently test readers.
Moreover, close readings led us to see how often we bring a set of
assumptions and projections to the words we read, words that just as

frequently do not endorse interpretive biases and sometimes contradict them.

An especially effective exercise involved having students think of single words transformed by repetition in different contexts through the course of a novel, reading it as if it were almost a poem. Asking them to make their own choice of a word, then to interpret its metamorphoses, they often came to class with revelatory posts of such examples as "key" or "candid" in *The Portrait of a Lady*, or "shadow" in *The Sound and the Fury*, or "remembering" in *Beloved* and "relics" in *Housekeeping*. The exercise has been made easier, moreover, in a digital age when texts are available online for word searches that quickly reveal their reappearance in passages one had overlooked. But this is only one way of attending closely to a literary text, and hardly the most exhaustive. There is, as the previous chapters have clarified, no single method to close reading nor any system other than sheer alertness to strange patterns.

And what are the benefits of this kind of attentiveness? Often as the question is asked, the answer lies not in any particular skill set or pre-professional training but in coming to appreciate verbal patterns more keenly, realizing the way in which words do not always mean what they first seem to, or otherwise contain disturbing ambiguities, or come together in sequences that at once defy and tantalize. In fact, close reading might best be understood as not only the very opposite of Woods's speed reading, or Franco Moretti's recent "distance reading," but more like a return to our earliest encounter with words on a page. As any parent knows, one secret reason for having children is the chance it gives to reread classic children's texts without apology—indeed, to share in those mysterious moments when the pronunciation of words from a bedtime picture book, the inky verbal scroll on a page, the colorful image accompanying it, all come together in the glow of a child's eyes as comprehension first occurs, then reoccurs in a steadily building drumbeat of delight. The magic of Margaret Wise Brown's *Goodnight Moon* (1947) or Maurice Sendak's *Where the Wild Things Are* (1963) lies in their ability to evoke wonder in four-year-olds finding their way into words, whether towards sleep or safety. And the teetering, unstable sense of those words registers the wavering sense of comprehension that slowly settles into an assurance about squiggly configurations that come to seem transparent, finally understood, now all too familiar. Yet close reading reawakens in us that earliest experience of wonder and instability, at least as we confront the singular quality of literary texts that makes them literary, by contrast with the normal round of customary discursive prose.

As well, paradoxically, close reading awakens us to the flat tones of so much discursive prose, not only in the way it too can work but just as often fails to, in unearned conclusions and half-baked judgments built on assertions that fall short of what they claim. For if the appeal of literature is to resonances we otherwise do not appreciate immediately, the value of close reading is to equip us as well to detect the failure of language in ill-supported claims and verbal sleights of hand. We become more practiced at spotting political grand-standing and mere propaganda for what they are, or pinpointing advertising slogans and sham assertions for what they are not. George Orwell announced that "the slovenliness of our language makes it easier for us to have foolish thoughts," but he also added: "The point is that the process is reversible." And close reading becomes the best means for reversing such slovenly habits. After all, to read Hemingway's "Up in Michigan" attentively is to realize that such situations—and as importantly, their representation—are less obvious than appearances might suggest, all as part of a larger process that alerts us to easy conformity and over-eager compliance.

The preceding chapters are intended to answer nothing more than the imperative to read literature attentively, tentatively, questioningly. They are certainly not meant as exhaustive or definitive; on the contrary, the very sequence of a mere handful of novels, with little connection to one another, written over eighty years, tells us only how arbitrary any such selection must always be. But the overall engagement should be exemplary of two major insights, the first of which is simply to register the multifarious ways in which fiction remakes itself anew. That should offer consolation for those concerned that the novel has written itself out. The inventiveness of American authors keeps surprising us as readers, in the way they themselves read earlier literature carefully, attending and reshaping ideas, images, narrative possibilities. The second insight accompanies those revelations available to listening closely to prose, reading it as slowly as one might read poetry, finding in the process how variously the "literary" defines itself. Neither insight is meant to imply a coherent "survey" of late modernist fiction, if only because so many other choices might have been included, and as well because as many possibilities exist for reading closely as there are texts to be read. The very absence of rules that might accompany close reading suggests that all one can rely upon is a certain ad hoc tentativeness of selection and judgment, both.[1]

Admittedly, this approach assumes an old-fashioned common reader, independent of gender or race, ethnicity or class, or any of the other distinguishing features of identity. Yet precisely what we separately share as readers (independent of such constitutive constraints) is what makes the literary at once so disarming and compelling, surprising us out of comfort zones and habitual notions of behavior, and fostering instead the beginnings of a decentered, destabilized consciousness. That also helps explain how different each of the readings above may appear, in deliberately not having been grouped according to a common theme or motif or pattern, or anything other than the literary merit that the chapters themselves are intended to demonstrate. All they share is a status as modernist and late modernist novels, with even their American status virtually ignored. What warrants attention is simply language that resists paraphrase or translation into another form, despite the need for interpretations that nonetheless do insist upon our interpretive conversions. That is the heart of close reading, forming part of the paradox of this book: of encouraging attention ever more closely and slowly to texts we consider literary, written by novelists who relentlessly test us with strategies meant to defy our readings, in sequences formally idiosyncratic, unexpected, perverse, new. But then, that paradox is what we always expect from literary performance. The alternative is simply generic and derivative, tired examples that fail to astonish or imbue us with a sense of wonder.

It is not enough, however, to end with formal considerations, since much as the aesthetic dislocates us, its only worthy effect is in nudging us into reconsidering habits of projection, into becoming more nuanced, more attentive, more open to possibilities than our judgments and settled values initially permit. The "lesson" that such reading provides is to transform us ethically, willing to reconsider the very expectations with which we began. We are born anew at those moments, in the momentary absence of strict rules for either reading or for life, awake to everything other than our own sensibility. At moments when slippery words entice us by being just beyond our grasp, we feel their "perversity" as well as their "seductiveness." They fiercely resist our efforts and yet subtly draw us back, luring us into seizing sense in their sounds, contested meanings in their stubborn arrangements, and in the process unmake us as we strive to understand.

Note

1   "There is a small but immitigable fallacy in the theory of close reading," Louis Menand has claimed; "The text doesn't reveal its secrets just by being stared at. It reveals its secrets to those who already pretty much know what secrets they expect to find. Texts are always packed, by the reader's prior knowledge and expectations, before they are unpacked. The teacher has

already inserted into the hat the rabbit whose production in the classroom awes the undergraduates" (72). Yet the surprise of literature is available as much to the teacher as the student, since classrooms are (or should be) settings where readings are contested, knowledge is unsettled, and words come undone. Occasionally, rabbits can be pulled out of hats, which is what makes teachers tenurable. But what keeps them going year after year is less job security than the promise that rabbits will appear mysteriously from "unpacked" hats.

BIBLIOGRAPHY

Adorno, Theodor. *Aesthetic Theory*. Trans. Robert Hullot-Kentor. Minneapolis, MN: University of Minnesota Press, 1997.

Alexandrov, Vladimir E. *Nabokov's Otherworld*. Princeton, NJ: Princeton University Press, 1991.

Altieri, Charles. 'Taking Lyrics Literally: Teaching Poetry in a Prose Culture.' *New Literary History* 32.2 (Spring 2001): 259–81.

Anders, John P. *Willa Cather's Sexual Aesthetics and the Male Homosexual Literary Tradition*. Lincoln, NE: University of Nebraska Press, 1999.

Arendt, Hannah. *Eichmann in Jerusalem: A Report on the Banality of Evil* (1960). Rev. edn. New York: Viking Press, 1964.

Aristotle. *The Complete Works of Aristotle*. Revised Oxford Translation. Vol. 2. Ed. Jonathan Barnes. Princeton, NJ: Princeton University Press, 1984.

Auden, W. H. *The Dyer's Hand and Other Essays* (1962). New York: Vintage Books, 1968.

Auerbach, Erich. *Mimesis: The Representation of Reality in Western Literature*. Trans. Willard Trask. Princeton, NJ: Princeton University Press, 1953.

Bal, Mieke. 'Over-writing as Un-writing: Descriptions, World-Making, and Novelistic Time.' In *The Novel*. Vol 2, 'Forms and Themes,' edited by Franco Moretti, 571–610. Princeton NJ: Princeton University Press, 2006.

Barthes, Roland. *The Pleasure of the Text*. Trans. Richard Miller (1973). New York: Hill and Wang, 1975.

Barthes, Roland. 'The Reality Effect.' In *The Rustle of Language*, trans. Richard Howard, 141–48. Berkeley, CA: University of California Press, 1986.

Beckett, Samuel. *Waiting for Godot* (1952). New York: Grove Press, 1954.

Bell, Michael. '*Lolita* and Pure Art.' *Essays in Criticism* 24 (April 1974): 169–84.

Bell, Vereen M. *The Achievement of Cormac McCarthy*. Baton Rouge, LA: Louisiana State University Press, 1988.

Benjamin, Walter. 'The Storyteller: Reflections on the Works of Nikolai Leskov.' In *Illuminations,* edited by Hannah Arendt, trans. Harry Zohn, 83–109. New York: Schocken Books, 1969.

Bennett, William (ed.). *The Book of Virtues: A Treasury of Great Moral Stories*. New York: Simon & Schuster, 1993.

Bergon, Frank. *Stephen Crane's Artistry.* New York: Columbia University Press, 1975.

Berlin, Isaiah. 'Two Concepts of Liberty' (1958). In *Liberty*, edited by Henry Hardy, 166–217. New York: Oxford University Press, 2002.

Best, Stephen and Sharon Marcus. 'Surface Reading: An Introduction.' *Representations* 108 (Fall 2009): 1–22.

Birkerts, Sven. *The Gutenberg Elegies: The Fate of Reading in an Electronic Age*. Boston, MA: Faber & Faber, 1994.

Bishop, Elizabeth. 'The Darwin Letter.' In *Elizabeth Bishop and Her Art*, ed. Lloyd Schwartz and Sybil P. Estess, 288. Ann Arbor: University of Michigan Press, 1983.

Blanco, Maria del Pilar. 'Reading the Novum World: The Literary Geography of Science Fiction in Junot Díaz's *The Brief Wondrous Life of Oscar Wao*.' In *Surveying the American Tropics: A Literary Geography from New York to Rio*, edited by Maria Cristina Fumagalli, Peter Hulme, Owen Robinson, and Leslie Wylie, 49–74. Liverpool: Liverpool University Press, 2013.

Bloom, Harold. *The Anxiety of Influence: A Theory of Poetry*. New York: Oxford University Press, 1973.

Bonheim, Helmut. 'Narration in the Second Person.' *Recherches anglais et américaines* 16 (1983): 69–80.

Boyd, Brian. *Vladimir Nabokov: The American Years*. Princeton, NJ: Princeton University Press, 1991.

Brailis, Matthew. Blackboard post for Princeton University course ENG363, December 10, 2012.

Brooks, Cleanth. *The Well Wrought Urn: Studies in the Structure of Poetry*. New York: Harcourt, Brace & World, 1947.

Brooks, Peter. *Reading for the Plot: Design and Intention in Narrative*. New York: Alfred A. Knopf, 1984.

Brower, Reuben A. 'Introduction' and 'Reading in Slow Motion' (1959). In *In Defense of Reading: A Reader's Approach to Literary Criticism*, edited by Reuben A. Brower and Richard Poirier, vii–x, 3–21. New York: E. P. Dutton, 1962.

Burke, William H. 'Border Crossings in Marilynne Robinson's *Housekeeping*.' *Modern Fiction Studies* 37 (1991): 716–24.

Butler, Sally. Blackboard post for Princeton University course ENG363, December 10, 2012.

Cant, John. *Cormac McCarthy and the Myth of American Exceptionalism*. New York: Routledge, 2008.

Carlin, Deborah. *Cather, Canon, and the Politics of Reading*. Amherst, MA: University of Massachusetts Press, 1992.

Carr, Nicholas. *The Shallows: What the Internet is Doing to Our Brains*. New York: W. W. Norton, 2010.

Cather, Willa. *On Writing: Critical Studies on Writing as an Art*. Lincoln, NE: University of Nebraska Press, 1976.

Cather, Willa. *Willa Cather in Person: Interviews, Speeches, and Letters*. Ed. L. Brent Bohlke. Lincoln, NE: University of Nebraska Press, 1986.

Cather, Willa. *The Professor's House*. New York: Vintage Classic, 1990.

Caver, Christine. 'Nothing Left to Lose: *Housekeeping*'s Strange Freedoms.' *American Literature* 68:1 (1996): 111–37.

Chabon, Michael. 'Dark Adventure: On Cormac McCarthy's *The Road*.' In *Maps and Legends: Reading and Writing along the Borderlands*, 107–20. San Francisco, CA: McSweeney's, 2008.

Champagne, Rosaria. 'Women's History and *Housekeeping*: Memory, Representation and Reinscription.' *Women's Studies* 20 (1992): 321–29.

Clifton, Gladys M. 'Humbert Humbert and the Limits of Artistic License.' In *Nabokov's Fifth Arc: Nabokov and Others on his Life's Work*, edited by J. E. Rivers and Charles Nicol, 153–70. Austin, TX: University of Texas Press, 1982.

Conrad, Joseph. *The Nigger of the 'Narcissus': A Tale of the Forecastle* (1897). Available at: http://www.gutenberg.org/files/17731/17731-h/17731-h.htm. Retrieved August 23, 2015.

Cooper, James Fenimore. *The Leatherstocking Tales: Volume I*. New York: Library of America, 1985.

Cooper, Lydia R. 'Cormac McCarthy's *The Road* as Apocalyptic Grail Narrative.' *Studies in the Novel* 43.2 (2011): 218–36.

Cooper, Lydia R. *No More Heroes: Narrative Perspective and Morality in Cormac McCarthy*. Baton Rouge, LA: Louisiana State University Press, 2011.

Crafts, Leland W., Théodore C. Schneirla, and Elsa E. Robinson. *Recent Experiments in Psychology*. 2nd edn. New York: McGraw Hill, 1950.

Crane, Stephen. *Great Short Works of Stephen Crane*. New York: Harper & Row, 1968.

Culler, Jonathan. *The Literary in Theory*. Palo Alto, CA: Stanford University Press, 2007.

Culler, Jonathan. 'The Closeness of Close Reading.' *ADE Bulletin* 149 (2010): 20–25.

Cunningham, J. V. 'Wonder.' In *Collected Essays*, 53–96. Chicago, IL: Swallow Press, 1976.

Dale, Alan. 'In the Shadow of the Tire Iron.' In *The Brokeback Book: From Story to Cultural Phenomenon*, edited by William R. Handley, 163–78. Lincoln, NE: University of Nebraska Press, 2011.

Damrosch, David. 'Auerbach in Exile.' *Comparative Literature* 47:2 (1995): 97–117.

de Man, Paul. 'The Return to Philology' (1982). In *The Resistance to Theory*, 21–26. Minneapolis, MN: University of Minnesota Press, 1986.

DelConte, Matt. 'Why *You* Can't Speak: Second-Person Narration, Voice, and a New Model for Understanding Narrative.' *Style* 37:2 (2003): 204–19.

Devereux, Cecily. '"A Kind of Dual Attentiveness": Close Reading after the New Criticism.' In *Rereading the New Criticism*, edited by Miranda B. Hickman and John D. McIntyre, 218–30. Columbus, OH: Ohio State University Press, 2012.

Díaz, Junot. 'Fiction Is the Poor Man's Cinema: An Interview with Junot Díaz.' Conducted by Diogenes Céspedes and Silvio Torres-Saillant. *Callaloo: A Journal of African-American and African Arts and Letters* 23.3 (2000): 892–70

Díaz, Junot. *The Brief Wondrous Life of Oscar Wao*. New York: Riverhead Books, 2007.

Díaz, Junot. Interview with Emily Raboteau. Princeton University, Princeton NJ, April 9, 2008. Transcribed by the author.

Díaz, Junot. 'Questions for Junot Díaz.' Interview conducted by Meghan O'Rourke. *Slate* Nov 2007. Available at: http://www.slate.com/articles/ news_and_politics/the_highbrow/2007/11/the_brief_wondrous_life_of_ oscar_wao.html. Retrieved April 8, 2008.

Díaz, Junot. 'Junot Díaz, Diaspora, and Redemption: Creating Progressive Imaginaries.' Interview conducted by Katherine Miranda. *Sargasso* II (2008–09): 23–40

Dimock, Wai Chee. *Residues of Justice: Literature, Law, Philosophy*. Berkeley, CA: University of California Press, 1996.

Donoghue, Denis. 'Teaching *Blood Meridian*.' In *The Practice of Reading*, 258–77. New Haven, CT: Yale University Press, 1998.

Donoghue, Denis. 'Teaching Literature: The Force of Form,' *New Literary History*, 30.1 (1999): 5–24.

Douglas, Mary. *Purity and Danger: An Analysis of the Concepts of Pollution and Taboo*. London: Ark, 1985.

Dreiser, Theodore. *Sister Carrie* (1900). Ed. Lee Clark Mitchell. New York: Oxford University Press, 1991.

DuBois, Andrew. 'Close Reading: An Introduction.' In *Close Reading: The Reader*, edited by Frank Lentricchia and Andrew DuBois, 1–40. Durham, NC: Duke University Press, 2003.

Eggers, Dave. *A Heart-Breaking Work of Staggering Genius*. New York: Simon and Schuster, 2000.

Ellis, Jay. *No Place for Home: Spatial Constraint and Character Flight in the Novels of Cormac McCarthy*. New York: Routledge, 2006.

Emerson, Ralph Waldo. *Essays: First and Second Series*. New York: Library of America, 1990.

Emerson, Ralph Waldo. *Essays and Lectures.* New York: Library of America, 1983.

Faulkner, William. *As I Lay Dying* (1930), The Corrected Text, New York: Vintage, 1990.

Faulkner, William. *Absalom, Absalom!* (1936). New York: Vintage, 1990.

Faulkner, William. *Light in August: The Corrected Text*. New York: Vintage Books, 1990.

Faulkner, William. Interviews by Jean Stein, 'The Art of Fiction No. 12.' *The Paris Review* 12 (Spring 1956): n.p. Available at: http://www.theparisreview. org/interviews/4954/the-art-of-fiction-no-12-william-faulkner. Retrieved August 16, 2015.

Fay, Sarah. Interview with Marilynne Robinson. *Paris Review* 186 (Fall 2008): 37–66. Available at: http://www.theparisreview.org/interviews/5863/ the-art-of-fiction-no-198-marilynne-robinson. Retrieved August 23, 2015.

Fish, Stanley. *Professional Correctness: Literary Studies and Political Change*. Oxford: Clarendon Press, 1995.

Fitzgerald, F. Scott. *The Great Gatsby*, edited by Matthew Bruccoli. New York: Scribner's, 1995.

Forster, E. M. *Aspects of the Novel*. New York: Harcourt Brace, 1927.

Foster, Thomas. 'History, Critical Theory, and Women's Social Practices: "Women's Time" and *Housekeeping*.' *Signs* 14.1 (1988): 73–99.

Friedan, Betty. *The Feminine Mystique*. New York: Norton, 1963.

Frye, Steven. *Understanding Cormac McCarthy*. Columbia, SC: University of South Carolina Press, 2009.

Funk, Wolfgang. *The Literature of Reconstruction: Authentic Fiction in the New Millenium*. London: Bloomsbury Academic, 2015.

Fussell, Paul. *The Great War and Modern Memory*. Oxford: Oxford University Press, 2000.

Galehouse, Maggie. 'Their Own Private Idaho: Transience in *Housekeeping*.' *Contemporary Literature* 41:1 (2000): 117–37.

Gallop, Jane. 'The Historicization of Literary Studies and the Fate of Close Reading.' In *Profession 2007*, edited by R. G. Feal, 181–86. New York: MLA, 2007.

Gallop, Jane. 'Close Reading in 2009.' *ADE Bulletin* 149 (2010): 15–19.

Gardner, Helen. *The Metaphysical Poets*. New York: Oxford University Press, 1961.

Gardner, John. *On Moral Fiction*. New York: Basic Books, 1977.

Gass, William H. 'Finding a Form' and 'Exile.' In *Finding a Form: Essays*, 31–52, 213–36. Ithaca, NY: Cornell University Press, 1996.

Gass, William H. *Tests of Time*. New York: Alfred A. Knopf, 2002.

Genette, Gérard. *Narrative Discourse: An Essay in Method* (1972), trans. Jane E. Lewin. Ithaca, NY: Cornell University Press, 1980.

Genette, Gérard. *Palimpsests: Literature in the Second Degree*, trans. Channa Newman and Claude Doubinsky. Lincoln, NE: University of Nebraska Press, 1997.

Geyh, Paula E. 'Burning Down the House? Domestic Space and Feminine Subjectivity in Marilynne Robinson's *Housekeeping*.' *Contemporary Literature* 34.1 (1993): 103–22.

Gingrich, Brian. 'Dream, Imagine, Say: The Passwords of Grammar and the Hinges of Fiction.' Seminar Paper, February 5, 2012. 18pp.

Gopnik, Adam. 'The Real Work: Our Far-flung Correspondents.' *The New Yorker* 84.5 (2008): 57–69.

Gossman, Lionel. *Between History and Literature*. Cambridge, MA: Harvard University Press, 1990.

Graulund, Rune. 'Fulcrums and Borderlands: A Desert Reading of Cormac McCarthy's *The Road*.' *Orbis Litterarum* 65.1 (2010): 57–78.

Gray, John. *Isaiah Berlin*. Princeton, NJ: Princeton University Press 1996.

Gray, Richard. 'Cormac McCarthy, *The Road*.' In *Still in Print: The Southern Novel Today*, edited by Jan Nordby Gretlund, 260–74. Columbia, SC: University of South Carolina Press, 2010.

Greenblatt, Stephen. *Renaissance Self-Fashioning: From More to Shakespeare.*
    Chicago, IL: University of Chicago Press, 1980.
Greenblatt, Stephen. *Marvelous Possessions: The Wonder of the New World.*
    Chicago, IL: University of Chicago Press, 1991.
Guillory, John. 'Close Reading: Prologue and Epilogue.' *ADE Bulletin* 149
    (2010): 8–14.
Harpham, Geoffrey Galt. *Getting It Right: Language, Literature, and Ethics.*
    Chicago, IL: University of Chicago Press: 1992.
Harpham, Geoffrey Galt. 'The Hunger of Martha Nussbaum.' *Representations*
    77 (Winter 2002): 52–81.
Hartman, Saidiya V. *Scenes of Subjection: Terror, Slavery, and Self-Making in*
    Nineteenth-Century America. New York: Oxford University Press, 1997.
Hawthorne, Nathanael. *The House of the Seven Gables.* Ed. Michael Davitt Bell.
    New York: Oxford University Press, 1991.
Hedrick, Tace. ' "The Perimeters of Our Wandering Are Nowhere":
    Breaching the Domestic in *Housekeeping.*' *Critique* 40:2 (Winter 1999):
    137–151.
Hemingway, Ernest. *Death in the Afternoon.* New York: Scribner's, 1932.
Hemingway, Ernest. 'Up in Michigan.' In *The Short Stories of Ernest*
    Hemingway, 81–86. New York: Scribner's 1953.
Herman, David (ed.). *The Cambridge Companion to Narrative.* New York:
    Cambridge University Press, 2007.
Hoberek, Andrew. 'Cormac McCarthy and the Aesthetics of Exhaustion.'
    American Literary History, 23.3 (2011): 483–99.
Holloway, David. *The Late Modernism of Cormac McCarthy.* Westport, CT:
    Greenwood Press, 2002.
Hopkins, Gerard Manley. 'The Windhover' (1918). Available at: http://www.
    bartleby.com/122/12.html. Retrieved August 18, 2016.
Huber, Irmtraud. *Literature after Postmodernism: Reconstructive Fantasies.*
    London: Palgrave Macmillan, 2014.
Hutcheon, Linda. *The Politics of Postmodernism.* New York: Routledge, 1989.
James, Henry. 'The Novels of George Eliot.' *Atlantic* 18 (October 1866): 485;
    reprinted in *Theory of Fiction: Henry James,* edited by James E. Miller, Jr.
    Lincoln, NE: University of Nebraska Press, 1972.
James, Henry. *The Portrait of a Lady* (1881). Harmondsworth: Penguin, 1984.
James, Henry. *The Wings of the Dove* (1902). Harmondsworth: Penguin, 1986.
James, Henry. *The Ambassadors* (1903). Harmondsworth: Penguin, 1986.
James, Henry. *Henry James, Literary Criticism: Essays on Literature; American*
    Writers; English Writers, edited by Leon Edel. New York: Library of
    America, 1984.
Jameson, Fredric. 'The Realist Floor-Plan.' In *On Signs,* edited by Marshall
    Blonsky, 373–83. Baltimore, MD: Johns Hopkins University Press, 1985.
Jameson, Fredric. *Postmodernism, or The Cultural Logic of Late Capitalism.*
    New York: Verso, 1991.
Jarrett, Robert L. *Cormac McCarthy.* New York: Twayne, 1997.

Jay, Martin. 'Two Cheers for Paraphrase: The Confessions of a Synoptic Intellectual Historian.' In *Fin-de-siecle Socialism and Other Essays*, 52–63. New York: Routledge, 1988.

Jay, Paul. 'Transnational Masculinities in Junot Díaz's *The Brief Wondrous Life of Oscar Wao*.' In *Global Matters: The Transnational Turn in Literary Studies*, 176–93. Ithaca, NY: Cornell University Press, 2010.

Johnson, Barbara. 'Teaching Deconstructively,' in *Writing and Reading Differently*, edited by G. Douglas Atkins and M. J. Johnson, 140–48. Lawrence, KS: University of Kansas Press, 1986.

Josephs, Allen. 'The Quest for God in *The Road*,' in *The Cambridge Companion to Cormac McCarthy*. New York: Cambridge University Press, 2013.

Kaivola, Karen. 'The Pleasures and Perils of Merging: Female Subjectivity in Marilynne Robinson's *Housekeeping*.' *Contemporary Literature* 34:4 (1993): 670–90.

Kandinsky, Wassily. *Concerning the Spiritual in Art and Painting in Particular* (1912), trans. by Ralph Manheim. New York: Wittenborn, Schultz, 1947.

Karlinsky, Simon (ed.). *The Nabokov-Wilson Letters: Correspondence between Vladimir Nabokov and Edmund Wilson, 1940–1971*. New York: Harper & Row, 1979.

Kauffman, Linda. 'Framing Lolita: Is There a Woman in the Text?' In *Major Literary Characters: Lolita*, edited by Harold Bloom, 149–68. New York: Chelsea House, 1993.

Keach, William. *Shelley's Style*. New York: Methuen, 1984.

Keats, John. *Selected Poems and Letters.* Ed. Douglas Bush. New York: Houghton Mifflin, 1959.

Kerouac, Jack. *On the Road*. New York: Penguin, 1999.

King, Kristin. 'Resurfacings of *The Deeps*: Semiotic Balance in Marilynne Robinson's *Housekeeping*.' *Studies in the Novel* 28:4 (1996): 565–80.

Kowalewski, Michael. *Deadly Musings: Violence and Verbal Form in American Fiction*. Princeton, NJ: Princeton University Press, 1993.

Kreml, Nancy. 'Stylistic Variation and Cognitive Constraint in *All the Pretty Horses*.' *Sacred Violence: A Reader's Companion to Cormac McCarthy*, edited by Wade Hall and Rick Wallach, 137–48. El Paso, TX: Texas Western Press, 1995.

Krutch, Joseph Wood. 'Nation' (12 October 1927). In *Willa Cather: The Contemporary Reviews*, edited by Margaret Anne O'Connor, 337. New York: Cambridge University Press, 2001.

Kunsa, Ashley. '"Maps of the World in its Becoming": Post-Apocalyptic Naming in Cormac McCarthy's *The Road*.' *Journal of Modern Literature* 33.1 (2009): 57–74.

Kunsa, Ashley. 'History, Hair, and Reimagining Racial Categories in Junot Díaz's *The Brief Wondrous Life of Oscar Wao*.' *Critique* 54 (2013): 211–24.

Lawrence, D. H. 'Why the Novel Matters.' In *Studies of Thomas Hardy and Other Essays*, 191–198. Cambridge: Cambridge University Press, 1985.

Leddy, Michael. '"Distant and Correct": The Double Life and *The Professor's House*.' In *Cather Studies*, Vol. 3, edited by Susan J. Rosowski, 182–96. Lincoln, NE: University of Nebraska Press, 1996.

Lee, Hermione. *Willa Cather: Double Lives*. New York: Pantheon, 1989.

Levenson, Marjorie. 'What Is New Formalism?' *PMLA* 122:2 (2007): 558–69.

Levenson, Michael. *Modernism and the fate of individuality: Character and novelistic form from Conrad to Woolf*. New York: Cambridge University Press, 1991.

Levenson, Michael (ed.). *The Cambridge Companion to Modernism*. New York: Cambridge University Press, 1999.

Lewis, Pericles. *The Cambridge Introduction to Modernism*. New York: Cambridge University Press, 2007.

Lilley, James D. '*Of Whales and Men*: The Dynamics of Cormac McCarthy's Environmental Imagination.' *Southern Quarterly* 38.2 (2000): 111–22.

Lindemann, Marilee. *Willa Cather: Queering America*. New York: Columbia University Press, 1999.

Longenbach, James. *The Resistance to Poetry*. Chicago: University of Chicago Press, 2004.

Love, Heather. 'Close but Not Deep: Literary Ethics and the Descriptive Turn.' *New Literary History* 41.2 (2010): 371–91.

Luce, Dianne C. 'The Road and the Matrix: The World as Tale in *The Crossing*.' In *Perspectives on Cormac McCarthy*, 2nd edn, edited by Edwin T. Arnold and Dianne C. Luce. 195–220. Jackson: University Press of Mississippi, 1999.

Mattessich, Stefan. 'Drifting Decision and the Decision to Drift: The Question of Spirit in Marilynne Robinson's *Housekeeping*.' *Differences: A Journal of Feminist Cultural Studies*. 19:3 (2008): 59–89.

McCarthy, Cormac. *Blood Meridian: or, the Evening Redness in the West*. New York: Vintage, 1985.

McCarthy, Cormac. *The Road*. Alfred A. Knopf, 2006.

McDermott, Sinead. 'Future-Perfect: Gender, Nostalgia, and the Not Yet Presented in Marilynne Robinson's *Housekeeping*.' *Journal of Gender Studies* 13:3 (2004): 259–70.

McGowan, John. *Postmodernism and Its Critics*. Ithaca, NY: Cornell University Press, 1991.

McGuiness, Patrick. *Maurice Maeterlinck and the Making of Modern Theater*. New York: Oxford University Press, 2000.

McHale, Brian. *Postmodernist Fiction*. New York: Methuen, 1987.

Meese, Elizabeth A. 'A World of Women, Marilynne Robinson's *Housekeeping*.' In *Crossing the Double Cross*, 55–68. Chapel Hill, NC: University of North Carolina Press, 1986.

Melville, Herman. *Moby-Dick*. Harmondsworth: Penguin, 1992.

Menand, Louis. 'Out of Bethlehem: The Radicalization of Joan Didion.' *The New Yorker* (August 24, 2015): 66–73.

Michaels, Walter Benn. *Our America: Nativism, Modernism, and Pluralism.* Durham, NC: Duke University Press, 1995.

Middleton, Jo Ann. *Willa Cather's Modernism: A Study of Style and Technique.* Rutherford, NJ: Fairleigh Dickinson University Press, 1990.

Mitchell, Lee Clark. 'Old Ethics, New Aesthetics, and the Problem of Late James.' *Raritan* 22.4 (2003): 69–89.

Moretti, Franco. *Distant Reading.* London: Verso, 2013.

Morgan, Wesley. 'The Route and Roots of *The Road*.' *The Cormac McCarthy Journal* 6 (Autumn 2008): 39–47.

Moseley, Ann. 'Spatial Structures and Forms in *The Professor's House*.' In *Cather Studies*, Vol. 3, edited by Susan J. Rosowski, 197–211. Lincoln, NE: University of Nebraska Press, 1996.

Mullan, John. 'As strange as a simile.' *The Guardian*, 3 June 2005. Available at: http://www.theguardian.com/books/2005/jun/04/featuresreviews. guardianreview30. Retrieved August 23, 2015.

Nabokov, Vladimir. *Nikolai Gogol* (1944). New York: New Directions, 1971.

Nabokov, Vladimir. *Strong Opinions.* New York: McGraw-Hill, 1973.

Nabokov, Vladimir. *Lectures on Literature*, edited by Fredson Bowers. New York: Harcourt Brace Jovanovich, 1980.

Nabokov, Vladimir. *The Annotated Lolita: Revised and Updated,* edited by Alfred Appel, Jr. New York: Random House, Inc., 1991.

Naiman, Eric. *Nabokov, Perversely.* Ithaca, NY: Cornell University Press, 2010.

Nussbaum, Martha C. *Love's Knowledge: Essays on Philosophy and Literature.* New York: Oxford University Press, 1990.

Nussbaum, Martha C. *Poetic Justice: The Literary Imagination and Public Life.* Boston, MA: Beacon Press, 1995.

O'Brien, Sean P. 'Some Assembly Required: Intertextuality, Marginalization, and *The Brief Wondrous Life of Oscar Wao*.' *The Journal of the Midwest Modern Language Association* 45:1 (2012): 75–96.

O'Brien, Sharon. '"The Thing Not Named": Willa Cather as a Lesbian Writer.' *Signs* 9:4 (1984): 576–99.

O'Connor, Margaret Anne (ed.). *Willa Cather: The Contemporary Reviews.* New York: Cambridge University Press, 2001.

O'Farrell, Mary Ann. 'Words to Do with Things: Reading about Willa Cather and Material Culture.' In *Willa Cather and Material Culture: Real-World Writing, Writing the Real World*, edited by Janis P. Stout, 207–17. Tuscaloosa, AL: University of Alabama Press, 2005.

O'Rourke, Meghan. 'Questions for Junot Díaz.' *Slate Magazine*, November 8, 2007. Available at: http://www.slate.com/articles/news_and_politics/ the_highbrow/2007/11/the_brief_wondrous_life_of_oscar_wao.html. Retrieved July 30, 2015.

Orwell, George. 'Politics and the English Language' (1946). Available at: http://www.orwell.ru/library/essays/politics/english/e_polit. Retrieved August 24, 2015.

Osen, Diane. 'Interview with Marilynne Robinson.' *National Book Foundation Archives*. Available at: http://www.nationalbook.org/authorsguide_ mrobinson.html. Retrieved August 17, 2016.

Otter, Samuel. 'An Aesthetics in All Things.' *Representations* 104 (2008): 116–25.

Page, Norman (ed.). *Nabokov: The Critical Heritage*. London: Routledge & Kegan Paul, 1982.

Parker, Patricia. *Inescapable Romance: Studies in the Poetics of a Mode*. Princeton, NJ: Princeton University Press, 1979.

Patteson, Richard. 'Textual Territory and Narrative Power in Junot Díaz's *The Brief Wondrous Life of Oscar Wao.*' *Ariel* 42:3–4 (2012): 5–20.

Peck, Demaree. *The Imaginative Claims of the Artist in Willa Cather's Fiction: Possession Granted by a Different Lease*. Selinsgrove, PA: Susquehanna University Press, 1996.

Phelan, James. *Reading the American Novel 1920–2010*. Chicester, Sussex: Wiley-Blackwell, 2013.

Phillips, Dana. 'History and the Ugly Facts of *Blood Meridian.*' In *Cormac McCarthy: New Directions*, edited by James D. Lilley, 17–46. Albuquerque: U of New Mexico Press, 2002.

Phillips, Dana. '"He ought not have done it': McCarthy and Apocalypse.' In *Cormac McCarthy: All the Pretty Horses, No Country for Old Men, The Road*, edited by Sara L. Spurgeon, 172–88. New York: Continuum, 2011.

Pifer, Ellen. *Nabokov and the Novel*. Cambridge, MA: Harvard University Press, 1980.

Piper, Andrew. *Book Was There: Reading in Electronic Times*. Chicago, IL: University of Chicago Press, 2012.

Platt, Cameron. 'Take a Shot: Choice in the Narrative Landscape of *The Road.*' Princeton University final course paper, December 2014.

Poe, Edgar Allen. *Selected Writings*. Harmondsworth: Penguin 2003.

Pollitt, Katha. 'Why Do We Read?' In *Debating P.C.: The Controversy over Political Correctness on College Campuses,* edited by Paul Berman, 201–11. New York: Bantam Doubleday Dell, 1992.

Pound, Ezra. *The Letters of Ezra Pound: 1907–1941*, edited by D. D. Paige. New York: Harcourt, Brace and Company, 1950.

Putnam, Hilary. 'The Craving for Objectivity.' *New Literary History* 15 (1984): 229–40.

Puttenham, George. 'Of Figures and Figuratiue Speaches,' Ch. 3.7 of *The Arte of English Poesie*. Available at: http://etext.virginia.edu/toc/modeng/public/ PutPoes.html. Retrieved August 23, 2015.

Quilligan, Maureen. *The Language of Allegory: Defining the Genre*. Ithaca, NY: Cornell University Press, 1979.

Rambo, Shelly L. 'Beyond Redemption? Reading Cormac McCarthy's *The Road* After the End of the World.' *Studies in the Literary Imagination* 41.2 (2008): 99–120.

Rampton, David. *Vladimir Nabokov: A Critical Study of the Novels*. New York: Cambridge University Press, 1984.

Rasmussen, Mark David. 'Introduction: New Formalisms?' In *Renaissance Literature and Its Formal Engagements*, edited by Mark David Rasmussen, 1–14. New York: Palgrave, 2002.

Ravits, Martha. 'Extending the American Range: Marilynne Robinson's *Housekeeping*.' *American Literature* 61.4 (1989): 644–66.

Richards, I. A. *Principles of Literary Criticism*. London: K. Paul, Trench, Trubner, 1924.

Richards, I. A. *Practical Criticism: A Study of Literary Judgment*. London: K. Paul, Trench, Trubner, 1929.

Richardson, Brian. 'The Poetics and Politics of Second Person Narrative.' *Genre* 24:3 (1991): 309–30.

Rivera, Catalina. '*Páginas En Blanco*: Transmissions of Trauma in Junot Díaz's *The Brief Wondrous Life of Oscar Wao*.' M.A. Thesis, University of North Carolina, Chapel Hill, 2011.

Robinson, Marilynne. *Housekeeping*. New York: Farrar, Strauss, 1980.

Robinson, Marilynne. 'My Western Roots.' In *Old West–New West: Centennial Essays*, edited by Barbara Howard Meldrum. Moscow, ID: University of Idaho Press, 1993. Available at: http://www.washington.edu/uwired/outreach/cspn/Website/Classroom%20Materials/Reading%20the%20Region/Northwest%20Schools%20of%20Literature/Texts/11.html. Retrieved August 23, 2015.

Rorty, Richard. 'The barber of Kasbeam: Nabokov on Cruelty.' In *Contingency, Irony, and Solidarity*. New York: Cambridge University Press, 1989.

Roth, Philip. *American Pastoral*. New York: Vintage, 1997.

Ryan, Marie-Laure. 'Toward a definition of narrative.' In *The Cambridge Companion to Narrative*, edited by David Herman, 22–36. New York: Cambridge University Press, 2007.

Sáez, Elena Machado. 'Dictating Desire, Dictating Diasporo: Junot Díaz's *The Brief Wondrous Life of Oscar Wao* as Foundational Romance.' *Contemporary Literature* 52:3 (2011): 522–55.

Saliba, Dawn A. 'Linguistic Disintegration in Cormac McCarthy's *The Road*.' In *Environmentalism in the Realm of Science Fiction and Fantasy Literature*, edited by Chris Baratta, 143–55. Newcastle upon Tyne: Cambridge Scholars Press, 2012.

Scarry, Elaine. *The Body in Pain: The Making and Unmaking of the World*. New York: Oxford University Press, 1985.

Scarry, Elaine. *On Beauty and Being Just*. Princeton, NJ: Princeton University Press, 1999.

Schwartz, Michael W. 'Defense of Reading.' *The Harvard Crimson*. August 2, 1962. Available at: http://www.thecrimson.com/article/1962/8/2/defense-of-reading-pin-defense-of/#. Retrieved August 23, 2015.

Sebald, W. G. *On the Natural History of Destruction* (1999), trans. Anthea Bell. New York: Random House, 2003.

Sedgwick, Eve Kosofsky. 'Across Gender, Across Sexuality: Willa Cather and Others.' *South Atlantic Quarterly* 88 (1989): 53–72.

Sendak, Maurice. *Where the Wild Things Are*. New York: Harper and Row, 1963.

Sepich, John. *Notes on 'Blood Meridian'*. (1993) Rev. edn. Austin, TX: University of Texas Press, 2008.

Shakespeare, William. *The Tragedy of Macbeth* (1606). Available at: http://shakespeare.mit.edu/macbeth/full.html. Retrieved August 18, 2016.

Shakespeare, William. *The Tempest* (1610–11). Available at: http://shakespeare.mit.edu/tempest/full.html. Retrieved August 18, 2016.

Shaviro, Steven. '"The Very Life of the Darkness": A Reading of *Blood Meridian*.' (1992). In *Perspectives on Cormac McCarthy*, edited by Edwin T. Arnold and Dianne C. Luce, 145–58. Jackson, MS: University Press of Mississippi, 1999.

Smit, David W. *The Language of a Master: Theories of Style and the Late Writing of Henry James*. Carbondale, IL: Southern Illinois University Press, 1988.

Smith, Carlota S. *Modes of Discourse: The Local Structure of Texts*. New York: Cambridge University Press, 2003.

Smyth, Jacqui. 'Sheltered Vagrancy in Marilynne Robinson's *Housekeeping*.' *Critique* 40.3 (1999): 281–91.

Snyder, Phillip A. and Delys W. Snyder. 'Modernisms, Postmodernism, and Language: McCarthy's Style.' In *The Cambridge Companion to Cormac McCarthy*, edited by Steven Frye, 27–38. New York: Cambridge University Press, 2013.

Steiner, George. *Language and Silence: Essays on Language, Literature, and the Inhuman*. New Haven, CT: Yale University Press, 1970.

Steiner, Wendy. *The Scandal of Pleasure: Art in an Age of Fundamentalism*. Chicago, IL: University of Chicago Press, 1995.

Stevens, Wallace. *Poems*. New York: Vintage, 1959.

Steward, Garrett. *The Deed of Reading: Literature, Writing, Language, Philosophy*. Ithaca, NJ: Cornell University Press, 2015.

Stewart, Garrett. *Novel Violence: A Narratography of Victorian Fiction*. Chicago, IL: University of Chicago Press, 2009.

Stout, Janis P. *Strategies of Reticence: Silence and Meaning in the Works of Jane Austen, Willa Cather, Katherine Anne Porter, and Joan Didion*. Charlottesville, VA: University Press of Virginia, 1990.

Stout, Jeffrey. *Ethics After Babel: The Languages of Morals and Their Discontents*. Boston, MA: Beacon Press, 1988.

Strychacz, Thomas. 'The Ambiguities of Escape in Willa Cather's *The Professor's House*.' *Studies in American Fiction* 14:1 (1986): 49–61.

Sundquist, Eric. *To Wake the Nations: Race in the Making of American Literature*. Cambridge, MA: Harvard University Press, 1993.

Swiss, Jamy Ian. EG5, Monterey 2011. Available at: http://www.youtube.com/watch?v=jjxeqyuSe_Y. Retrieved August 23, 2015.

Tanner, Tony. *The Reign of Wonder: Naivety and Reality in American Literature*. New York: Cambridge University Press, 1965.

Tanner, Tony. 'The Watcher from the Balcony: Henry James's *The Ambassadors*.' *Critical Quarterly* 8 (1966): 35–52.

Tatum, Stephen. 'Cormac McCarthy.' In *Updating the Literary West*, 475–88. Fort Worth, TX: Texas Christian University Press, 1997.

Thoreau, Henry David. *A Week on the Concord and Merrimack Rivers, Walden; or, Life in the Woods, The Maine Woods, Cape Cod*. New York: Library of America, 1985.

Ting, David. 'Understanding Beli's Scar as Post-Atomic: How Allusions to Japan in *The Brief Wondrous Life of Oscar Wao* Internationalize Trauma.' Princeton University course paper, December 18, 2014.

Trilling, Lionel. 'The Last Lover.' *Encounter* (1958): 9–19.

Trilling, Lionel. 'On the Teaching of Modern Literature.' In *Beyond Culture: Essays on Literature and Learning*, 3–27. New York: Harcourt Brace Jovanovich, 1965.

Trilling, Lionel. 'Review.' In *Willa Cather and Her Critics*, edited by James Schroeter, 154–55. Ithaca, NY: Cornell University Press, 1967.

Twain, Mark. *Adventures of Huckleberry Finn*. New York: Penguin, 2014.

Wallace, David Foster. *Infinite Jest*. Boston, MA: Little, Brown and Company, 1996.

Weigel, Emily. Blackboard post for Princeton University course ENG362, September 24, 2008.

Welty, Eudora. 'The House of Willa Cather' (1974). In *The Eye of the Story: Selected Essays and Reviews*, 41–60. New York: Random House, 1977.

Wharton, Edith. *The House of Mirth*. Ed. Martha Banta. New York: Oxford University Press, 1994.

Whiting, Frederick. '"The Strange Particularity of the Lover's Preference": Pedophilia, Pornography, and the Anatomy of Monstrosity in *Lolita*.' *American Literature* 70:4 (1998): 833–62.

Whitman, Walt. 'Song of Myself' (1882). In *Leaves of Grass*, 22–78. New York: Penguin, 2013.

Whitman, Walt. 'Song of the Open Road.' In *Leaves of Grass*, 125–34. New York: Penguin, 2013.

Widiss, Benjamin. 'See Monkey, Do Monkey: *Lolita* (aping).' In *Obscure Invitations: The Persistence of the Author in Twentieth-Century American Literature*, 76–108. Palo Alto, CA: Stanford University Press, 2011.

Wilcox, Leonard. 'Baudrillard, Delillo's *White Noise*, and the End of Heroic Narrative.' *Contemporary Literature* 32 (1991): 346–65.

Williams, Bernard. *Ethics and the Limits of Philosophy*. Cambridge, MA: Harvard University Press, 1985.

Winfrey, Oprah. Interview with Cormac McCarthy. June 1, 2008. Available at: http://www.oprah.com/oprahsbookclub/Oprahs-Exclusive-Interview-with-Cormac-McCarthy-Video. Retrieved August 23, 2015.

Witek, Terri. '"He's Hell When He's Well": Cormac McCarthy's Rhyming Dictions.' *Myth, legend, dust: Critical Responses to Cormac McCarthy*, edited by Rick Wallach, 78–88. Manchester: Manchester University Press, 2000.

Wood, Michael. '*Lolita* Revisited.' *New England Review: Middlebury Series* 17 (3) (1995): 15–43.

Wood, Michael. *The Magician's Doubts: Nabokov and the Risks of Fiction.* Princeton, NJ: Princeton University Press, 1994.

Woodward, Richard B. 'Cormac McCarthy's Venomous Fiction.' *The New York Times* (April 19, 1992): 28–31. Available at: http://www.nytimes. com/1992/04/19/magazine/cormac-mccarthy-s-venomous-fiction. html?pagewanted=all&src=pm. Retrieved August 23, 2015.

Woolf, Virginia. *Mrs. Dalloway.* New York: Harcourt, Brace & World, 1925.

Wordsworth, William. 'The Tables Turned' (1798). Available at: https://www. poetryfoundation.org/poems-and-poets/poems/detail/45557. Retrieved September 29, 2016.

INDEX

Eliot, George, *Adam Bede*, 58 n.16
Eliot, T. S., 59 n.20, 60 n.21, 64, 182, 186
Ellington, Duke, 37
Ellis, Brett Easton, 163
Ellison, Ralph, 47
Emerson, Ralph Waldo, 121, 144, 145 n.2,
    186; Robinson and, 129, 135, 136,
    138, 139, 142 n.2, 144, 147 n.12,
    147 n.13; wonder and, 39, 63;
    "Compensation," 135; "Nature," 139,
    147 n.12; "The Poet," 136, 147 n.13
error, as literary conceit, 28–33; classical
    literature and, 29–30; James and
    30–2; modernism and, 30–3;
    Roth and, 28–9, 31, 32
Escher, M. C., 113
Esperanto, 34
ethical readings, 16, 19–21, 35–6; literary
    predispositions, 19–21. *See also*
    ethics of reading, symptomatic
    readings
ethics of reading, 17–25, 34–5, 114–16,
    238
    aesthetics and, 18, 20–4; authorial
    responsibility, 49, 98, 100; awe as
    ethical position, 24–5; cultural
    work, 23; desensitizing literature,
    17–18; James on, 21–2; Nabokov
    and, 22–3, 48–9, 114–16; value
    pluralism, 15–16, 34, 54, 58 n.14.
    See also ethical readings

Faulkner, William, 36, 39, 47, 73, 90, 149,
    235; McCarthy, influence on, 150,
    158, 159, 163, 169; Robinson and,
    124, 134, 144; *Absalom, Absalom!*,
    124, 134; *As I Lay Dying*, 40; *Light
    in August*, 124, 163; *The Sound
    and the Fury*, 236
Ferry, Ann Davidson, 58 n.13
Fish, Stanley, 6–7, 35, 37, 56 n.6
Fitzgerald, F. Scott, 64, 186; and wonder,
    46; *The Great Gatsby*, 46
Flaubert, Gustave, 170, 172 n.9
Foer, Jonathan Saffron, 60 n.23, 175,
    230 n.2
Ford, Richard, 175
formalism, 5–6, 11–12, 13, 60 n.26,
    119 n.18 150. *See also* close

reading, New Critics, new
    formalism
Forster, E. M., 31–2; *Aspects of the Novel*,
    23
Foster, Thomas, 124, 147 n.17
Foucault, Michel, 27
Franzen, Jonathan, 175, 230 n.2
Friedan, Betty, 125
Frost, Robert, 27
Frye, Steven, 201 n.11
Funk, Wolfgang, 60 n.22, 60 n.23, 230 n.2
Fussell, Paul, 170 n.1

Gaddis, William, 90
Galehouse, Maggie, 124, 146 n.7, 147 n.16
Gallop, Jane, 8, 53
Gardner, Helen, 172 n.12
Gardner, John, 16
Gass, William, v, 23, 38, 46, 90; *Tests of
    Time*, 1
Genette, Gerard, 67–8, 71, 80, 87 n.7,
    88 n.9, 187, 206, 228
Geyh, Paula E., 124, 146 n.7, 147 n.16
Gingrich, Brian, 133
Glanton, John Joel, 50
Godden, Richard, 11
Gogol, Nikolai, 113, 115–16; *Dead Souls*,
    101
Gopnik, Adam, 8, 54
Gossman, Lionel, 26–7
Grauland, Rune, 200 n.6
Gray, John, 15, 34, 58 n.14
Gray, Richard, 202 n.15, 202 n.17,
    203 n.18
Greenblatt, Stephen, 13, 56 n.10, 65, 70,
    80, 85
Grey, Zane, 75
Gupta, Nikhil, 44

Hardy, Thomas, 58 n.20
Harpham, Geoffrey Galt, 36, 58 n.18
Hartman, Saidiya, 171 n.3
Hawthorne, Nathaniel, 58 n.20, 73; *The
    House of the Seven Gables*, 123
Hedrick, Tace, 124, 145 n.2, 146 n.7,
    147 n.16
Hemingway, Ernest, 39, 50, 64, 73, 90,
    218, 235; Cather and, 68–9, 73;
    influence on McCarthy, 159, 163,